EURIPIDES

THE RATIONALIST

CAMBRIDGE UNIVERSITY PRESS
London: FETTER LANE, E.C.
C. F. CLAY, Manager

Edinburgh: 100, PRINCES STREET
Berlin: A. ASHER AND CO.
Leipzig: F. A. BROCKHAUS
New York: G. P. PUTNAM'S SONS
Bombay and Calcutta: MACMILLAN AND CO., Ltd.
Toronto: J. M. DENT AND SONS, Ltd.
Tokyo: THE MARUZEN-KABUSHIKI-KAISHA

EURIPIDES

THE RATIONALIST:

A STUDY IN THE HISTORY OF ART AND RELIGION

BY

A. W. VERRALL Litt.D.

FELLOW OF TRINITY COLLEGE, CAMBRIDGE

Cambridge:

at the University Press

1913

First Edition 1895
Reprinted 1913

PRINTED IN GREAT BRITAIN

TO

HENRY JACKSON Litt.D.

THIS BOOK
WRITTEN IN RESPONSE TO HIS SUGGESTION
IS OFFERED
AS A SMALL ACKNOWLEDGEMENT
OF MANY DEBTS

INTRODUCTION

THE purpose of this book is to explain and account for, perhaps also to diminish or to abolish, but at any rate to account for and explain, the great and surprising difference of opinion between ancient readers and modern respecting the position and merits of Euripides. That this difference exists is not, so far as I know, disputed, and certainly cannot be disputed with reason; in many modern works of authority it has been justly marked and emphasized. From Euripides' death to the decline and fall of pagan learning there never was, so far as we have evidence, any noteworthy dissent from the view that Euripides, however he, like any other artist, might be variously estimated by personal taste, stood at all events in the very first rank of artists, superior to all but the elect, and not demonstrably or confessedly inferior to any. Such is the opinion depicted, variously but harmoniously, by the highest representatives of literary culture in succession down to the very end, by Plato, by Cicero, by Lucian, and by all the voices who fill up that tract of time. There is not a sign that by any one commanding attention the question was ever raised whether Euripides had really deserved the honour of standing with Sophocles and with Aeschylus. The opinion which groups them as 'different but equal' is given by Cicero, for example, not as his own judgement, but as a commonplace. The polemic of Aristophanes, if and in so far as it tends to impeach Euripides as an artist (for almost all of it, that can be taken as serious, is aimed not at his art but at his opinions), failed with the ancient world completely. By the side of Aeschylus and Sophocles—and if distinctions must be made, not lowest assuredly of the three—Euripides stood securely. It is on the other hand notorious that in modern times this position of his has been incessantly contested, and by the weight as well as the majority of voices has been with increasing emphasis denied. The contradiction is no matter of detail ; it goes to the whole tone and substance of judgement. No one in modern times, since Greek has been well understood, has said that his dearest desire beyond the grave would be to meet Euripides ; not this nor anything like it. No one in the ancient world, so far as we know, ever said that much of Euripides' work might seem to have been composed in a fever ; not this nor anything like it. Agreeing generally, with remarkable but not surprising exactness, in their estimate of the great writers Greek and Roman, about this one man the ancient readers and the modern are out of accord. The most cultivated men of the ancient world (I do not except or forget Aristotle, who shall be specially considered in due course) speak of Euripides regularly and habitually as modest men would now speak of Shakespeare or Goethe, and sometimes as reverent men would now speak of Dante or St Paul. The modern remarks, whether of censure or defence, are pitched in another key and confined to a different range. The ancients do not defend Euripides. In our time a defence, cordial sometimes or fervent, but still a defence, is the utmost that he obtains. By Menander, or Ennius, or Ovid, to judge from their own practice, such a defence would have been heard with amazement. There are some names which must not be so praised, and in the ancient world among such names, high among such, stood the name of Euripides.

The explanation of this discrepancy which will here be offered, has at least one advantage. The reader will not be

asked to dissent, as a matter of taste and aesthetic judgement, either from the ancient opinion or from the modern.
Scarcely even the scorn of Schlegel is too much for many of
the works of Euripides, read as they were by Schlegel and
are by the modern world in general. Scarcely even the
adoration of the admirer pourtrayed by Philemon is too
much for Euripides, read as he was read certainly by Lucian
and presumably by the ancient world in general. The works
of Euripides, almost all of them, depend for their interpretation on a certain broad conventional principle, probably not
ever applicable to many writings except his, and applicable
to no others now extant. This principle is stated (as we
shall see before we conclude) by an excellent authority in
the clearest terms; but nevertheless it has never in modern
times been steadily applied, and for the most part has been
simply ignored. The effect of this one error can be compared only to that of changing, in a mathematical expression,
the positive sign for the negative; and the result is a body of
criticism of which a large part is really not more pertinent or
more reasonable than it would be to put a statue upon its
head, and then to complain of the statuary for representing
a man with his feet in the air.

ALCESTIS

'Cela vous apprendra,' dit d'Artagnan, 'à traiter d'une façon plus courtoise les hôtes que Dieu vous envoie.'

DUMAS.

APOLOGY, if I am not mistaken, is no longer due from an enquirer who, in approaching the study of Euripides, will start, as he has done before, from the assumption that in this region no high road of authority has yet been laid out. It is still a case of exploration; we are not bound, and shall scarcely be wise, to follow religiously in tracks of which one thing only can be said with certainty, that they do not lead to the goal. " Nothing is more certain," as I read with satisfaction in the *Preface* to the welcome *Euripides in English Verse*, of which the first volume has just now[1], opportunely for me, been issued by Mr Way, "nothing is more certain than that the old fashion of disparaging his genius (in which Schlegel led the way, giving all the weight of his authority to a sentence which others were too uncritical or too timorous to revise) is now utterly discredited, and that we have ceased to regard the generations of Greeks and Romans who loved and reverenced him, as degenerate fools and blind, *and are at last making some humble efforts to understand them and to recover their point of view*." Whether Mr Way is justified or not in his expectation of general sympathy, he has at least himself the credit of setting a good example. The right view of Euripides, the capacity of understanding him, is a thing which

---

[1] Aug. 1894. Most of this first essay had been written; but I have remodelled some parts.

we moderns have yet to *recover*; and our only way is to begin
with recognizing that somewhere in our notions about the
poet there must be something fundamentally wrong.   It
should not be possible, as it was not long ago (and notwithstanding the assurance of Mr Way the thing is conceivable
still), for an English poet, bound to the poets of Greece by
mutual obligations, to pronounce Euripides no peer of his
peers, a dramatist not to be ranked as the equal of those with
whom he was actually ranked by the judgement of Athens
and all the ancient world, without perceiving that he condemns,
not the object of his criticism, but simply his own comprehension.   Even to apologize for Euripides, or to patronize
him, is to show that we mistake our position.   Until we can
admire him heartily and wholly, the " humble effort " recommended by Mr Way is our only rational course.

It is indeed not a bad attitude to be taken by the student
in all cases ; and for myself at any rate I am ready to adopt
it in dealing with the criticism of Mr Swinburne.   Making a
humble effort, and with no affected humility, to understand
the grounds of his judgement, I have found instruction in a
term of contempt which, after his trenchant manner, he has
thrown out by way of summary.   Euripides, he has told us,
was a ‘ botcher.’   Deserved or not by the poet, the phrase is
apt enough to indicate the nature of modern objections.   It
appropriately describes the sort of dissatisfaction which we
feel after reading, with the modern expositions, some of
Euripides’ best known and best appreciated works.   There is
plenty of excellent material ; single scenes, or it may be all
the scenes, are wrought with undeniable and astonishing
power.   The murmurs begin when we contemplate the work
as a whole ; and then the ‘ botcher ’ can no longer be kept out
of our minds.   After all, it would seem, the thing is a patch-
work.   The excellences of the parts do not seem to subserve
any common design, nay, even are mutually repugnant.   The
author is doubtless a master of his tools, but still, to speak
familiarly, he ‘ does not know what he is driving at.’   Or at
all events we do not know, and are left with a sense of puzzle,
which is of all things the most fatal to the pleasures of art.

If, as I have heard said with too much vigour but also too much truth, 'Euripides has ceased to count,' here, where Mr Swinburne places it, is the cause or a frequent cause of the common disappointment. And we may illustrate it by the case of the *Alcestis*.

Excepting perhaps the *Andromache*, the *Alcestis* of all the plays has provoked most frequently and thoroughly this contradictory judgement of parts and whole which in modern times has been the dominant note of criticism. These two belong neither to that very small list of which we are able to say that, with no reservations or insignificant reservations, we comprehend and admire the whole work, nor to that very large list, where comprehension is so much at fault that, to say the plain truth, they have ceased to have any general importance, being relegated to the school-room and lecture-room. In the *Medea* we have scarcely any fault to find ; the faults, whatever they may be, of the *Ion* and the *Madness of Heracles*, can be left to be disputed by scholars. But the *Alcestis* cannot so be dismissed. We love Alcestis well enough to be jealous for her. The play of Euripides, so far as it is concerned with her wifely devotion, has told enough on our hearts to make us warmly sensible of what we find in it to offend us ; and the complaints which otherwise might simmer in obscurity, are stirred by this interest to vigour and fulness of expression. The more closely and impartially these complaints are examined, the more clearly it will appear that either the author of the play is, or we ourselves are, singularly unfortunate in the view we take of the subject. If modern criticism has not mistaken the matter, Euripides in the *Alcestis* shows himself at once master and tiro, master in the execution of details, tiro, or something less, in the lack of taste and judgement by which the elements are so incongruously and inharmoniously combined.

The history of Alcestis, like many other legends whose origin is doubtful or lost, had been drawn before recorded times into the great circle of religious belief whose centre was the oracle of Delphi. It is possible that Heracles, who as a semi-divine agent retains in the version known to us an

important though subordinate part, once figured as an independent deity, and that with his worship, not that of Apollo,
the story was associated at some earlier stage. But in its
existing shape it belongs to the deity of Pytho. In its general
outline it is almost too familiar for repetition. Apollo, being
condemned by Zeus to serve for a time among the herdsmen
of a mortal man, and having found in Admetus, prince of
Pherae in Thessaly, a kind and gentle master, not only
rewarded the house with vast increase of riches, but when
Admetus, yet young, was doomed by the Fates to die, obtained
their consent to accept a substitute. Alcestis, the wife of
Admetus, undertook to redeem his life by the sacrifice of her
own, and died accordingly on the day predicted. But the favour
of heaven was not to be thus frustrated of its completeness ;
for Heracles, as Apollo willed and foresaw, rescued the heroic
wife from the grave and the arms of death, and restored her
alive again to her husband. If the roots of the legend are
obscure, and descend into a stratum of thought and feeling
which can hardly now be penetrated, the religious instincts to
which it appeals as a whole are plain and universal. Accepted
in the simplicity of faith, it offers, in the first place, a comforting
answer to that question of questions with which the mind of
mortality is for ever occupied, an assurance that the spirits of
the just are in the hand of God. The form is foreign to us,
but the substance familiar and intelligible, so much so that to
believe, even for one imaginative instant, in the truth of the
history is to feel, for that instant, its profound religious importance. The virtues by which this manifestation of divine
goodness is earned,—in the husband humanity towards the
unhappy and helpless, in the wife the utmost unselfishness of
love,—are virtues to some extent of all ages and pre-eminently
of the Christian ages. If the modern attempts to deal with
the subject in dramatic and other forms have not been highly
successful, this is explained sufficiently by the absence of one
indispensable condition, a genuine or at least, if I may so put
it, a practically efficient faith on the part of the spectator and
reader. The theme is too solemn for play ; but if (to make a
bold hypothesis) it were possible for a modern audience to

retain for the space of two hours a belief in the miracle, there would be no remaining difficulty in the way of an impressive representation. At Athens in the fifth century before Christ this one impediment did not exist. The belief was a part of public religion[1]; and even those who had ceased to share it by personal conviction could have no difficulty in re-assuming it temporarily for the purpose of artistic enjoyment. In one respect the subject was peculiarly fitted for the newly-founded stage of tragedy. Aeschylus, from whose mind the new art had taken its stamp, is nowhere more profound or more attractive than when he touches such problems of life and death, such mysterious links of union between the seen and the unseen, as are involved in the history of Alcestis. If a poet of that day mis-handled the theme, it was not for want of a model. Even now with the help of Aeschylus it would not, I conceive, be impossible for Mr Swinburne to compose in English, or for Professor Jebb to compose in Greek, a drama in which the spirit of the legend should be fairly preserved and reflected. What is not easy to conceive is that now or then any man should suppose himself to have tolerably executed the design by a piece so cast and constructed as the *Alcestis* of Euripides. A brief sketch will suffice to remind the reader what the construction is, and to account for the general dissatisfaction. In order to clear the framework of the piece, we will disregard for the moment the *prologue* or *introduction*, which has its own personages and separate action ; and in the play proper we will attend only to the strictly dramatic portion, the scenes in dialogue. Of these the topics and proportions are as follows :—

Sc. i. It being the day on which Alcestis is to die, some friends of Admetus come to make enquiries of her condition. A servant describes to them her preparations for death ; she is now sinking, and desires to be brought into the open air, which is accordingly done (*vv.* 77—243 : number of verses, 167).

Sc. ii. Alcestis bids farewell to her husband and children, and receives from her husband assurances of fidelity to her

---

[1] *Alc.* 452.

memory. She dies. The corpse is carried into the house, and Admetus retires to complete the preparations for burying it (*vv.* 244—434 : 191).

Sc. iii. While he is within, his friend Heracles, travelling through Pherae, arrives at the house in the expectation of rest and refreshment. Admetus, who appears now in mourning, contrives by a false account to conceal from him the identity of the person whose funeral is about to be performed. He is thus persuaded to enter, and some of the servants are ordered to entertain him (*vv.* 476—567 : 92).

Sc. iv. The funeral is about to proceed, when Pheres, the father of Admetus, presents himself as if to take part in it. Admetus repels him, with a fierce invective against both him and his wife, Admetus' mother, for their cowardice in having refused, though advanced in years, to redeem the life of their only son, and having left the sacrifice to be made by a woman in her prime. Pheres retorts the charge : it is Admetus who, by shirking his proper destiny, has been in fact the murderer of his too devoted victim. The theme, notwithstanding the interference of the friends, is pursued on both sides in a duel of taunts, after which Pheres retires, and the funeral procession sets forth (*vv.* 606—740 : 135).

Sc. v. A man-servant, coming from the house, describes with indignation the behaviour of Heracles at his meal, his indifference to the decencies of a house in mourning, un-seasonable exactions, noise, and drunkenness. Heracles follows; he lectures the servant on the certainty of death, and presses him to drink ; the servant is provoked into disclosing the deception practised by Admetus ; Heracles, shocked and horrified, declares his intention of rescuing the deceased from death, and is directed by the servant to the grave (747—860 : 114).

Sc. vi. Admetus returns accompanied by his friends. His despair, repentance, and self-reproach (861—961 : 101).

Sc. vii. Heracles returns, leading Alcestis veiled. He pretends that she is a slave, won by him as a prize in an athletic contest which fell in his way as he was setting out. He proposes that Admetus shall keep her for him till he returns from his journey. Admetus reluctantly consents, and Alcestis is unveiled. Tableau and conclusion (1006—1158 : 153).

Such is the play which was offered (we are to understand) by Euripides as the best he could do by way of presenting in the forms of the stage the death and resurrection of Alcestis. It would be strange indeed if, while praising him for the dramatic skill displayed in the separate scenes, his critics could have refrained from murmuring at the discord between theme and treatment which characterizes the whole conception. If my object were to make out a case, it would be easy to quote respectable authorities who have expressed this objection with acrimony; but it will be safer to cite the gentle and apologetic complaint of Paley, whose merits and even defects as a commentator made him an excellent reflector of average opinion :—

As for the characters in the play, that of Alcestis must be acknow-ledged to be pre-eminently beautiful....But, if we except the heroine of the piece, the rest are hardly well-drawn, or, at least, pleasingly por-trayed. The selfish Pheres, the unfilial Admetus, the boisterous Hercules, are not in themselves proper characters for tragedy; but then they serve to set off and bring out in relief the beauties which the poet has laboured to concentrate upon one person....The dispute between Admetus and Pheres is calculated, as Hermann observes, and as was very probably designed, to please a contentious and law-loving audience. The poet might perhaps, had he pleased, have represented Admetus in a more amiable point of view. But he preferred to take the legend as he found it; and we must in fairness admit that the faults are those inherent in the subject itself rather than in the poet's manner of treating it.

It should be noted that when Paley describes Admetus, Pheres, and Heracles as 'not well-drawn,' he means, as appears by the correction 'not pleasingly portrayed,' that they are not drawn well for the general effect of the picture. Regarded merely as studies from life they are drawn only too well. And when he says that they are 'not proper characters for tragedy,' he must be taken to mean that they are not proper for *this* tragedy, for a play on this particular subject, since no one could dispute that characters equally unpleasing in them-selves, equally 'selfish,' 'unfilial,' and 'boisterous,' are to be found in dramas and even in tragedies of which the total effect is nevertheless both pleasing and consistent. And if we ask why then these traits are objectionable here, the answer is first, that they are *useless to the conduct of the story*, and secondly that, according to an instinct which not without reason we assume to be universal, they are *repugnant to the solemnity of the topic*. You cannot make a good play, nor anything fit to be called a play, out of incidents which have no moral or necessary connexion, no other connexion in short than that they *might* succeed one another in the way represented ; and you ought not to make a trifle out of a theme so full of tenderness and awe as the death and resurrection of Alcestis. We will consider the scheme for a moment in these two points of view, and will confine our attention for convenience to the scenes numbered fourth and fifth, upon which the objections may be concentrated. It should be noted that these two scenes form between them a full fourth part of the action, and that a survey of the whole work would only confirm our impressions.

Of these two scenes then in particular we have to say, in obedience to the general verdict, that they are mechanically useless and aesthetically repulsive. It will be seen that these charges, though separable, are in reality two sides of the same. An incident not agreeable in itself becomes pardonable and even acceptable, if it contributes essentially to the progress of the story. But in the two examples before us, the altercation with Pheres and the intoxication of Heracles, it is not the least curious part of the author's offence, though it is commonly the less insisted on, that they contribute nothing to the movement of the drama. The progress of events towards the proposed conclusion is not forwarded, arrested, or in any way explained by the fact that Admetus and his father regard one another with a contempt which they succeed in making not altogether incomprehensible, and that neither of them has decency enough to refrain from waging a battle of taunts over the corpse of the wife and daughter, and in the presence of vainly expostulating friends. The altercation leaves us, so far as the story is concerned, exactly where we were. Of the next scene indeed this cannot be said, for here the story does take a step; Heracles discovers the deception practised upon him with regard to the identity of the corpse. But to make this discovery it was not requisite that he should get very drunk, in circumstances which make such behaviour not merely contemptible but grossly offensive, and thus expose himself to the scorn and indignation, the merited scorn and merited indignation, as most people have thought and will continue to think, of the servant who waits at his table. To produce the disclosure was not a difficulty needing to be cut in this heroic fashion. On the contrary the difficulty, if any, was to keep Heracles so long in ignorance of the truth ; but neither on this side nor on the other is there anything in the dramatic requirements of the situation to account for the manners which he is made to exhibit.

Mechanically therefore these scenes are useless ; and considered aesthetically, as exhibitions of character, they are worse. The finale of the play consists entirely of a dialogue between Heracles and Admetus, and must depend therefore largely for its effect upon the impression of these two personages which in the course of the piece has been stamped on the mind of the spectator or reader. Admetus is there to figure as a man who for his virtue receives from heaven a miraculous boon, perhaps the most astonishing and affecting which human imagination can conceive. Heracles is to figure as the chosen agent, himself something more than man, by whom the divine purpose is carried into effect. As the examination of the finale itself will fall more fitly in another place, we will for the moment assume, what the reader who may have the scene in mind will not be inclined to dispute, that the interlocutors in it do little to clear themselves of any untoward association which they may have previously contracted. What then, we have to ask, is contributed to the final effect by the reflected light of the episodes which we are now considering? That Admetus is not more but less likely to obtain sympathy after his encounter with Pheres, Heracles not more but less likely to appear a worthy deputy of divine power after his interview with the manservant, are propositions which may be defended when they have been denied ; and I do not think that the apologists for either, to whom we will come in due course, have gone so far. In the case of Heracles the point is particularly important, because it is only in the fifth scene that we are permitted to make acquaintance with him, before he appears finally as the conqueror of Death.   In the third scene, which exhibits his first arrival, his part is secondary and reveals little of him.   The benefit of the fifth scene is entirely his own.

How strong and inevitable is the persuasion that to compromise the moral dignity of Admetus and Heracles is to strike at the heart of the story, and that by these powerful scenes, as well as by much else in the play, their dignity is compromised to a degree which, as the author should have seen, is incompatible with the purpose that he professes, appears in nothing more plainly than in the efforts which have been frequently made to defend the character of one or the other; laudable efforts, as proceeding on the assumption that what is patent to us is not likely to have been invisible to Euripides, but as appears to me with the standing majority, desperate nevertheless.   In saying that these defences are unsupported by the majority, I must make an exception of one plea put forward for Admetus which among modern critics has had nearly if not quite universal support. Admetus (it is said), though we may give up as insufficiently ' amiable ' his attitude as a husband and as a son, is redeemed by his generosity as a host.   The hospitality which in the midst of his grief he extends to Heracles, must be set off against his demerits, and leaves an adequate balance in his favour. We will postpone for the present this plea of ' confession and avoidance' and consider those answers which directly traverse the indictment.

I mention only to put aside as here irrelevant all excuses offered not for the *dramatis personae* but for the author, as for instance that since the play, it appears, stood last among the four exhibited together in the same year, it was designed to replace the ordinary 'satyric drama,' which accounts for the prevalence of elements unsuitable to tragedy.   Manifestly this is only the accusation itself in another form. If the author wanted something in a light style, it was his business to select a theme suitable for it[1]. Or again (this appears in Paley as above cited), that the unamiable characters are foils for Alcestis. In that case, since Alcestis takes part in only one scene, the work is composed mainly of 'foil'; and indeed we are forbidden by the author himself, as we shall see hereafter, to suppose that the character of 'the heroine' is meant to be the dominant interest. Nor again would it affect our present question if we were to admit, what according to Paley we must in fairness admit, "that the faults are those inherent in the subject itself rather than in the poet's manner of treating it." Admit it however we neither must nor can; for it is refuted by Paley himself when he says (after Hermann) that "the dispute between Admetus and Pheres was very probably designed to please a contentious and law-loving audience." Whatever be the value of this excuse (if it is meant for an excuse and not an aggravation, for this is not very clear), it assumes, what is surely certain, that the dramatist himself invented the scene in question. Neither this, nor the intoxication of Heracles, is "inherent in the subject." Both incidents must have been chosen, if not engrafted, by the poet, and he is directly responsible for the effect. At any rate all these are defences for the author, not for the *personae*, and therefore are not now in view.

Coming then directly to the point, and taking first the case of Admetus—is it the fact that the son of Pheres and husband of Alcestis, as presented by Euripides, appears as a selfish, unattractive, and rather contemptible person; and may we assume—for this of course is material—that such would be the view of the Athenians in the time of the author? The first part of the question, about which there has been

---

[1] Such as the legend of *Death and Sisyphus*, on which a 'satyric drama' was composed by Aeschylus, and which seems to have been exactly suited for treatment as a grotesque. Whether the legend of Alcestis could be so treated satisfactorily appears to me more than doubtful, nor does it matter, since Euripides at all events has made no attempt to treat it so. His picture is purely realistic (to the utmost extent which the Greek stage permitted) and must be defensible as realism or not at all.

little dispute, has perhaps been set at rest by Browning in *Balaustion's Adventure*. Browning, for reasons which will present themselves later, was or conceived himself more free than most readers have felt to express, without abating his respect for the play or the author, the sentiments excited in modern minds by the behaviour of Admetus not only in the encounter with Pheres but also at the death-bed of Alcestis. To us at least it appears 'childish' (the word is Browning's) in a man who has deliberately accepted the sacrifice of another life for his own, to spend the moments of parting in beseeching his substitute 'not to abandon him' and 'asking for impossibilities.' And it is worth notice, as bearing on the probable opinion of the Greeks, that this shrewd comment, 'asking for impossibilities,' is furnished by Euripides himself[1]. To us it appears that one who in such a position blusters about the inconceivable things that he 'would have done, had they been possible,' to rescue his substitute from death, must be stupefied by 'passionate egoism' (the phrase is George Eliot's), if he cannot perceive that he is making the worst of his delicate case, like the coward who pretends to dignify retreat by muttering about 'another time.' And as between him and his father we hold that, whatever might be said in decent privacy for the view that the elder man 'has had his time' and ought, for the greatest happiness of the greatest number, to have accepted death in the place of his son, the son must be wanting in sense, stupefied as before by passionate egoism, not to apprehend without the humiliation of experiment that to argue in this sense with his father is to make himself ridiculous, and to attack his father upon this ground is logical suicide. Moreover we think that, apart from such particular breaches of taste and sense, the act of Admetus in accepting, much more in soliciting, the sacrifice of his wife, could be dignified and justified only if it were his duty to live, if his life were important to others, and much more important than hers, which nevertheless Euripides does not show us, or indeed give us reason to suppose. To all this, as representing the

---

[1] *v.* 202 : cf. 250, 388 etc.

modern view, the reader will probably assent or, if he should doubt, may fix his sentiments by the perusal of *Balaustion's Adventure*. But it may still be maintained that such were not the sentiments with which Euripides had to count; and such is the contention recently developed, much more fully and positively than by previous critics, by Mr Way[1], who is on every ground entitled to respectful consideration.

According to Mr Way " it is certain that the modern view is diametrically opposed to that of the Athenian audience. In their eyes (1) Admetus was a noble character : (2) he was in the right in respect to the *motif* and incidents of the play : (3) he reaped the just reward of the good man." Now if it is certain that such would be the view of the Athenian audience, the opinion of Athens, that is to say, in the time of Euripides, upon what society, we must ask, did the poet model the public opinion of his imaginary Pherae and his imaginary Iolcus? For strangely enough, it is certain that in these places the prevalent view was again diametrically opposite, differing not perceptibly from the modern. As to what would be thought in Iolcus, the original home of Alcestis, we have the undisputed assertion of Pheres[2] :—

> I go: her murderer will bury her.
> Thou shalt yet answer for it to her kin.
> Surely Akastos is no more a man,
> If he of thee claim not his sister's blood.

Pheres is not an admirable old man; he has, as Browning puts it, a truly paternal resemblance to Admetus, he is Admetus aged into cynicism; but he is not a fool. If it be true that in those days, " failing the substitute who shirked his duty," that is to say, Pheres, "Alcestis would be regarded as simply fulfilling hers in yielding her life," how is it that this very Pheres can threaten Admetus with the vengeance of her friends, whose anger must on that hypothesis have been directed altogether against himself? How does Admetus miss this obvious retort, and answer only with irrelevant reiteration of his own implacable hatred? And if it be said

---

[1] *Translation of Euripides*, Vol. I. App. A.
[2] *v.* 730. The translations here are Mr Way's.

that Pheres is blinded by selfishness, and the family of Alcestis not impartial—though as between father and son they may, it would seem, judge as fairly as any one else—we may turn from Iolcus to Pherae and hear, in a cooler moment, the testimony and confession of Admetus[1].

> All this within: but from the world without
> Shall bridals of Thessalians chase me : throngs
> Where women gossip; and I shall not bear
> On those companions of my wife to look.
> And, if a foe I have,—

We pause to note that this tone of emphatic hypothesis is introduced, unconsciously and instinctively, by the translator: "whoever happens to be hostile to me" says the Greek :—

> thus shall he scoff:
> " Lo, there who basely liveth—dared not die,
> " But whom he wedded gave, a coward's ransom,
> " And 'scaped from Hades. Count ye him a man?
> " He hates his parents, though himself was loth
> " To die !" Such ill report, besides my griefs,
> Shall mine be. Ah, what profit is to live,
> O friends, in evil fame, in evil plight?

Such is the reception which Admetus expects from his world; and his own particular friends, who are present for the very purpose of consoling him, dare not, or at least do not, say a word to relieve his fears. But his fears are idle, if to the average Pheraean Admetus would still be "a noble character." The tongue of malice is impotent against public opinion. Pherae therefore held the modern view, not a view diametrically opposite; and if Pherae, why not Athens?

Very clear indeed should be the testimony which is to over-balance such passages as these. The evidence adduced is the old evidence in favour of Admetus' hospitality, "the highest social virtue recognized by a Greek."

The hospitable man embodied for them the virtues, not only of the modern philanthropist, but also of the enlightened diplomatist: he established and maintained friendly relations with other states, gaining for his city allies, and for her people friends and protectors in foreign lands, and

---

[1] *v.* 950.

that in days when without such, not only was travel perilous, but even commerce was difficult and precarious....Conjugal affection shrank into insignificance beside such a trait....It was his duty to his country to neglect no means of prolonging his usefulness.

The nature and merit of Admetus' hospitality, as actually exercised towards Heracles in the play, will be considered hereafter. Here we will only remark that the public benefit of his function as host would have been more clearly perceived, and the sympathy of the audience on this ground better secured, if it had obtained some notice upon the stage; if for example the gratitude of Pherae had been alleged by his friends as likely to protect him from the obloquy which he anticipates. The statements of Mr Way's paragraph have much truth as generalities about Greek life, but when we ask whether the action and character of Admetus were such as to bring him within the benefit of the doctrine, nothing explicit can be produced, nothing but "considerations which presuppose" the paramount value of his life. Surely this is unsatisfactory.

But although Mr Way, so far as I can judge, has by no means proved that an Athenian jury would have acquitted his client, he does not leave the matter where it was. In the first place he has pointed out with desirable precision what the Admetus of Euripides lacks. The paragraph above cited indicates excellently the sort of beneficence by which an Admetus might have been justified in the eyes of a Greek audience, and which Aeschylus or Sophocles would, we may presume, have made prominent. That Euripides omits to notice or provide such a trait is among the things which show either that he has ill-executed his design, or that we misconceive it. And further, as against Browning, who is cited as representing the enemies of Admetus, Mr Way assuredly has a case, though not perhaps exactly on the issue which he puts foremost. *Balaustion's Adventure* involves two propositions about the Euripidean Admetus; first, that he is not exhibited for our admiration, and secondly, that Euripides deserves no censure for not making him admirable. Mr Way contends formally against the first, not, as I think, with

success ; but his statement implies a hypothetical decision,
that *if* Euripides has not made Admetus admirable, Euripides
must be excused, if at all, by some other method than that of
Browning.   And here I am entirely with Mr Way.   If in
reading *Balaustion's Adventure* we are able to forget that,
according to the legend and according to Euripides, as
Mr Way properly reminds us, Admetus was a favourite of
the gods, specially chosen to receive the reward of virtue,
if his want of what is commonly thought virtue comes at last
to seem no drawback but rather an advantage to the total
effect, that is because in the joint production of Euripides
and Balaustion Admetus becomes a mere foil, and his whole
story scarcely more than an opportunity, for displaying the
grandeur of the fair collaborator's hero, *Heracles.*   Here
therefore we will abandon the husband as apparently indefensible, and consider the case offered by Browning on
behalf of the other incriminated personage, the semi-divine
deliverer.

It is, if I may say so without impertinence, very much to
the credit of Browning's poetical and dramatic instinct, that
he should have fixed so decisively upon *Heracles* as the true
nodus of the literary problem presented by the *Alcestis* ; and
Balaustion's Adventure is a striking proof how instructive may
be the criticism of artist by artist, even when it results, as it
is not unlikely to do, in a thorough-going recomposition of
the subject.   Browning, it is needless to say, was no more
likely than Goethe to repose complacently in such a theory of
Euripides as satisfied the vigorous but narrow and unimagina-
tive mind of Schlegel and has infected too many who were
capable of knowing better.   The conclusion at which Balaustion arrives[1] is the assumption from which Browning started,
that the *Alcestis* is the work of a true artist and a man of
sense, justifiable as a whole upon ordinary principles, like the
work of Sophocles or another.   It must have then some
general ruling purpose.   From the tradition of commentaries
he borrowed the further assumption that this general purpose
is to illustrate the religious legend.   And he saw, or rather

[1] p. 110, ed. 1889.

felt—for I do not of course mean that he said such a thing to himself or put it consciously as a step in an argument—he acted, let us say rather, on the truth which he perceived instinctively, that, given these premisses, a noble, beautiful, and thoroughly admirable *Heracles* is an indispensable necessity. With a selfish, unmanly, unwise, and half-contemptible Admetus it would just be possible—Browning has shown this—to present the legend of Alcestis so as still to preserve the religious hypothesis. The gods, it might be said, though the theology is not very Hellenic, are merciful to the repentant; and the Euripidean Admetus repents, if it be repentance to perceive your folly, as heartily as could be desired. On the whole he might do. But that Heracles should be exposed to any just contempt, Heracles the son of the highest god, the minister of life, privileged to wrestle victoriously with the power of darkness and corruption, to bring quick out of the grave a body upon which the mortal change had actually been accomplished, that Heracles should be semi-comic, or comic at all in the least degree—this seemed, as it is, intolerable, a thing as repugnant to the organic laws of art as a centaur or a chimaera to those of nature. Accordingly since the Heracles of Euripides, as the expositors agree, is in fact semi-comic and liable to much just contempt, Browning simply made another, enveloping and dressing, literally as well as figuratively, the original man in robes, trappings, and appurtenances, material and moral, of which in the Greek play there is not the least suggestion, until once at least, so complete is the transformation, he has to be unwrapped again as it were, before the words of Euripides can find their way to his mouth.

The thing is done (with what perfect unconsciousness and good faith is proved by the audacity of it) by means of copious stage-directions and interpolated remarks. The form of Browning's poem, as will be remembered, is a recitation of the play, with occasional comments by the reciter. The comments are largely pictorial, explaining how the personages looked and moved, replacing in short the action. It is noticeable that at one time Browning seems to have felt,

or come near to feeling, the peril of such a form, and the
temptation of the poet-commentator to abound in his own
sense, instead of following his author.   There is an unpleasant,
suspicious tartness in the reply of Balaustion to a certain
" critic and whippersnapper," who at a previous recitation
seems to have objected to her use of such phrases as " Then
a fear flitted o'er the wife's white face " on the ground that no
fear could be seen to flit over a mask[1].   So silly a pedant
was really not worth quoting, and had better have been
answered, if at all, without needless quibbling upon the true
import of the word *poetry*, as signifying "a power that *makes*."
If the whippersnapper had rejoined to this that Euripides and
Balaustion are not one " maker " but two, two of a trade, and
liable to disagree, he would have said something much to the
purpose ; and possibly it was a hint of this kind, lurking in
his ill-stated objection, which caused Balaustion to note and
resent it.

However it must be confessed that Balaustion not only
makes very well, but also in general remembers her office and
fairly makes to order.   Now and then she paraphrases in
narrative instead of reproducing, and when she does, it may
be taken for a note that the original here contains something
worth particular attention ; but such changes are rare.   Her
chief activity is in additions, and here she mainly goes by her
text.   Not only the visible accessories, such as the bow of
Apollo, the black robe of Admetus in mourning, and the
wreath of Heracles after his feast, are warranted by the
dramatist, but in things less directly perceptible by a reader
Balaustion is found right upon reference.   For instance,

> that hard dry pressure to the point,
> Word slow pursuing word in monotone,

does really appear in the language of the dying Alcestis, and
merits, if it does not demand, Balaustion's sympathetic explanation.   Or again, the leap of Pheres out of decorum into
nature under the unexpected attack of Admetus is lawfully
prefaced by this admirable simile :—

[1] p. 17.

> He came content the ignoble word, for him,
> Should lurk still in the blackness of each breast,
> As sleeps the water-serpent half surmised:
> Not brought up to the surface at a bound,
> By one touch of the idly-probing spear.

The vivid, coloured, Miltonic image, though not found in the scene as spoken, fits the words like a glove, and properly compensates for the loss of appropriate action. But when the reciter comes to Heracles, and wherever she has him in view, her invention soars regardless. Without a hint from Euripides, and even against his command, masses of mythology and theology, scenery and portraiture, are rolled in; motives are imputed, facts bluffed, and the whole business of exposition carried on with the fascinating iniquity of a feminine partizan.

Immediately upon his entrance[1], and before he has said anything but " Pheraean friends," Balaustion stops the action to assure us that in his tone, bearing, and appearance you perceived 'the friend of man,' 'the Helper,' 'the God,' as her style is :—

> Himself, o' the threshold, sent his voice on first
> To herald all that human and divine
> I' the weary happy face of him,—half God
> Half man, which made the god-part God the more.

And as soon as he has asked whether Admetus is within, she stops again to point out

> all the mightiness
> At labour in the limbs that for man's sake
> Laboured and meant to labour their life long.

In both places her worship flows over the page, and many other eloquent pages are given to repeating and re-enforcing this first impression; so that as long as we keep to the *Adventure*, it scarcely matters what exactly is said or done in the brief scenes by a personage so stupendous. Like Pindar's Hiero, 'whatsoever he lets drop, falls great because from him.' But if the enchanted reader seeks Euripides, for the pleasure of seeing how his *making* has *made* all this, he finds with

---

[1] p. 49.

dismay that it is pure Balaustion, every word of it; the 'God'
and 'the half-God,' the 'great voice,' 'weary happy face,'
'happy weary laugh,' 'love of men,' 'many grandnesses,' 'arm
which had slain the snake,' 'lion's hide,' 'interval 'twixt fight
and fight again,' 'snatched repose,' 'dust o' the last encounter,'
'breathing space for man's sake,' 'unimaginable shaft,' 'plate-
mail of a monster,' 'pest o' the marish,' 'world-weary God,'
'solemn draught of true religious wine,' 'grand benevolence,'
'the God surmounting the man,' 'tree-like growth through
pain to joy,' and all the rest of it ; every thing put in which
Euripides might have attached to the conception of Heracles,
but has in fact resolutely and consistently left out.

The labours, for example, the unflinching incessant labours
on behalf of humanity ! Balaustion recalls them to us incessantly ; they are Heracles ; he personifies the great love,
'careless of self where others may be helped,' which reproves
by its mere presence the littleness of Admetus, his counsellors,
servants, and the rest of the crew.   In Heracles everything
must be praised, anything forgiven.   If he says, 'Is Admetus
at home?' you must revere him : think of his labours !   If he
drinks till he 'howls discordance,' you must not call him a sot,
nor let any one do so unrebuked.   Poor man, he wanted it ;
think of his labours ! Well then, if we are to think so much
of them, why do we get no help from Euripides ?   Certainly
the myths of Heracles offer abundant material for presenting
him as the friend of humanity and reliever of the distressed.
Many of them, such as the slaying of the lion in Nemea or
the serpent in Lerna, were adapted if not designed for the
very purpose; and Euripides, like Balaustion here, can find and
use them, *when he wants them*.   Why did he pass them over
in the *Alcestis* ?   The 'labours of Heracles,' in the sense put
upon the phrase by Balaustion here and by Euripides *elsewhere*, his services to humanity, are in this play ignored
completely ; and nothing is said by any one to show that for
his previous career he enjoys or deserves gratitude any more
than an ordinary man.   The enterprise upon which he is
bound at the time of the action is to seize, on behalf of
Eurystheus king of Tiryns, a famous team of four horses

belonging to Diomede the Thracian. He expects a fight, and is ready to kill Diomede, if necessary. No benefit is intended or can accrue from the achievement to anyone except Eurystheus; nor is it pretended that Eurystheus is prosecuting a right. The matter lies altogether between two fierce chieftains, one of whom covets the property of the other; and the aggressor has the advantage of commanding the services of Heracles. Courage and gallantry he certainly shows, but as 'a friend of humanity' he must be ranked with Hawkins or Sforza. The visitors of Admetus, who know his name and presumably his history, treat him without distinguishing particularity; and from Admetus we learn only that Heracles upon various occasions has received him hospitably at Argos, which is satisfactory but scarcely sublime. What impression of his character an unflattering and uninterested observer might derive from his present employment, as he describes it, and from previous performances (of the same kind so far as appears) to which he alludes, we hear from the servant commissioned by Admetus to make him comfortable :—

> And so here am I, helping make at home
> A guest, some fellow ripe for wickedness,
> *Robber or pirate!*

It is curious that Balaustion, so prompt in observing the superhuman way in which Heracles says 'Yes,' 'No,' and 'How do you do?' should have heard this pointed remark without any reflexion more precise than broadly to label the speaker a 'creature' and condescendingly dismiss him as one who 'had been right if not so wrong.'

As it is with the 'labours,' so it is with all the divine attributes accumulated upon the hero in Browning's enlarged and amended version. They are not to be found in the *Alcestis* of Euripides. And to prove this absence not accidental we have only to compare the author's *Madness of Heracles*, where the moral nobility of the hero as the friend of man really is a part of the hypothesis, and all the flowers of Balaustion's ornamentation, labours and trophies, generous toil and grateful world, can be illustrated *ad libitum*. In fact what Browning has done is just to take the Heracles of the one play and put him, to make a figure of suitable height, on the top of his namesake in the other, 'the God surmounting the man' (as Balaustion says), with what stifling compression of the unlucky 'man' we will see in a moment. To set out the whole detail would be tedious; but the reader with the three poems before him can easily satisfy himself.

Down to his very dress the Heracles of Balaustion is not the personage of the *Alcestis* but of the *Madness*. It is she, not Euripides, who tells us that when he goes forth to encounter Death, he picks up his lion-skin and leaves behind his club; she who by other allusions takes care to keep before our eyes these consecrated symbols of beneficent power. The arrows too, the 'unimaginable shaft,' she manages to get in by a side-glance; and it seems a mere accident that these also are not brought upon the stage. Now of course from the nature of the case it cannot be proved directly that Heracles in the *Alcestis* does not wear the spoil of Nemea, does not carry the club which smote the giants, or the bow which put an end to the outrages of Nessus. No one notes their absence; it were impossible, except in a burlesque, that any one should. But neither is there any trace of their presence; which of itself proves that the author on this occasion attached no importance to them, and when taken in connexion with the corresponding omission of all the mythical and doctrinal matter associated with them, goes far to prove that he did not allow them to be used. In the *Madness* all are mentioned, and not only mentioned but brought tragically into play. In the *Alcestis* the skin of the lion would be as irrelevant as the lion itself. If worn on the stage (which I do not believe) it must have been merely as a conventional mark of the person; and the author, who wrote, we must remember, for a public of readers as well as of spectators, has done his best to protect a reader at all events from the intrusion.

How hopeless is the well-meant effort to deify a swash-buckler appears when Balaustion ceases to describe and begins to quote. She indeed, like a good girl, having given her heart sticks at nothing; and since Browning—with a poet poetizing it could not be otherwise—has given his heart to her, we, so long as we keep in their company, can perhaps believe what they tell us. But go to Euripides, and the charm is lost. Here is the behaviour of the hero at table, as described by Euripides—Mr Way, not Balaustion, shall recite, as it will save the trouble of noting a few little coquetries of hers :—

> He first, albeit he saw my master mourning,
> Entered and passed the threshold unashamed ;
> Then nowise courteously received the fare
> Found with us, though our woeful plight he knew,
> But what we brought not, hectoring bade us bring.
> The ivy-cup uplifts he in his hands,
> And swills the darkling mother's fiery blood,
> Till the wine's flame enwrapped him, heating him.
> Then did he wreathe his head with myrtle-spray,
> Dissonant-howling,

and so on. It seems scarcely credible, when we are not under Browning's control, that what Balaustion infers from this description is the peevishness of the servant (whom without warrant she talks of as 'old') and the magnanimity of the guest. She is indeed a little hard-pushed by the tone which his 'grand benevolence' adopts when he presently appears, and she feels the need of a fresh make-up :—

> Then smiled the mighty presence, all one smile,
> *And no touch more of the world-weary god*,
> Through the brief respite.

No touch indeed ! 'The Helper' has recovered so thoroughly that he 'helps' the poor servitor (whom he knows and sees to be deeply afflicted by the recent bereavement) with a sort of maudlin sermon, asking him 'whether he is aware' that all men are mortal, and leading to the moral that one should drink and kiss the girls. This, thinks Balaustion, is the way to 'soften surliness' and 'bridle bad humours.' Such idolatrous devotion is beyond the reach of argument.

The truth is that the Heracles of the *Alcestis*, though he has his good qualities, is as far from moral sublimity as he well could be. Nor is he by any means strong in religion, presenting in this respect an instructive contrast to his friend

Admetus, whose piety is his *forte*. Their diversity produces an awkward clash of opinion, and puts the politeness of Admetus to a trial, when Heracles will not see that a person doomed to death by prophetic fiat is as good as dead already[1]. The tone he takes would be simply cruel, unless intended to imply doubts about the weight of the prediction; and it is clear that if he had known (which he does not) that an actual day had been named for Alcestis to die on, he would still not have shared the absolute assurance of Admetus and his household, that on that day she would inevitably die. Much in the same way the old Pheraean, the leader of the Chorus, makes no impression on Heracles whatever by telling him (what he has never heard) that the horses of Diomede, the horses which he proposes to steal, eat human flesh. Heracles derides the story, and when the other persists, parries him with the sneering question, ' And whose son does the breeder *brag himself*?' ' Son of Ares.' ' Still my hard fate! I have fought two *sons of Ares* already[2]!' The attitude is intelligible and intelligent; but it certainly suggests a suspicion that, however he might feel in moments of peculiar mental and physical stimulus[3], this cool-headed fighter must often have known misgivings about the superhuman parentage attributed to himself.

But perhaps the most striking revelation of Heracles is given us in the story told by and about himself to account for his possession of the disguised Alcestis and his return with her to the house of Admetus. Here it is—Mr Way is more exact, for Balaustion as usual drags in the ' labours,' but somehow a little too weighty—in the version of Browning :—

> Take and keep for me
> This woman, till I come thy way again,
> Driving before me, having killed the king
> O' the Bistones, that drove of Thrakian steeds:
> In such case, give the woman back to me!
> But should I fall—as fall I fain would not,
> Seeing I hope to prosper and return—
> Then I bequeath her as thy household slave.

[1] *v*. 521 ff.   [2] *v*. 494 ff.   [3] *v*. 839.

She came into my hands with good hard toil!
For what find I, when started on my course,
But certain people, a whole country-side,
Holding a wrestling-bout? *as good to me*
As a new labour:

—for which read simply 'worth exertion'—

                    whence I took, and here
Come keeping with me this, the victor's prize.
For such as conquered in the easy work[1]
Gained horses which they drove away: and such
As conquered in the harder,—those who boxed
And wrestled,—cattle; and to crown the prize
A woman followed. Chancing as I did,
Base were it to forego this fame and gain!
Well, as I said, I trust her to thy care:
No woman I have kidnapped, understand!
But good hard toil has done it: here I come!
Some day, who knows? even thou wilt praise the feat.

Such is Heracles as he paints himself, delineating the part
from his knowledge of himself and of other people's opinion
about him. It should be remembered that Admetus, as
Heracles now knows, is in the first agony of a widower, and
that Heracles has many other friends in Pherae. Further
comment seems superfluous: and if, dismissing the question
how Euripides came to make him such, we ask simply what
he is, we need not after this passage hesitate about the answer.
He is drawn from a type well known in the age of the poet,
the athlete-adventurer, the class of which a specially brilliant
specimen was his supposed descendant the Heracleid Dorieus
of Rhodes, the high-born ill-starred enemy whom the
Athenians, having taken him prisoner, spared and liberated
for his personal beauty and Olympian renown. The story of
Dorieus presents the romance of such a career; the portrait of
Heracles in the *Alcestis*, omitting for the moment his encounter with Death, offers the prose of it. Such persons, the
less well-endowed or less fortunate members of the aristo-
cracies formerly hymned by Pindar, were driven, by an
education which fitted them for nothing else, to pick up what

---

[1] More exactly 'nimble work,' *i.e.* running.

they could in a life of shifty wandering service, sometimes rising as in the case of Dorieus to the level of the *condottiere*, more often probably sinking, like our Heracles, to something nearer the bravo. The Athenians, notwithstanding their generosity to the Rhodian, whose singularly splendid misfortunes marked him as a proper object for a theatrical act of generosity, were by no means in the latter part of the fifth century indiscriminating cultivators of the athlete in general, and Euripides in particular had no great love for them. What he has given us in his Heracles is a portrait drawn, as it would seem, without flattery and without caricature—a high-born athlete-soldier of Argos, engaged in the service of the 'despot' Eurystheus. All that he does, still excepting his miraculous achievement in the case of Alcestis, fits perfectly together and exhibits the man. The virtues of his breeding, or at least some of them, he has and retains; he is brave, warm-hearted, sensitive in that sort of honour or pride which dislikes to have made a blunder, to lie under an obligation, or in any way to cut a poor figure. When master of himself, and so long as he is under the eye of those whom he respects, he can behave like the 'gentilhomme' that he is. He is shrewd, but not quick-witted. In the pursuit of his calling he is as free from scruple as from fear, perfectly ready to rob and to murder without any other reason than the interest of his master for the time being; and if occasion offered, he would rob for his own appetite (we have his own word for it) with as little remorse. Living irregularly and by shifts, he is greedy of gain, though not poor, and ready to stoop for it. In his personal tastes he is jovial, sensual, and coarse; and when he feels himself at liberty, he is liable to degrade himself by rudeness and even gross indecency. He will be sorry for it afterwards. Such in brief is the semi-divine deliverer.

To palliate the ruin which this bull-headed apostle makes among the Delphian porcelain of the legend, by clapping on him the mask of an angel, and then crying to us, whenever he plunges into the pots, 'But look at his face!' is an expedient practicable only for an expositor like Browning, who incorporates the work of his author in original poetry of his

own. What Browning really shows us, with regard to
Heracles, is not that the Euripidean personage is fit for the
story, but that we ought to be more moved, than some would
seem to be, by his extreme and incredible unfitness. 'He
cannot,' says Browning virtually, 'be such as you suppose!'
He is nevertheless just that; but to say so is to give Browning
only half an answer. 'I meant of course,' he might rejoin,
'that if he is such, you, before you pretend to understand
Euripides, are bound to say why.' And to that no answer is
at present offered. It does not help to call him a 'comic
element': let him be comic or tragic, that does not matter;
the question is, 'Is he relevant?'

So far as I am aware, no one has yet essayed in this case
the suggestion of a difference between ancient and modern
sentiment. It has not been contended that though, from the
modern English point of view, to get very drunk in the house
of a gentleman who has treated you with marked courtesy
seems an odd preparation for wrestling victoriously with the
Angel of Death, an ancient Athenian would not have been
displeased. For the satisfaction however of possible doubts,
it may be said that beyond all question the ancient Athenians
must have been far more displeased. Even to us, among
whom (to our shame be it said) it is still widely held that
drunkenness is in itself highly amusing, and always excusable
(considering the temptation) unless very gross, even to us the
behaviour of Heracles seems not easily pardonable. But the
abuse of wine was not a popular vice among the Greeks ; and
they were not disposed to make light of it. They reserved
the main benefit of their indulgence, as we ours, for the
excesses to which they were addicted. A comic tale like
Pickwick, in which the male characters, good and bad alike,
are sopping and swilling daily and hourly throughout, would
probably have been read by Aristophanes with the same
sense of 'allowance for the ethics of the age,' which we make
in the case of the *Lysistrata*. An Athenian could of course,
under suitable circumstances, enjoy the grotesqueness of a
drunkard as well as of a glutton. For example, the figure of
Heracles himself, in his character of 'strong man' and huge

feeder, was familiarly so exhibited on the comic stage; but
then he was exhibited *as a grotesque*, intentionally contemptible. But that will not help the *Alcestis*, where the
question that arises is this, 'Can a man make himself tipsy,
and this at a time and place specially unfit, *without deserving
contempt?*' It is certain that an Athenian would have been
not more but less likely than an Englishman to answer this
question in the affirmative.

Before we part finally with Balaustion's encomiums upon
Heracles, we should perhaps give a separate word to one of
her *ex parte* judgements, which proceeds on an assumption
not peculiar to Browning, but mistaken nevertheless and
injurious to the play. We are invited by Balaustion more
than once to contrast the bravery of Heracles, who 'held his
life out in his hand for any man to take,' with the cowardice
of other persons, the Chorus and the servants, who did not
save the much-praised Alcestis by taking her place as victim
of the Fates, and thus redeeming the king at less expense.
The old men of Pherae, says she, are ashamed to tell Heracles
on his arrival that the queen is dead, for fear of his scornful
'Why did you let her die?' Now as between Heracles and
the others this distinction (saving her respect) is plainly
untenable, acceptable only to the blindness of her partiality.
If the Pheraean friends of Admetus were really admissible as
substitutes, then so was Heracles. He knew the stipulation
of the Fates, and knew that Alcestis had undertaken to fulfil
it; he did not know before his visit that a date had been
fixed for the fulfilment; but why did he wait for this? Here
was just the occasion, if ever, for 'holding his life out in his
hand,' and bestowing on his friend Admetus both life and
wife at once. So far Balaustion's error is personal and easily
disposed of. But her charge against the friends of Admetus
generally is a separable point, and deserves attention. If, for
instance, any one of the Chorus could have redeemed Admetus,
there is, as Browning felt, something tasteless in their laudation
of Alcestis for consenting, and downright fatuity in their
denunciation of his parents for refusing. And the case of
the household is worse; for if Admetus had a *claim* upon

anyone, it was surely on the serfs whom, as Apollo experienced, he treated with such remarkable kindness. But
in truth the whole charge rests on a misconception. According
to Euripides, who presumably follows tradition, the bargain
of the Fates was not, as is often stated or assumed, to take
instead of Admetus *anyone who consented to die.* Upon such
terms a Greek gentleman of wealth and rank would have got
off easily. It would have been strange if not one could have
been found, among the many families of human beings
absolutely dependent on him, to purchase his good-will for
those they left behind them by *giving* the life which he could
take. But Euripides expressly says that Admetus, "having
tried *all* his loved ones, *that is to say* his father and aged
mother, found none willing to die, except his wife[1]." The
Greek will not bear the sense, which we should expect if
every substitute was admissible, "having tried all his loved
ones, *including even* his father and aged mother"; and this is
so clear, that corrections have been proposed to get rid of the
difficulty. But the truth is that according to the bargain
none was admissible except *the family of Admetus.* What
the Fates promised was, in the words of Euripides, that
Admetus should escape "if he gave *another corpse* instead
of his own *to those below*[2]." This does not mean "if another
person would die instead," but something much more precise.
The language used refers to that simple conception of 'the
other life' according to which the dead were not ghosts at
large in another world but persons 'living' together in the
burial-place where they were put. Antigone in Sophocles
uses similar language, and assumes the same conception,
when she says, as a reason for giving funeral rites to her dead
brother even at the cost of offence against the living, "I shall
rest a loved one with him whom I have loved, sinless in my
crime; for it will be longer needful for me to please *those
below* than those here : *there* I shall lie for ever[3]." The

---

[1] *vv.* 15–17   πάντας δ' ἐλέγξας καὶ διεξελθὼν φίλους,
                    πατέρα γεραιάν θ' ἥ σφ' ἔτικτε μητέρα,
                    οὐχ ηὗρε πλὴν γυναικὸς κ.τ.λ.

Nauck proposed καὶ πατέρα γραῖάν θ' in *v.* 16. Others omit the verse.

[2] *v.* 14 ἄλλον διαλλάξαντα τοῖς κάτω νεκρόν.   [3] *v.* 73 ff.

persons described as *those below*, to whom Admetus is to give *another corpse* instead of his own, are those who, his hour being come, are entitled to his company, that is to say, *the dead of his family*. The death of a person of another family, who would be buried with *his* 'loved ones,' in a different burying-place, and worshipped with other and alien rites, would be no compensation at all. Now it happened that at the time Admetus' whole family (excluding his young children, who of course could not consent, nor be sacrificed) consisted of his father, mother, and wife. He applied to all of them, "all his loved ones" as Euripides says, and only his wife would consent. Thus, and thus only, can we understand the freedom with which the Chorus, as well as Admetus, assail the selfishness of the father and mother. No one else had refused, because no one else was admissible. The modern misconception has arisen from the brevity with which the story, being familiar, is told in the prologue, and from our want of acquaintance with the religious beliefs and formularies presupposed. However this is a small matter and a side-matter. Let us return to the main issue.

The moment is convenient for looking round us and considering where we are arrived. We set out from the observation that, with individual varieties of tone, the expositors of the *Alcestis* all agree in expressing surprise and dissatisfaction at the incongruity between the nature of the supposed story and the characters of Admetus and Heracles. The depth of this dissatisfaction, we said, might be measured, even better than by the outspoken scoffs of malevolent critics, by the efforts of benevolent critics to explain the incongruity away. We have now considered the allegations of two benevolent critics, Mr Way and Browning. They, if they do not stand alone in their respective classes, may be taken as typical of those who, seeing that for the purpose designed the defence of the impeached characters, or of one at least, must be complete and thorough-going, have tried to make it so. Mr Way says that the Admetus of the play is altogether noble *from a Greek point of view*. Browning says that the Heracles of the play is altogether noble, because

he is Heracles, and Euripides has shown how sublime
Heracles is. But when we go back to the text we find in the
case of Admetus an express statement that Greeks would not
take the favourable view attributed to them, and in the case
of Heracles none of those traits, actions, and symbols which
Euripides (as we see in another play) thought proper to show
his sublimity, but instead of them other lineaments which
are manifestly ignoble and noted as such by the author. In
such circumstances the thorough-going style of defence is
impracticable for the average composer of continuous commentary, bound or safeguarded by the necessity of weighing
all that the author has said, and the impossibility of putting
anything in.

But the instinct which Browning and Mr Way by their
several methods attempt to satisfy, is imperious and universal.
If the play, and especially the conclusion of it, is to harmonize
at all with the supposed design, then something of heroic
dignity, something above the commonplace, must be attached,
if not both to Heracles and to Admetus, at least to one of
them, and to Admetus rather, since, though the part of
Heracles is more important to the religious legend, that
of Admetus bulks larger in Euripides. An expedient, which
avoids the impracticable extreme of a thorough-going admiration, has been found for making a tolerable hero out of the
Euripidean Admetus, and has been adopted, I think, universally. Having said this, I naturally feel some reluctance
and embarrassment in saying, what nevertheless after long
consideration I must say, deliberately and respectfully, that
this expedient exhibits the most extraordinary proof conceivable of our human capacity for ignoring what we do
not wish to see, and believing not what we know but what
we like.

It has been said in book after book, that the character of
Admetus as presented by Euripides, however unattractive
and undignified in other respects, is redeemed by one trait of
true nobility, the ideal of friendship and hospitality which he
exhibits, at the expense of his tenderest feelings, in the
reception and entertainment of his guest. As a husband he

is perhaps not up to the standard, but then what a host! How worthy of the prince whose prosperity was founded upon his kind treatment of Apollo as a servant in his house, is the suppression of self which enables him, by concealing the truth, to open his door to the traveller in the very instant of his bereavement! Here lies the unity of the whole play, the moral of which "undoubtedly is, that *disinterested hospitality never fails of its reward.*" So, and with such emphasis of type, says Paley[1]; and so say the rest in a chorus. Let us then contemplate for a little the act of virtue to which our reverence is thus powerfully invited.

The case, it will be remembered, is this. Heracles, on his way from Argos to the north, is passing through Pherae, in which town he has many friends, Admetus being one of the number. He is on an errand imposed by authority, and so pressing as not to admit of more than a few hours' delay[2]. With the purpose of requesting this temporary entertainment he selects the house of Admetus, who tells us that he has been very well entertained himself by Heracles on the occasion of visits to Argos. It happens that he arrives at the palace just when the master of it is on the point of carrying his wife to the tomb. Admetus, to account for his emotion and mourning garb, declares that he is about to perform the funeral of a girl who had been entrusted to him by her deceased parents and has died in his house. Heracles expresses his regret at having arrived so inopportunely, and is about to go elsewhere, but Admetus protests that there is no reason for this : 'the dead are...dead ; his guest will be put in a part of the house quite separate from that in which the funeral preparations are proceeding'; and he finally cuts short his objections by handing him over to a servant, who receives orders to take care that the provision is ample, and to keep the doors shut between the respective apartments, while Admetus himself retires to continue the obsequies of the supposed orphan.

And this is hospitality! This is the ideal of friendship! This is the act which not only redeems a man from the

---

[1] On *v.* 1147.   [2] *v.* 1152.

imputation of selfishness, but by its high nobility explains and recommends a story designed to show us how heaven rewarded it with a benevolent miracle! I venture to say on the contrary that the behaviour of Admetus to Heracles is just of a piece with the rest of his proceedings, inconsiderate, indelicate, and unkind; that no one in his own case, and no one in any case, unless compelled by some supposed necessity, would esteem it otherwise; and that this view, if it were not provable by the common sense and sentiments of mankind, would still have to be accepted as the view of Euripides, inasmuch as the act is condemned by every one of his mouth-pieces, the personages of the drama, not excepting Admetus himself.

Be it observed in the first place that, if the entertainment thus bestowed upon Heracles is to be reckoned a proof of kindness, this must be on some other ground than the mere material benefit of shelter and food, for these he did not lack. We are told repeatedly[1], whenever in fact Admetus refers to the subject, that Heracles had other friends at hand, from whom, if allowed to depart, he could and would have obtained refreshment. And it is evident that, unless it were in the quality of the viands, almost any entertainment must have been more comfortable than that which is forced upon him by Admetus, a solitary meal consumed under the eyes of unwilling servants, while the so-called host is engaged in conducting a funeral. Indeed, to do Admetus justice, he never does pretend that his motive in the matter is solicitude for his friend. The ground on which he defends himself against objections is that, if Heracles had gone elsewhere, his own character for hospitality would have suffered:—

> So adding to my ills this other ill
> That mine were styled a house inhospitable.

From whom under the circumstances this reproach was to be apprehended, and why any one should take a view of the case so different from that of Heracles himself and of the protesting

---

[1] *e.g. vv.* 538, 1044.

Chorus, Admetus does not explain; but we will assume for
the moment that the apprehension is real and not groundless.
In that case the conduct of Admetus, though not in the least
noble or even disinterested, is prudent and so far justifiable:
he protects himself against possible censure, which any man
has a right to do, provided that he can do it without wronging
another.

But how can Admetus be brought within the limits of
this proviso? And does then Heracles sustain no wrong?
What of the deceit which is practised upon his confidence
in Admetus' loyalty? What of the false position in which he
is thus led to place himself, what of the mortification and
self-reproach which he thereby incurs? The deceit in itself
would have been sufficiently offensive, even if it had led to no
worse consequence than the unpleasantness of recollection,
when sooner or later he made the inevitable discovery. When
one friend demands and another renders a trivial service of
little intrinsic value, the pledge of friendship is not in the
thing bestowed, as in this case the victuals and drink, but
in the mutual confidence and goodwill, which makes it seem
natural to each that he should thus ask or be asked. Common
free consent is the essence of the matter, and the only estimable
part of it. But if there is on one side no consent, or if,
which is the same thing, the consent of one party is only
secured by the fraud of the other, so that he asks and accepts
on a misrepresentation what, not needing it, he would not ask
or accept if he knew the truth, the substance of friendship
is sacrificed to the mere appearance and form of it. The
friendship of Admetus and Heracles is so strong that Admetus
cannot possibly allow Heracles to take a meal in another
house instead of in his own; and yet this same friendship
is so slight, that Heracles has no claim to share the sorrow of
Admetus when his wife is lying dead in the house! Admetus
insists that Heracles, if he had been told the truth, would
have gone elsewhere. Whether this would in fact have been
so, we have no means of judging. It would depend on the
real relations between the two men, or rather on Heracles'
opinion of those relations: he might have been moved to go,

ALCESTIS

and he might have been moved to remain. But one thing
surely is manifest, that if Admetus conjectures truly, he
thereby condemns his trick. So much for the deceit in itself,
for the mere offence against loyalty. But the offence goes
deeper than this. Being thus admitted or rather entrapped
into the house, Heracles behaves there in such a way, that on
learning the truth from a servant he is overwhelmed with
horror and self-disgust. For the full extent of this mis-
adventure Admetus is not solely responsible. He could not
perhaps be expected to guess that his excellent friend would
console himself for the want of society by getting drunk,
especially as the circumstances, even as pretended, would
have sufficed to restrain most men from this extremity. But
neither is Admetus excusable. The actual sequel does but
emphasize the predictable risk to which he exposes his un-
suspecting guest, who, without going as far as he does, might
have done many things unsuitable to the awful situation in
which the household is found. What right or approvable
reason has Admetus for thrusting another upon this danger,
merely because it consists with his opinion of his own interests
that his bread should be eaten and not the bread of his
neighbours; and where is the nobility of this economical
purchase? I say nothing about the quality, in regard to the
dead wife, of the particular lies by which the noble result is
achieved.

Such, as it seems to me, would be the judgement on the
case, if argued from the sentiments of mankind in general.
But what we are concerned with after all is the sentiment
of the Greeks as conceived by Euripides. Let us see how
he represents it. The first to pronounce an opinion are the
Chorus, from whom, as the especial friends of Admetus,
accustomed by long respect and affection to regard him with
uncommon indulgence[1], we may expect the best that can be
said for his conduct. But they expostulate vehemently :—

> Admetus! what, with such a sorrow here
> Hast heart for entertainment? Why so mad?

[1] *v.* 212, and passim.

3—2

And when Admetus pleads the importance of sustaining his reputation, and the high claims of Heracles as a friend, they reply :—

> If he be e'en so dear, *how was it then*
> *That thou didst not impart thy present case?*

It will be seen that they put simply and sharply the precise dilemma which we have already expounded in the foregoing remarks. Either Heracles is very near and dear to Admetus, or he is not. If he is not, it is needless and improper to admit him at such a moment ; if he is, it is needless and improper to deceive him. That Euripides thought this dilemma, as I think it, unanswerable, I infer from his making Admetus not solve it but silence the discussion :—

> He never would have willed to cross my door
> Had he known aught of my calamities.
> And probably to some of you I seem
> Unwise enough in doing what I do;
> Such will scarce praise me : but these halls of mine
> Know not to drive away or slight a guest.

And thereupon he retires. Since he has added nothing to his case as he put it before, except the assumption, both gratuitous and damaging, that Heracles, if treated frankly, would not have come in, he naturally supposes the others to maintain their unanswered objections ; and if they were nevertheless represented by Euripides as convinced, that would affect not the truth but our estimate of their intelligence. But in fact they retract nothing. Since their admired prince will not hear them, they set themselves, like loyal courtiers, to make the best of what he chooses to do. They remind themselves that the house always was, as Admetus has said, a most liberal and hospitable house. Had not Apollo consented to live in it, graced it with miracles, and rewarded it with immense increase of substance and land ? Upon this encouraging theme they are made to dilate with a fulness which has been noted as exceeding the occasion[1],

---

[1] Prof. Paul Decharme, *Euripide et l'esprit de son théâtre*, p. 436. I shall have occasion to refer again to this excellent book.

and justly so noted, were it not that irrelevance is the only
way of escape for those who desire to applaud what they
have rationally condemned. Between the treatment of Apollo
and the treatment of Heracles there is neither analogy nor
connexion; but the speakers assume that, strange though
it seems to them, from the glory and blessing thus earned
must be traced the sensitiveness of Admetus towards possible
injury to the reputation of his house as a place of reception.
"It is a part of high breeding" they say "to *tend exceedingly*
to the point of honour"; and they add with generous breadth
of allowance that "upon the noble all the virtues rest," or
in other words, the actions of princes are presumably right
because theirs. "It is amazing: but we have a settled
confidence that the god-worshipping man *will fare well and
do well*," a double inference which Greek enables them to
express in a single term of convenient ambiguity[1]. With
this pious *petitio principii* they conclude, and the king re-
enters. How they might have reviewed their doctrine in the
light of subsequent events we do not learn, for as we shall
see, at the close of the play it is not found convenient by the
author that they should explain their sentiments; but it will
be consistent with their attitude throughout, if we suppose
them to acquiesce, as before, in the final pronouncement of
Admetus.

It is curious and instructive to note that Browning, who,
having discovered (as he supposed) a satisfactory hero for the
play in Heracles, was little concerned for the honour of
Admetus, and could judge without prejudice what Euripides
really says of him, has a comment here on the inadequacy
of the language put in the mouth of the Chorus to express
what (*ex hypothesi*) the situation requires. It is, I think, the
only occasion on which Balaustion goes so far as to suggest
a correction.

---

[1] *vv.* 600—605.

> τὸ γὰρ εὐγενὲς ἐκφέρεται πρὸς αἰδῶ,
> ἐν τοῖς ἀγαθοῖσι δὲ πάντ' ἔνεστιν σοφίας.
> ἄγαμαι· πρὸς δ' ἐμᾷ ψυχᾷ θάρσος ἧσται
> θεοσεβῆ φῶτα κεδνὰ πράξειν.

And on each soul this boldness settled now,

she says, citing in indirect form the terms of the original,

> That one, who reverenced the Gods so much,
> Would prosper yet: (or—I could wish it ran—
> *Who venerates the Gods, i' the main will still*
> *Practise things honest though obscure to judge*).

Exactly so : if Euripides expects us to admire the behaviour of Admetus as a host, and has founded his play upon this expectation, the Chorus, whose first judgement is unfavourable, should have been made to disprove and retract their opinion, or at least to acknowledge in unequivocal terms that, however the thing may look, *they must be mistaken*.   It is strange (*ex hypothesi*) and unsatisfactory, that all their inspiriting reminiscences should bring them no nearer to the point than this, that with a man so pious all will assuredly...*be right*.

It appears then that at this point the sentence upon Admetus' action remains in suspense ; and there it is left, till we come to the concluding dialogue between the prince and the traveller.   For as to the ejaculations and speeches of Heracles in the moment when he discovers the fact concealed from him, and resolves to recover Alcestis from the grasp of Death, they are from the circumstances inadmissible as matter of judgement.   He is then speaking under the double excitement of wine and remorse.   He is filled, as any man would be, when his eyes are thus suddenly opened, with the sense of his own misbehaviour and loss of respect.   His one impulse is to put himself right forthwith and recover his dignity, "to approve himself," as he says, "for a son of Zeus " by a signal service rendered to those whose hospitality he had claimed and certainly, as he perceives, has abused.   He is thus in no condition to estimate or to consider the behaviour of his friend to himself ; and in fact his exclamations, so far as they touch this side of the matter, betray by their inconsistency that he has not yet reflected on it.   At the first moment of suspecting a deceit he cries out against it as an incredible injury :—

> Have I been outraged by my friend and host?[1]

> [1] *v.* 816.

And in the same spirit he reproaches the slave, in language broken with indignation, for having complied with Admetus' order that he should be kept in the dark. On the other hand in the course of the wild and startling tirade which precedes his exit, he works himself up to the opposite point of view, and expresses it with an energy and assurance far exceeding that of Admetus. As the speech is for many reasons important, as it contains the only unequivocal commendation bestowed in the drama upon the act which we have to consider, and as Browning, cheered, we may well suppose, by finding here, for the first and last time, something like the tone of religious confidence which the Heracles. of *Balaustion's Adventure* might be expected to use, has discarded for the moment the somewhat stumbling style of his average dialogue, and has produced a version of excellent spirit, I should like to quote the whole of it.

> O much-enduring heart and hand of mine
> Now show what sort of son she bore to Zeus,
> That daughter of Electruon, Tiruns' child,
> Alkmené! for that son must needs save now
> The just-dead lady: ay, establish here
> I' the house again Alkestis, bring about
> Comfort and succour to Admetos so!
> I will go lie in wait for Death, black-stoled
> King of the corpses! I shall find him, sure,
> Drinking, beside the tomb, o' the sacrifice:
> And if I lie in ambuscade, and leap
> Out of my lair, and seize—encircle him
> Till one hand join the other round about—
> There lives not who shall pull him out from me,
> Rib-mauled, before he let the woman go!
> But even say I miss the booty,—say,
> Death comes not to the boltered blood,—why then,
> Down go I, to the unsunned dwelling-place
> Of Koré and the King there,—make demand
> Confident I shall bring Alkestis back,
> So as to put her in the hands of him
> My host, that housed me, never drove me off:
> Though stricken with sore sorrow, hid the stroke,
> Being a noble heart and honouring me!
> Who of Thessalians, more than this man, loves

> The stranger? Who, that now inhabits Greece?
> Wherefore he shall not say the man was vile
> Whom he befriended—native noble heart!

A fine declamation, amazingly fine—and not the less so, or less suited to the state of the speaker, that it cannot possibly be reconciled with his indignant condemnation of the same 'noble host' pronounced but a few minutes before. But if we want his fixed and deliberate opinion, we shall plainly do well to consult him at some hour when he is...more himself. And this Euripides permits us to do. For when Heracles comes back from the tomb with the disguised Alcestis, and faces Admetus for the first time since the discovery of the deception, he goes to that subject forthwith, and treats it in a manner as sober as we could possibly desire.

The tone indeed of his opening so little satisfies Balaustion, that before she begins to quote she puts in, as her fashion is at such places, a more than commonly eloquent description of her own. This, though excellent as original poetry, suffers as an exposition of Euripides from the unlucky fact that it does not accord with the speech which it introduces, as Balaustion herself ingenuously confesses by directing us to put the description out of sight again before we come to the speech itself. The whole passage is so interesting an example of Browning's method that, though his version is here not so good as in the last citation and wants altogether the polish of the original, we will cite it nevertheless together with his preamble. The version is substantially faithful, and free at any rate from the suspicion of serving unduly any purpose of mine.

> Ay, he it was advancing! In he strode
> And took his stand before Admetos—turned
> Now by despair to such a quietude,
> He neither raised his voice nor spoke, this time,
> The while his friend surveyed him steadily.
> *That friend looked rough with fighting: had he strained*
> *Worst brute to breast was ever strangled yet?*
> *Somehow, a victory—for there stood the strength*
> *Happy, as always; something grave perhaps;*

The great vein-cordage on the fret-worked brow
Black-swollen, beaded yet with battle-dew
The yellow hair of the hero!—his big frame
A-quiver with each muscle sinking back
Into the sleepy smooth it leaped from late.
Under the great guard of one arm, there leant
A shrouded something, live and woman-like,
Propped by the heart-beats 'neath the lion-coat.
When he had finished his survey, it seemed,
The heavings of the heart began subside,
The helpful breath returned, and last the smile
Shone out, *all Herakles was back again,*
As the words followed the saluting hand.
"To friendly man behoves we freely speak,
Admetos!—nor keep buried, deep in breast,
Blame we leave silent. I assuredly
Judged myself proper, if I should approach
By accident calamities of thine,
To be demonstrably thy friend: but thou
Told'st me not of the corpse then claiming care,
That was[1] thy wife's, but didst instal me guest
I' the house here, as if busied with a grief
Indeed, but then, mere grief beyond thy gate:
And so, I crowned my head, and to the Gods
Poured my libations in thy dwelling-place,
With such misfortune round me. And I blame—
Certainly blame thee, having suffered thus!
But still I would not pain thee, pained enough:
So let it pass!"

Here by way of parenthesis I would ask the reader to
compare carefully this speech with the foregoing picture;
to remark the device by which the one is linked to the other;
to note that Euripides has nothing anywhere to warrant one
stroke of the picture, and nothing in this place but a remark
from the Chorus that the person approaching the house
appears to be Heracles; to consider how easy it could have
been to suggest such a picture by common dramatic means—
and then to believe, if he can, that Browning and Euripides
have here the same conception and purpose. To proceed

---

[1] *That 'twas* would better express the meaning. Is *was* perhaps a misprint or
slip of the pen?

however with our immediate subject. The reply of Admetus, so far as it relates to the present matter, runs in Browning's version as follows :—

> Nowise dishonouring, nor amid my foes
> Ranking thee, did I hide my wife's ill fate;
> But it were grief superimposed on grief,
> Shouldst thou have hastened to another home.
> My own woe was enough for me to weep!

Now it is evident that these two speeches, allowing for the difference of speaker, decide the main question—whether the behaviour of Admetus to Heracles was right or wrong, kind or unkind—in the same sense, and that is, against Admetus. The language of Heracles is frankly that of reproach, tempered but not substantially modified by compassion. He had a *claim*, he says—and surely this is the pith and sense of the whole affair—having come as a friend, to be treated and allowed as a friend, by receiving confidence and returning sympathy; instead of this, he was betrayed by deceit into behaviour which it is painful to remember. And Admetus frankly apologizes, defending not his act, but his intentions; he did not mean a slight, he had no ill-will to Heracles. In explaining what then his motives were, he is lamer and weaker than ever; but one thing at least is clear, that he no longer pretends to have done right. And as this is the last word which we hear on the subject, we may and must conclude that it is the verdict not only of Heracles, and Admetus, and his friends, and his servants, but of the poet himself, and that whatever the object of his play may have been, it was certainly not to recommend, as an example of supreme and divinely rewarded kindness, an act for which he finds nothing more to be said than that it was not designed as an injury.

In saying that we hear no more on the subject, I should not and do not forget a passing allusion, which occurs a little later, almost at the end of the play, and upon which the reader, if he depended on the interpretation of Browning and some others, might certainly found some remarkable inferences.

It is the farewell of Heracles to Admetus, and is rendered by Browning thus:

> Lead her in meanwhile; good and true thou art,
> Good, true remain thou! Practise piety
> To stranger-guests the old way![1]

If Heracles did indeed say this, we should be driven to suppose that, in spite of all the contrary evidence, Euripides meant us somehow to conclude in favour of the hospitality which Admetus has just exhibited. But in fact he says nothing of the sort. In Browning's version the words *good and true thou art* are a mistranslation, while the words *good, true remain thou,* and the still more important words *the old way,* are additions for which the original has nothing at all. The error is not originally Browning's, but has crept into commentaries because of the very prejudice which it serves to sustain. The true English is: "Now lead her in; and as thou art bound, henceforth, Admetus, behave duly to guests." That Admetus, after his present experience and the generosity of Heracles, is under a particular obligation to observe the duties of friendship and hospitality in future, is true; and so he is plainly told: but so far from commending his recent conduct for an example, Heracles would seem rather, by this very injunction, to regard it as a warning, and in the light of his previous reproof, he cannot be otherwise understood. And so Admetus does understand him; for his final declaration is not that he will persevere in his virtue, but that "from this time forward his life is transformed for the better," a transformation which among other things would include, it is to be hoped, a better theory and practice in the way of dealing with persons who accept his friendship.

---

[1] *v.* 1147.   ἀλλ' εἴσαγ' εἴσω τήνδε· καὶ δίκαιος ὤν,
τὸ λοιπὸν, "Αδμητ', εὐσέβει περὶ ξένους.

Mr Way writes:

> But lead her in, and, just man as thou art,
> Henceforth, Admetus, reverence still the guest.

This is not so loose as Browning's, but betrays the same misconception by inserting *still*, which is not in the Greek and makes all the difference. Nor does it, though this is of less importance, rightly represent δίκαιος ὤν, which, to be connected with the rest of the sentence, must have the meaning assigned by others δίκαιος ὤν (ποιεῖν τοῦτο), *i.e.* εὐσεβεῖν περὶ ξένους.

Before quitting the subject of Admetus' 'hospitality,' we may observe that this unanimity of condemnation among the *dramatis personae* must determine our opinion, so far at least as concerns the play, not only with regard to the act in itself, but also as to the pretext for it which is pleaded by Admetus. When he says—and it is all that he has to say—that if Heracles had gone away from his door it would have affected injuriously the reputation of his house, we must understand that this excuse is not only (as it is) irrelevant, for reasons which, if not apparent before, become so at any rate after the rebuke of Heracles, but is also untrue. We must view this "excess of susceptibility" with the wonder, and something more than the wonder, which it excites at the moment in the indulgent minds of the Chorus. If Euripides had thought it possible that any one in Pherae or in Athens should seriously maintain the opinion of social obligation which Admetus pretends to fear, he would have shown us at least some one person actually so maintaining it. But in fact he assumes and implies that every one then would think what in a case unprejudiced every one now would think. The obvious, natural, and only permissible course for the master of the house was to acquaint his friend and visitor with the facts as they really were ; and whether after that the visitor stayed or went, whether he took his meal in that house or the next, was a thing indifferent, to be settled between the parties according to their mutual feelings, but not touching the duty or affecting the character of either in the slightest degree. And indeed we see that even Admetus, when he has to face not his obsequious inferiors but Heracles, does not venture to make this plea a part of his apology, but says merely that to let the visitor go elsewhere would have been *painful to himself*, a needless addition to the grief of his bereavement[1]. I will not waste the time of the reader by explaining what he doubtless perceives, that in this altered form the excuse is still as vain as ever, or worse, involving the same false assumption about the facts, the same evasion of the issue, and adding fresh absurdity at which we have full liberty to

[1] *v.* 1039.

laugh. Only fancy the widower 'weeping,' as he pictures himself, 'not only' because his wife was dead 'but also' because the cup and plate of his friend were being filled by the slaves of some other Pheraean!

The common attempt, therefore, to educe a unity and moral for the play from the nobleness of Admetus as a host, can as little be approved or allowed as the attempt of Browning to introduce a unity and moral by ennobling the conception of Heracles. The 'hospitality' of Admetus is an offence, which he is compelled to confess, and for which his real motives, since those which he chooses to allege are neither credible nor intelligible, must be supposed such as he does not care to avow. But although he does not avow them, they may nevertheless be discoverable or even obvious; and so we shall find that they are, if, putting aside all presumptions about what Euripides must have meant and therefore should or should not have said, we will but attend to what he does say, and allow ourselves to learn what he did mean. But for this purpose we must quit for the present this particular topic of 'hospitality': we must widen the scope of our consideration to take in the action of the play as a whole, and must observe a certain element in the facts presented, of which if we take no heed, we ourselves are responsible for the oversight, and not the author, who has omitted no available means of keeping it steadily before us.

The modern reader, having arrived at ancient Greek drama, as he commonly must, through a course of modern commentary and criticism, approaches it as a rule under a general prepossession, that among the things which he must not expect from the dramatist is a regard for the relation of events to one another in the article of time. Time (it is understood and occasionally asserted) is an element of reality which the Greek dramatist, in his imitation, did not pretend to account for. It was covered, obliterated, ignored by a general agreement between artist and audience. Time in a Greek tragedy is 'ideal,' or to speak more plainly, insignificant. Whether the scenes of the story are supposed to pass slowly or rapidly, or by how long an interval one incident is separated from another, are questions which the Greek dramatist never entertained, nor the Greek audience either. By a convention (it is said) the incidents of a Greek tragedy were supposed, whether this were in fact possible or not, to occupy a day or thereabouts, and within this 'ideal' day they may be distributed as you please. If, ignoring this conventional treatment, you try to translate the story into terms of real time, you will become aware of your error by finding yourself involved in contradictions, compelled (for example) to suppose that one and the same interlude represents for one purpose an interval of a few hours but for another purpose an interval of as many weeks. This 'systolé and diastolé,' with many other remarkable things, is a natural effect of the convention. Now I do not propose here to investigate this theory, as it does not directly concern us. Its development is a curious chapter in the history of opinion, and I have tried to relate it elsewhere[1]. Under the name of 'the unity of time,' a term now happily, if slowly, going out of use, it has had in its day an immense influence both on dramatic composition and on the archaeology of the drama. So that although it is utterly untrue, the traceable product of mere blunders committed in the sixteenth and seventeenth centuries, and although these errors, or part of them, are now widely recognized and the theory decadent, some of the parasitic errors to which in the nature of things it gave rise, are still flourishing or alive ; and the study of Greek tragedy is still influenced by vague but efficient presumptions which have no higher or better credited origin.

To some such cause I should attribute the fact that, so far as I am aware, in none of our commentaries or studies on the *Alcestis* is any note taken of an element in the story presented which, if the play were treated as liable to the ordinary judgement of our senses, would certainly strike a reader at the first view as one of the most startling in the whole remarkable narrative. I refer to the haste and precipitancy, irregular and indecent in any case, and in this particular case nothing less

---

[1] In the *Introduction* (Essay III.) to the edition and translation of Euripides' *Ion*.

than outrageous, with which the corpse of the noble heroine is conveyed to the grave.

Strange enough in itself, even if this were all, and sufficiently offensive to the customs imposed by nature and necessity upon mankind, would be the performance of the funeral on the day of the death. It is perhaps needless to say that this was no more the practice in Athens, and there-fore no more likely there to seem probable to the inventor of a fiction or to pass with an audience for satisfactory, than it is or would be among ourselves at the present time. In ancient Athens, as a matter of fact, the general sentiment, so far as it differed from ours, differed rather in the other direction. The primitive doctrine which associated the personality of a dead man as much or more with the visible body than with an unseen spirit, had by no means, in the time of Euripides or even later, yielded the field to the more refined and spiritual doctrine which places personality al-together in a soul; and there was still therefore a disposition to extend the observance bestowed upon the corpse, in respect of time, magnificence, and otherwise, much beyond the limit which enlightened and practical regulators would have liked to establish. Plato in a curious passage of the *Laws*[1] lays down that the funeral may safely take place, and therefore should take place, on the next day but one after that of the decease, and that a statute to this effect should be accompanied by public instruction in the true doctrine of personality, calculated to appease the sentimental opposition which he evidently anticipates. There were indeed, or perhaps rather had been, some who, by a more crude application of what we may call the corporeal doctrine of the dead, arrived at the conclusion that a corpse should be buried as soon as con-veniently might be, so that the dead might pass entire into the other world. The doctrine appears in Homer[2]. The actual practice in historical times seems to have been much the same as our own, except that the performances in the house and about the dead body were much more elaborate

[1] p. 959.
[2] *Il.* 23. 71. See Smith's *Dict. Ant.* 'Funus.'

and indispensable, as indeed in most countries they still are. As to the mere question of time there is little range for choice, so far as the mass of mankind are concerned: within narrow limits it is settled, without regard to sentiments or doctrines, by the laws of physical fact.

It is to be presumed then that an Athenian, if told that a certain corpse was buried on the day of the death, would have felt exactly the same shock of surprise, suspicion, and displeasure as an Englishman in the like circumstances; and that the same effect would be produced by the representation of such a proceeding on the stage. Why should the dramatist make his personages do an outrageous thing, except in order that its impropriety might be observed? There was no compulsion on him. It is true that there were practical reasons, arising from the arrangements of the Greek theatre and company, why the action of a play should not, if it could be avoided, be such as to occupy more than a day or thereabouts[1]. And it could be avoided in most cases by a little ingenuity. For example, it would have been perfectly easy to present a story like that of Alcestis, a story of death and revival, without introducing any funeral at all, and so that a day or a few hours should naturally cover events from first to last. But the dramatist, if he chose, might sacrifice theatrical convenience to some other consideration, and make his action as long as he pleased. Euripides himself, for instance, in his *Suppliants* presents an action which would occupy from first to last something like a month, and he does so without any disguise, leaving the imagination of the audience to leap the necessary interval at the proper time. And similarly if he or any playwright had presented within one action a death and burial, and had meant the proceedings to appear natural and regular, he could and must have allowed a time sufficient for them; he would have shown us where we should suppose the lapse of that interval which could not be denied without affronting the reason and feelings of humanity. There are of course exceptional cases, in which prompt and hasty burial is a sign not of negligence but of love, inasmuch as the rite, if

---

[1] See the essay on ‘The Unity of Time,’ cited above.

delayed, is likely to be prevented. We have an instance in the *Ajax* of Sophocles[1]: but such is not our present affair. The *Seven against Thebes* of Aeschylus is something nearer, though even there the circumstances are highly peculiar, the dead having been slain in the assault and defence of a beleaguered fortress from whose walls the enemy have just fallen back. It is not improbable that in such a situation no time would be lost. However the dramatist does not demand the supposition, but leaves us to settle the procedure for ourselves, providing us by the regular means of a choric ode with an opportunity for interpolating as much time as we think necessary. Such *a fortiori* would have been the natural representation of an ordinary case.

And what of the actual case, the case of Alcestis? If the omission of these universal dues would be noticeable in itself, what is it when the dead is an Alcestis? That we should forget her surpassing claim to every possible sign of love and respect is certainly not the intention of the poet. From first to last the subject of the honours which ought to be and must be paid to her, is prominent in the minds of the speakers. Twice in beautiful songs[2] the Chorus dilate on the worship which she will receive; how as the noblest of womankind she will be celebrated in the religious feasts of Hellas, and her heroism will be annually sung at Sparta or at Athens; how when travellers pass her tomb, they will pray to her spirit (which doubtless they did) as to a guardian angel. All Pherae is filled with admiration of her; and as to the household, the men-servants and maid-servants, their reverence and affection is altogether inexpressible. The slaves who wait upon Heracles are almost ready to rebel because they thus miss the chance of saying a ceremonious farewell to the corpse[3]. But none is more eloquent upon this theme, as indeed none has more cause, than the husband for whom she dies, Admetus himself. In the promise of mourning observances he is inexhaustible; the utmost efforts of imagination seem, as we note with sympathy, insufficient to answer his intentions. No common

---

[1] See *v.* 1040, and the finale from this point.
[2] *v.* 435, *v.* 991.   [3] *v.* 767.

widower's year of black, he says while still the ears of his wife are open to his assurances[1], will content his grief. His whole life will be spent not merely in cherishing but in acting his regret. Never an entertainment any more in the house which has been so hospitable. No garlands, no music ever again ; where would be the pleasure of them ? The very bed of the wife will be occupied only by a graven imitation of her, upon which the husband will bestow his embraces, as if it were indeed herself. Nor when she has ceased to hear him does he cease to promise ; rather his anticipations take a wider range[2]. It is his command that the public celebration, like the private, shall be on a scale almost incredible. All his subjects are to put into mourning their persons, their households, and (if they have them) their carriages ; nor is this injunction limited to any period of time. Even the severe ordinance that 'neither flute nor lyre shall be heard'—an ordinance which in a Greek town would have had an effect something like that of a papal interdict in the middle ages, curtailing or suspending every office of social and religious life and practically closing the schools—even this refinement of severity is expressly extended to 'twelve full months.' No burial, as he justly adds, could better deserve such recognition than that of his queen deserves it from the king of Thessaly.

But all this predicted, prospective, and promissory magnificence, this more than liberal estimate of what shall be, must be, done by himself and his people in the future to show forth by outward signs their eternal memory and worship of the heroic dead, does not in the least affect, except so far as to illuminate by the light of contrast, the visible fact that Alcestis is actually buried not like a heroine, not like a queen, not even with the commonest offices of love, nor the barest observances of humane precaution, but with just such perfunctory haste as might be thought permissible in the case of a corpse infected with the plague : and that this arrangement of her obsequies is due to the express prevision and persistence of the king her husband. What he ought to have done, what he feels and

---

[1] *v.* 336.   [2] *v.* 425.

knows that he ought to have done, we are perpetually reminded by the eloquent outpourings of his uneasy conscience. But what he does, we see; and strange is the comparison.

For if it would be surprising and unsatisfactory that without grave cause a body should be entombed on the day of the death, what shall be said of a funeral which is commenced not merely within the same hour, but at the very minute of the death itself, while the corpse is yet as warm as in life, and almost before the departed voice has ceased to vibrate upon the ear ; a funeral which from that moment to its completion is pushed forward in spite of hindrance with all the speed that forethought and ingenuity can secure? Such is the funeral of Alcestis. The extraordinary scene which ensues upon her death would prove of itself, even if we had not had previous intimations to the same effect, that nothing is or has been more near to her husband's thoughts than the importance of performing her obsequies without the smallest delay. Scarce a minute has passed since her last 'Farewell!' was spoken, the wail of her frightened child has scarcely sunk into sobbing, and the friend who stands by has barely proffered his first word of condolence, when Admetus, dismissing these commonplaces with the remark, on this occasion uniquely appropriate, that the subject has been long the burden of his thoughts, runs on, as it were in one sentence, to invite the immediate assistance of his visitors in conveying 'this corpse' to the cemetery[1]. That this amazing suggestion is not a birth of the moment, but prearranged with their complicity, is evident not only from the way in which it is launched, but from their own behaviour in acting upon it without so much as the form of an acceptance ; and in fact the audience also has already been made privy to their expectations.

The first scene of the action proper[2] (first after the prologue) consists of a curious conversation which passes between these visitors upon their arrival at the door. Although they come in the fore-part of the day (as appears shortly afterwards from the account of what has passed in the house, and would in any

[1] *v.* 422.　　　[2] *v.* 77 foll.

4—2

case have been assumed by Greek spectators from the habitual
and almost inevitable practice of the choric dramatists[1]) they
are so possessed by the unwonted sensation of fore-knowledge
and by the prophetic announcement of the date[2], that their
first feeling is surprise at not perceiving about the house the
signs which according to custom would have marked that the
decease had actually taken place ; they are surprised at not
seeing before the entrance the holy water and stationary
servant, nor hearing from within the shrieks and beaten hands
of women performing the ceremonial lamentation over the
corpse. (We may observe in passing that, although the whole
action proceeds before this same gate, we find no indication
in dialogue or ode that any of these regular things are afterwards done ; the servant, if she takes her station, does so in
silence and unheeded ; the cries, if any are heard, excite no
remark or echo; nay more, at the time when such demonstra-
tions would naturally appear, we have, in the conversation of
Heracles who happens just then to arrive, a positive proof
that nothing of the sort was exhibited.   It is from the entrance
of Admetus, and the marks on his person, that he receives the
first intimation of anything amiss[3].)   However, in the midst
of their conjectures the Chorus agree, though not without a
significant doubt, that at least 'the corpse cannot have left
the house,' and the reason is startling.   ' Why so ? ' says some
one, ' I dare not say.   What makes you sure ? '   ' Oh, because
surely Admetus could not have performed the funeral of such
a wife *without attendance !* '   Manifestly this remark is intelligible only on the supposition that, to the knowledge of
the speakers, the funeral, if performed before their arrival,
could have had no attendance, or in other words, that they
are themselves the invited mourners, and are alone apprised
of the intention, which certainly no uninformed person was
likely to anticipate, that the ceremony shall proceed as soon
as ever there is a body to bury.   Noticeable moreover is their
conviction of the king's determined haste.   It does *not* seem
inconceivable to some of them that, if the death has occurred

---

[1] *v.* 158 foll.   See 'The Unity of Time,' already cited
[2] *v.* 105.   [3] *vv.* 476—512.

before their arrival, Admetus *may have dispensed with a convoy altogether*; for instead of accepting the contrary suggestion as conclusive, they continue their inferences from the state of the house—'no holy water, no lock of hair' and so on—inferences which, as appear from the sequel, do less than justice to the king's unity of purpose and indifference to needless detail.

They suppose him therefore ready to commit, if necessary, what to Greek minds was more repugnant than a crime. Even among ourselves and with the 'psychical' doctrines now prevailing, a prince, who conveyed the corpse of his wife to the grave with no other attendant than himself, would be censured severely. What Greeks with their 'corporeal' doctrines would think of him, we may see in Aeschylus. Even the guilt of a Clytaemnestra, murderess of her lord, can take a blacker shade from the fact that she buried him 'without the lament of a husband *or the train of a king*[1]': and this it is which, more than anything else in the story, arouses the frenzy of the avenger.

But Admetus is not driven to this extremity. The queen's procession, such as it is, happily arrives at the palace before she is actually dead. From the report of a maid-servant, who presently comes out of doors to weep, we learn among other things both why these few persons have been selected for invitation and why others would not have been welcome. 'I will go,' she says, 'and say that you are here. It is not by any means all, who feel for my lord[2] so kindly as to bring to his griefs a sympathetic presence. But you have been from of old the master's friend.' That Admetus just at this time is not popular in his realm any more than in his household, we hear without surprise. By requesting and accepting the sacrifice of his more amiable lady, he would have somewhat dimmed in the general eye the glory of his liberal housekeeping, religious habits, and other unquestioned virtues. Indeed he is

---

[1] *Cho.* 429.

[2] *v.* 210. The Greek has the plural, but only, according to frequent usage, as a term of respect. Admetus plainly, and Admetus only, is meant. Towards Alcestis there could be no feeling but admiration and respect.

himself obliged to acknowledge, when all is over and his choice apparently irrevocable, that this disadvantageous impression is only too likely to be permanent[1]. We can therefore well understand his wish that the persons before whom he was to exhibit himself in the position of chief mourner for the victim (as the less 'kindly' might put it) of his own cowardice, should be those whose loyal attachment had been proved by long experience.

The mourning-train, then, is provided, and so also, as far as circumstances permit, is the rest of the funeral. It was the Greek custom that a corpse should be adorned not only with elaborate wreaths and other such decorations, but also, when the condition of the family permitted, with jewellery and the like, which was buried or burnt with it and thus appropriated to the use of the dead. In reply to a question from the friends—or should we not rather say, the accomplices?—of Admetus, the maid-servant informs them and us that this matter has not escaped his prevision: the articles are selected and prepared; 'Yes, the tiring which her lord intends to bury with her, is in readiness[2].' Something, much indeed, Alcestis herself contributes to preparation; for knowing that 'the appointed day' has dawned for her, she performs upon herself, with pathetic patience and forethought, the needful washing and robing, and happens even to conceive the desire of looking once more upon the open sky, for which purpose she is carried out, apparently on a litter, to the front of the palace. Nor does she, living or dead, ever re-enter her own chamber until after she has lain in the grave. After her death the body is carried into the house; at least it seems so, though in the absence of stage-directions we cannot be sure of this; but it remains, in the brief interval before the departure, at the entrance, ready for bearing out, as appears in the indignant and sneering allusion of the servant who waits on Heracles. 'But the corpse,' says Heracles, 'was only that of a stranger to the family!' 'O yes,' replies the man, playing upon an ambiguous word, 'O yes, it was out of the family *and out of*

[1] *v.* 954.   [2] *v.* 149.

the door, too much so!' This man has no love for the pious Admetus, and does not conceal his sentiments[1].

That Alcestis is apprised of the plan to precipitate her burial, or acts under suggestion from those who are, is neither indicated nor likely; it is conceivable that, had she known it, she would have seen her self-sacrifice in a new light. Rather it is an enhancement of our pity, that without any suspicion she is furthering by all that she does the plan of a husband who, in the midst of professing eternal gratitude, is preparing so promptly to insult her memory. However that may be, it is the joint result of his proceedings and hers that, when she lies inanimate at the portal, there is literally nothing left to be done before the funeral starts, except to shave her husband and slip on his black; and this is the whole programme of the pomp as it is actually carried out. In no way perhaps can the monstrosity of the performance be more clearly realized, than by asking ourselves what is the proper costume for the Chorus. It is certain that they follow the corpse in the same which they wear when first they come as visitors. They have no chance of changing. Admetus does change and, as was the custom of the Greek dramatists for practical reasons, matters are so arranged that verbal as well as visible intimation should be given of the significant alteration[2]. But what of his friends? When they come to the house ostensibly to enquire of the queen's condition, do they come with close-cut hair and sable vest? We are informed of the contrary— 'Must we *change to black*? Is the time already come[3]?' exclaims one of them oddly, as an expression of despair; and we should presume it without information. What could be more repugnant to humanity and decency, than to surround with anticipatory emblems the couch of the dying heroine? Or what more offensive to the public, than to parade the street clad in mourning for a benefactress for whom it was still

[1] *v.* 811 (refer to *v.* 532 and *v.* 828, and also to *v.* 771).

HP. οὐ χρῆν μ' ὀθνείου γ' οὕνεκ' εὖ πάσχειν νεκροῦ;
ΘΕ. ἦ κάρτα μέντοι καὶ λίαν θυραῖος ἦν.

The reading λίαν θυραῖος is clearly right: λίαν οἰκεῖος, the facile but pointless variant, is merely an unintelligent guess.

[2] *v.* 512.   [3] *v.* 215 ff.

possible to hope and to pray, and whose death, however it might appear to Admetus and other such devotees, would be thought by at least five persons in ten, as it is by Heracles, not at all necessarily imminent because it had been predicted by a prophet? But on the other hand, since the Chorus are *not* in mourning, what sort of figure must they make in the character of a funeral procession?

It has been already said that the action of Admetus, in thus abridging the honours of the deceased, is emphasized and made conspicuous by the largeness of his promises; and this we see by the manner in which these promises are introduced. Browning notes, and we all note with him, the 'childishness,' to use the most charitable expression, of the redeemed husband when he assures the redeeming wife how courageously, if he had been an Orpheus, he would have fronted Cerberus, Charon, and all the terrors of the underworld, in order to bring back her soul. How much more simple, as Balaustion observes, to say

> what would seem so pertinent,
> 'To keep this pact, I find surpass my power.
> Rescind it, Moirai! Give me back her life,
> And take the life I kept by base exchange!'

And just the same futility, by comparison with what we know to be planned and doing, appears in those other assurances which make the rest of his speech:—

> And I shall bear for thee no year-long grief[1],
> But grief that lasts while my own days last, love!......
> For I will end the feastings—social flow
> O' the wine friends flock for, garlands and the Muse
> That graced my dwelling. Never now for me
> To touch the lyre, to lift my soul in song
> At summons of the Lydian flute; since thou
> From out my life hast emptied all the joy!—

and so on, with invented observances even more extravagant. How much more simple to begin observance with the present

---

[1] 'Mourning' would be a more exact rendering. The word refers to outward manifestations, not mere feeling; 'grief' somewhat changes the colour, and impairs the point of the sequel. See *v.* 336 foll.

day, to let the corpse lie its fair time in the hall, bewailed with
a fair lament, and go forth, when it must, with a fair and pro-
portionate train! And when later he reverts to the same
subject, the self-contradiction is stronger still, rises almost to
the grotesque, and like much else in the play is distinguished
from sheer comedy only by painfulness. His wife (be it
remembered) has been dead something less than five minutes.

> You have to stay, you friends,
> Because *the next need is to carry forth*
> *The corpse here* : you must stay and do your part,
> Chant proper paean to the God below ;
> Drink-sacrifice he likes not. *I decree*
> *That all Thessalians over whom I rule*
> *Hold grief in common with me; let them shear*
> *Their locks, and be the peplos black they show!*...
> *And through my city, nor of flute nor lyre*
> *Be there a sound till twelve full moons succeed.*
> *For I shall never bury any corpse*
> *Dearer than this to me, nor better friend:*
> *One worthy of all honour from me, since*
> *Me she has died for, she and she alone.*

With what feelings would this proclamation have been received
by the people of Pherae and the neighbourhood, when it
reached them together with the intelligence that the beloved
queen was not only dead but already entombed, buried within
an hour of her death, and with a ceremony which, excepting
a few private friends who 'happened' to present themselves,
no single person, far or near, had been asked or allowed to
attend? It seems to me that in the resurrection of Alcestis
Admetus was not so much 'supremely blest'—that way of
putting it is Balaustion's—but rather, in all the simplicity of
Euripides, 'fortunate[1].' It seems to me that, if she had not come
back, he would have run some risk of being pelted out of his
palace.

But if in the earlier scenes of the play, up to and including
the death of the victim, the considerate speed of the plans for
her burying is a feature not to be overlooked, it is made more
prominent still by the scene which next follows, and brings us

---

[1] *v.* 1158, οὐ γὰρ εὐτυχῶν ἀρνήσομαι.

now back again to our previous topic, the arrival and reception
of Heracles. What, we have asked, was the king's real motive
for an act which he himself, whether he boasts of it as he does
at first, or excuses it as he does at last, is alike and always
unwilling or unable to explain? Why, instead of frankly
communicating his sorrow to his sympathetic visitor, does he
force upon him a graceless entertainment by means of a
deception which sooner or later must needs be discovered and
resented? Why does he do it? The situation itself presents
the wretched reason. It is because by his own devices he has
put himself in such a position that he dares not, cannot tell
the truth. The arrival of Heracles at this instant is an embarrassment for him at once ludicrous and horrible. The
Chorus, waiting before the door, at once perceive the difficulty
and stand on reserve. 'Is Admetus within?' 'Yes,' they reply,
'he *is* within; but....' But what? Why do they not say
plainly and naturally 'But you cannot have heard, and we
have to tell you, that he is in mourning for his wife, who died
a few minutes ago'? Instead of this they engage him in
conversation about himself and his journey, which continues
till Admetus comes out and they resign the lead to him[1].
Now what is Admetus to do? In the dialogue which ensues,
his wriggling, quibbling, and lying are those of a criminal on
the point of detection; for such and no better he feels himself
to be. It would have been humiliating enough, had there
been nothing more in the circumstances, to say to this gallant
friend, who is so far from believing that Alcestis is really to
be sacrificed by and for her husband, that he prefers rather to
make light of the anxiety which the prediction of her fate has
raised in more impressionable minds,—to meet him with the
words ' But it is certainly true. It has come to pass. I have
accepted her self-immolation, and with my consent she has
actually died in my stead.' This, for a man 'excessive,' as we
are told, 'on the point of honour,' would have been bad
enough. But that would not have been the end nor the worst,

---

[1] That the Chorus are unwilling to tell Heracles the truth is well brought out
by Browning. But he does not see why, and has to find a reason by mis-stating
the facts. See above, p. 28.

for the next word must have touched on the funeral, and
whatever it was, must have abased him further. Should he
confess to the noble Argive, 'descendant of Perseus and son
of Zeus,' that the company before him, a few old friends of the
house, are engaged as a minimum to make a following for the
queen of Thessaly, who is dead indeed, just dead, and for
certain reasons (what reasons?) is to be buried forthwith? Or
on the other hand should he turn to the Pheraeans and confess
to them, in the presence of the new-comer, that since the
intended celebration must now be deferred, or else disclosed
to this respectable personage so inaptly arrived,—it had best
be deferred? The position of Admetus is such that he is
driven to lie, not for hospitality, but for shame. Nor does he
dare to let Heracles go, as he proposes, elsewhere. Partly he
is afraid lest after all it should be suspected by Heracles that
the bereavement is something graver than he has represented,
and this should somehow lead to an exposure aggravated by
the deceit. Partly he has, it may be supposed, a vague hope
that Heracles, if he can be kept at the house, may be got
out of Pherae without yet knowing what has occurred,
and weakness loves postponement. But above all it is clear
that, if the visitor repairs to another host, there will be no more
privacy for what is done and doing at the palace. Now
Admetus is resolved as ever—it is the only point on which he
is consistent—that the clandestine funeral shall proceed, and
proceed immediately. This is the cause of his crowning
blunder in remitting his guest to the uncontrolled charge of
the servants, thus making it practically certain that he will be
undeceived in some such scandalous and distressing fashion
as he presently is. The brief visit of Heracles might perhaps
have been got through tolerably, if the funeral had been put
off even till the evening. But no; Heracles must stay and
Admetus must go; an upshot reasonless and senseless,
except so far as it explains and is explained by the pre-occu-
pation which this scene and those which precede it are con-
trived to exhibit.

Meanwhile we have naturally been asking ourselves, and not
without receiving from the dramatist the means of anticipating

the answer, what is the motive which induces a man like Admetus, hitherto known as generous, kindly, honourable, and particularly pious, to persist in this union of meanness with falsehood for the purpose of impoverishing, obscuring, degrading the solemnities of religion and love. To complete the answer is the object of the next ensuing scene, which shows us as it were by a specimen, in case we could not for ourselves imagine it, what sort of torture it is that Admetus, by these premature and surreptitious obsequies, is scheming to avoid, and what it would have been for him to go through the only alternative. No man of sensibility, who had acted as he has done, could fail to be aware that, however he might gloze or bluster, to all impartial eyes he must make a sorry figure. Admetus is perfectly aware of it. After the burial, in the cold forlornness of his return to the house, he vividly depicts the advantage which malice would take of him, and the effect that it would produce. I have cited the passage before, but I will cite it again (it is worth while), this time in the version of Browning :—

> And then, whoever is a foe of mine,
> And lights on me—why, this will be his word—
> 'See there! alive ignobly, there he skulks
> That played the dastard when it came to die,
> And giving her he wedded, in exchange,
> Kept himself out of Hades safe and sound,
> The coward! Do you call that creature—man?
> He hates his parents for declining death,
> Just as if he himself would gladly die!'
> This sort of reputation shall I have.

'That,' subjoins Balaustion aptly, 'was the truth.' Perhaps in supposing that such hostility would be quite and for ever invincible, he is carried by remorse somewhat beyond the truth. It is, I fear, conceivable that a year or so later his banquets might, by the favour of the gods, have been as well attended as ever. But while the affair was fresh, the opinion of the world would undoubtedly have been such as he describes. And this truth, though Balaustion may not be wrong in saying that it is fully realised only when it is confessed, is *felt*, palpably felt as a determining motive, by his instincts all along.

It is impossible that Admetus should not shrink, as one would shrink from flaying, even although one had never been flayed before, from the thought of walking after the bier of Alcestis, first of a noble train, before the assembled townsfolk of Pherae, in the presence of the parents whom he so preposterously maligns, of the kin of his wife (Euripides does not forget them), and of all the curious who could manage to reach the place, knowing that all were saying, to themselves if not audibly,

See there! alive ignobly, there he skulks!

His plan is, and all his actions up to the burial have no other object, to escape this horror in the only possible way, by interring his wife with such ceremony or lack of ceremony as the case might admit, but anyhow instantly, before any one except his household and his chosen associates could know that she was dead. Whether even in the circumstances this was a wise thing to do, Euripides does not ask us to decide. We may think if we like, as I do, that it was rather a leap into the fire, and that, if things had not taken an unexpected turn, Admetus would soon have realised a little more 'truth.' Euripides only says and shows, that for a man such as the husband of Alcestis must have been, quicker to grasp relief than to imagine consequences, this was a natural thing to do. In showing this he has done, as we shall find, all that is required for his ultimate purpose.

The execution of the plan is for the moment almost perfectly successful, but not quite. If the procession had started, as it might have done but for the arrival of Heracles, at the time when Admetus, coming out ready dressed from the house, finds that innocent intervener at the door, it would have got comfortably away, and the king's sensibility would have escaped irritation. When Heracles is installed, he comes out again, and gives the word for setting forth. It is still impossible that his proceedings should be generally known. But unhappily there is one of his neighbours who can readily divine his feelings, inasmuch as in his own breast there is a faint reflexion of them, who has reason to anticipate his design, and even to approve it strongly, on the condition that he himself be not excluded from participation. At the first news that Alcestis is dead and her burial fixed for the present hour, Pheres the father hurries to the palace with his offering. Except Admetus, he is the only person who, having been in a position to save Alcestis if he had chosen, and being also liable to follow her corpse, has cause to think that on the whole the ceremony may as well be private, that is to say, speedy. His conscience is indeed much quieter than his son's, not only, as Browning says truly but with perhaps too exclusive an emphasis, from the more hardened selfishness of old age, but also because his share of reproach would be so much the lighter. It is Admetus, not Pheres, who has devolved upon another his own proper fate; and whatever may be said by the satellites of the son, for the general eye his disgrace would completely outshade his father's. Pheres arrives then calm and decorous, resolved, as we see, to show that he at least has no reason to avoid the ceremony, and well-pleased, as we may imagine, that he can do this with so little discomfort. That his son will make a scene he naturally cannot suppose. But Admetus is too sore and too undisciplined to reason. The unreason of his self-refuting invective measures for us how intensely his conscience hates and fears an unfriendly eye; or, as Browning excellently puts it,

> So in old Pheres young Admetus showed
> Pushed to completion: and a shudder ran,
> And his repugnance soon had vent in speech:
> Glad to escape outside, nor, pent within,
> Find itself there fit food for exercise.
> "Neither to this interment called by me
> Comest thou, nor thy presence I account
> Among the covetable proofs of love...."
>
> You see what all this poor pretentious talk
> Tried at—how weakness strove to hide itself
> In bluster against weakness—the loud word
> To hide the little whisper, not so low
> Already in that heart beneath those lips!
> Ha, could it be, who hated cowardice
> Stood confessed craven, and who lauded so
> Self-immolating love, himself had pushed
> The loved one to the altar in his place?

The exposition of this scene is indeed the best part of *Balaustion's Adventure* regarded as a commentary, and so far as the scene itself is concerned leaves nothing to add. But beyond the mere situation, and not less essential for a complete understanding, is the bearing of it on the action of the play as a whole: and this is, that when we have heard the retorts of Pheres, turning as they do insistently upon the disgrace and contempt attaching to the appearance of Admetus in the character of mourner, we understand, if we did not before, why he has schemed to elude, even at the cost of an offence against humanity, a performance in which he must have borne, without even the consolation of reply, to read such things on the eyes and the lips of a thousand malign spectators.

> So good words, henceforth! If thou speak us ill,
> Many and true an ill thing shalt thou hear!...
>
> And dost not thou too, all for love of life,
> Carry out now, in place of thine, this corpse?...
>
> Meanwhile woo many wives—the more will die!...
>
> Die when thou wilt, thou wilt die infamous!
>
> *Thou buriest her whom thou didst murder first.*

Such would have been the missiles which, worded or not, must have gone to the heart of Admetus with every flower flung by assembled Thessaly upon the bier of Alcestis. And that is why, at the very instant when she is declared to be dead, "the next need is to carry forth this corpse."

Here, at the pause in the action which follows the retirement of Pheres and departure of the convoy, it will be convenient to review our road. We set out to investigate certain detractions, on the face of them serious, which are commonly made from the praise of Euripides, and notably from that of the *Alcestis*. These detractions, we find, are not ill summed up in the epigrammatic phrase, pronouncing the poet a 'botcher,' and meaning that in his works the single pieces, however smart or well-wrought, are merely tagged together; the scenes do not grow out of one another in the way of progress towards a common end, and do not contribute to any one sentiment which may be regarded as the outcome of the whole; sometimes on the contrary, as is the case of the *Alcestis*, there is between parts and whole a marked repugnance; a vital defect, as it is rightly thought, and killing to the merits which might be allowed in the details, if only they had belonged to another scheme. Now as regards the scenes which we have been considering, we have got some way, though at present only part of the way, towards disproving this charge. The first half of our play is at all events coherent within itself. The altercation between Admetus and Pheres is not dragged in 'to please a contentious and law-loving audience'; it was not written because the dramatist saw his way to play the pair smartly against one another, and was blind or indifferent to the effect which his damaged puppets might make when it came to the finale. The reception of Heracles does not stand upon the hollow and artificial plea that it is an occasion for redeeming the character of Admetus, otherwise so unsuitably ignoble, by exhibiting his sublime hospitality. These scenes, taken in their place and with what we can see at present, are proper exponents of the main action, the theme of which up to this point is the death *and burial* of the heroine, and the purport of it to show how, for reasons deducible from the data of the legend, the latter event succeeds the former with a strange and unexampled rapidity. We have next to consider how, if at all, this bears upon the sequel and particularly upon the conclusion, where we expect to find reflected the general aspect of the whole.

Of the two next scenes, that in which Heracles, under the effects of his too copious feast, discovers the real bereavement and declares his resolve to wrestle for Alcestis with Death, and that in which Admetus, returning with his friends, bewails the situation to which he has brought himself and confesses the error of his choice, we have already had occasion to speak, and may now pass over them. Each is separated from what precedes by a supposed interval of time, expressed probably, since the Chorus are absent, simply by the emptiness of the stage. These two intervals are, we may say, the only breaks in the action; for in this play the choric odes stand, as appears from the adjoining scenes, for spaces of time scarcely longer than they might well represent without assistance from the imagination of the spectators. During the first interruption, Heracles is occupied with his eating and drinking, for which we are to allow whatever time is indicated by the fact that he does not overtake the procession, the corpse having been left in the tomb, and the mourners having gone away, before he arrives there. Considering his habits, and that the tomb is near[1], and that the performers of the ceremony have strong reasons for expedition, all this fits together naturally enough. The second interval, which must be something longer, is loosely defined by the story of Heracles, who arrives before the palace soon after Admetus and his friends. He is able to pretend without detection that the disguised Alcestis is a slave, won by him as a prize in a gymnastic competition which he found going on in the neighbourhood. As to this imaginary incident, which to our notions comes in rather oddly, it was to the Greeks an obvious sequence, particularly in a story supposed to imitate, however vaguely and inexactly, poetic antiquity. As the news spread that the queen was gone, the first thing that the Pheraeans would be expected to do was to 'keep holiday' and to improvise 'games,' by way of showing honour to the occasion. We moderns, regarding the play as an antiquarian document, would have been glad to hear how the interval has been spent by Admetus and his party; but for the original audience, who knew the customs presumed, this was unnecessary. It is manifest that the mourners, on this occasion at least, do not come straight back from the tomb to the house; this is excluded not only by the lapse of time, but also by other facts implied, such as that they and Heracles have not met, that the Chorus have now changed their dress for black[2], and that the approach of the company to the palace painfully reminds Admetus of that escorting 'home

---

[1] *vv.* 835—836.   [2] *v.* 923; see above, p. 55.

to bed' which ended the antique wedding-day[1], a picture not
likely to be associated with the fore-noon. It should be
noticed however, if we were now concerned with the antiquarian view of the matter, that the husband is in a condition
of mind which, even for a widower on the day of his loss,
and even among the demonstrative Greeks, can scarcely be
figured as normal. The sight of his house inspires him with
such horror that he cannot advance, and his companions
struggle in vain against his reluctance to enter[2]. It is
possible therefore that the delay of his return is to be explained not by customary occupation elsewhere, but as part
of the natural extravagance which belongs to his singular
and singularly distressing situation.

Be that as it may, in this way Heracles, returning with
the wife disguised, is brought again face to face with Admetus
before the door, and we enter upon the finale, commonly
regarded as one of the most unsatisfactory parts of the play.
Speaking broadly, its most noticeable quality is negative. It
is the absence of solemnity; the absence, not only of those
particular phrases adapted to the creed of the age, which
from the piety attributed to some of the personages we
should have expected to hear in the circumstances, but also
of all attempt to pourtray or suggest that kind of instinctive
emotion which any mortal creatures, as such, might be expected to feel at the return of a fellow-mortal from the dead.
Nothing is done, nothing conceded, by way of satisfaction to
the feeling of awe, or even to the vulgar love of the ghostly
and 'eerie' as a means of imaginative pleasure. Excepting
a few lines of bald *ex officio* statement, just sufficient to make
the slight perceptible, nothing passes in the long dialogue
which would not have been equally appropriate if Alcestis,
instead of dying and being buried, had been lost in a mist
or had drifted out to sea, and Heracles had been the shepherd
who found her or the boatman who picked her up, and had
now brought her back to friends who had ceased to hope. It
is true, and it is not the least remarkable feature of the case,
that scarcely anything at all is allowed to pass, when the queen's

[1] *vv.* 911—925.   [2] *vv.* 861—872.

identity has been revealed; but even in the earlier and longer
part of the scene, while she is yet unrecognized, the incongruity of treatment is sufficiently apparent. What it would
be like to encounter a living man fresh from a wrestle with
Death, and bringing with him as prize of the contest a
human being restored to earthly state after body and soul
had passed through the mortal crisis, none of us, I suppose,
are qualified by experience to judge. But this is certain,
that not one man in ten thousand would shape such a scene
in imagination after the fashion chosen by Euripides. Certainly we should not suppose, and for reasons presently to be
noticed the audience at an Athenian drama would be even
less likely to suppose, that the victor and the rescued could
walk in like any two people from the street, and without
suggesting by appearance, tone, or otherwise the suspicion of
anything transcending the habits of everyday life. We have
already remarked[1] the striking contrast between this entrance
as it appears in the original, and as it appears when modified
by the fine but unwarranted interpolations of Browning, and
the almost laughable difficulty which he has betrayed, as it
were involuntarily, of adjusting the demand of his feelings to
the obstinate refusal of the poet. That 'shrouded something,
live and womanlike,' which Balaustion saw leaning 'under
the great guard' of Heracles' arm, is so far from receiving
such notice from those who are compelled to speak only the
language of Euripides, that until she is actually put forward
by Heracles (and he is in no hurry to do it) they do not
seem to see her. She stands to all appearance unremarked,
like the slave she is said to be, among the unnamed attendants
by whom Heracles, as a traveller, was presumably accompanied. If in his aspect the hero showed, as Balaustion
informs us, the signs of his appalling contest, Euripides has
been curiously negligent of impressing any such marks upon
his speech. Here we find, to quote once more Balaustion's
true conclusion, 'all Heracles back again,' that is to say, if we
keep to the veritable lines of the dramatist, a hearty fellow,
generous in his way but coarse, the high-born athlete-bravo,

[1] See p. 40 f.

5—2

who combines the pride of a prince with the grossness of a man-at-arms.

We may question whether in itself, however it had been treated in detail, the common theatrical trick by which the recognition of Alcestis is deferred, could have been made acceptable to such feelings as the supposed situation would naturally excite in a serious mind. A certain value it has, as Browning points out. It enables Heracles to extract from Admetus, for the benefit of his wife before she is restored to him, assurance of the genuine impression which has been made upon him, at least for the time, by the lesson which he has received. Nevertheless I cannot believe that Aeschylus, for example, or Sophocles, or Shakespeare, or Browning himself, would have thought it tolerable in the ostensible circumstances ; and certainly one of these four, the only man perhaps who could have dramatized a resurrection with success, would have done his utmost, if he had allowed the prank to be played at all, to lift it by every art of solemnity in the treatment above the nature of such a thing and into something near the level of the stupendous theme. It is worth while just to imagine for a moment the finale of an *Alcestis* as it might have been presented by the author of the *Choephori*, if only to remind ourselves that the Athenian audience were not without the means of estimating by comparison what it was that Euripides had done. For if the trick was perilous in itself, what is it when Euripides, availing himself of the traits with which he has chosen to invest the ' Helper' and 'Saviour,' has lowered it instead of elevating, until one of the feelings, and not the weakest, which it would inspire in a sensitive spectator, is a feeling of thankfulness that the heroine is veiled ?

In the opening sentences of Heracles, and before the subject of the woman is touched, all chance of solemnity is deliberately thrown away. I have quoted already the rebuke which he addresses to Admetus, exactly as if nothing of importance had occurred since they parted, upon the subject of his treachery as a host. It is a very proper rebuke, and deserves more attention than it commonly gets.

' But O good gods ! '—such must have been the thought of
sundry honest auditors, who shared the prejudices but not
the acuteness of Aristophanes—' what, in the name of Persephoné, is this to the purpose? Here at the man's back
is a woman *risen from the dead*, pulled by his own hands out
of the hands of Death. And he reads a lecture on manners !'
When in this way the strings of our thoughts, tuned perhaps
by the previous meditations of the Chorus to the pitch not
indeed of piety but at least of pensiveness, have been slacked
again and flattened to the common tone, Heracles introduces
the matter which has caused his return. Will his friend take
charge of this woman till he comes back from his adventure
in the north? He has picked up some cattle as a prize, and
the woman into the bargain. Admetus makes objections,
objections which come practically to this, that by obliging
Heracles he may possibly incur some annoyance. After all
he is not so much altered but that he still thinks first of
' number one.' He even reproduces in this new connexion,
by one of those exquisite turns in which Euripides is unsurpassed, his important point that Heracles ' has many other
friends in Pherae.' The grand difficulty is how and where to
give the woman a suitable room in the palace. If he places
her within his own protection, may it not be said that the
widower consoles himself? If elsewhere, may not the consequences be injurious to the rights of her owner? A
charming argument for a man to expound, with antique
plainness of speech, in the presence of the noble lady who
furnishes the matter of it, and she an Alcestis ! The truth
is that in this scene, admirable as comedy but comedy pure,
Heracles is Heracles still, Admetus still Admetus, the one
indelicate and the other selfish ; and between them they
make it impossible to contemplate the situation, whatever
elements of pathos it may contain, as anything out of the
common, and impossible to believe that the author, if he
knew what he was doing, is preparing us to accept it as an
answer to the deepest of human questionings.

After a final altercation, ingenious and striking as a stage-
device, but not otherwise affecting the posture and colour of

the facts, Admetus consents to give his hand to his future inmate, and is persuaded to look her in the face. At last then the truth is out, the awful, thrilling, soul-penetrating truth. The king and his friends know now, that they have before them a mortal who has passed from death into life, and the heaven-born saviour who has brought her through. Here then, if faith or hope in the author's sympathy with his subject has survived in us under the shocks which he has given, we wait for our satisfaction; we wait to hear from Heracles the account of his tremendous experience, and from the others the outpouring of their belief and thankfulness. I will give in words of my own, as exactly as I can, the whole of what is said from this point to the end.

Admetus.	Gods, what is this? Oh marvel passing hope!
	Is it my wife that I behold indeed,
	Or mocks me heaven with a madding joy?
Heracles.	Nay, not so. What thou seest is thy queen.
Adm.	Perchance an apparition from below.
Her.	Hold'st thou thy friend for conjurer of ghosts?
Adm.	She whom I buried...visible...here...my queen?
Her.	Aye; 'tis no marvel that belief is hard.
Adm.	May I touch her...speak to her as alive...my queen?
Her.	Aye, *speak to her*; for all thy will thou hast[1].
Adm.	Ah, dearest, face and form of thee, that ne'er
	I thought to see! Oh wonder! Art thou mine?
Her.	Aye. Jealous heaven, forgive this happiness!
Adm.	O son of Zeus Supreme, his noble son,
	Blest be thou: may the father that begat
	Protect: for thou hast raised me, thou alone!...
	How didst thou bring her from beneath to day?
Her.	*By wrestling with the power that rules herein.*
Adm.	*A bout with Death! Where didst thou close with him?*
Her.	*At the tomb. I lay in wait, rushed out, and gripped....*
Adm.	*Why stands, oh why, the woman speechless thus?*

[1] προσειπ'· ἔχεις γὰρ πᾶν ὅσονπερ ἤθελες. The point of this line is lost in English, because the phrase *speak to*, *address* (προσειπεῖν) has not with us the secondary limited sense of *saying farewell*, especially to the dead, the πρόσρησις or *farewell* being a regular part of the burial-office (*Alc.* 609—610). The Greek hints that Admetus is to have just what he chose to have (by consenting to her death) *and no more*, that he may speak but Alcestis will refuse to answer. It thus anticipates the sequel and the sarcasms of *vv.* 1144—1146, on which see below.

Her.	*To hear her salutation is not yet*
	Permitted thee.. First to the nether gods
	She must acquit her, and the third day dawn.
	Now lead her in; and deal, as thou art bound,
	Henceforth, Admetus, piously with thy guests.
	Farewell! For me, I go to execute
	For King Eurystheus the appointed task.
Adm.	*Remain with us, a partner of the feast[1].*
Her.	*Another time; the present bids me speed.*
Adm.	*Good fortune then be thine, and safe return.* [*Exit Heracles.*
	In Pherae and in all the Marches Four
	For this good hap be dances set afoot
	And worshipped altars steam with sacrifice.
	This hour transforms us to a better life,
	Being fortunate, as I shall not deny. [*Exeunt.*
Chorus.	*Many a guise hath deity,*
	Doth surprises oft decree,
	Cunning for the expected end
	Unexpected close to send,
	By such way as this doth wend. [*Exeunt.*

'Quite unexpected! And is that all?' must have been the
comment of those in the Athenian audience (and there were
probably not a few) who had followed the play so far with
the desire to see in it a *bona fide* version of the sacred legend.
'If it is unexpected, why then it is all!' might have been the
reply of those (and even as early as the date of the *Alcestis*
they must have been a large majority) who understood the
attitude of Euripides, and sympathized with him sufficiently
to desire that he should be allowed, so far as might be, the
means of public expression. The conclusion of the piece,
from the moment when Heracles is asked for a narrative of
his enterprise, is on the face of it a mere ironical mystifica-
tion, representing no conceivable reality, felt to be incredible
even by readers who have not been tempted to enquire
further, and signifying nothing, except that the dramatist
and his *dramatis personae* have agreed to drop the subject.
Strange and inexplicable, to begin with, is the behaviour of

---

[1] συνέστιος : see Eur. *El.* 784. As this example shows, *partner of the hearth*,
though literally right, implies in English far too much, and the remarks of
Browning are unfounded. What Admetus gives is simply an invitation to the
feast (see *v.* 1156) which would naturally follow.

Heracles in evading without cause alleged the natural and blameless desire of Admetus to learn the manner of this astounding achievement. Why—to put the point in a practical way—should so admirable a narrator as Euripides defraud himself and the audience of this fine opportunity? What is his motive, and what is that of his hero? 'Heracles,' thinks Balaustion, 'said little but enough.' Little it is; but enough it apparently is not, when it leaves so many readers to exclaim, with Dr Munk, 'That the poet should expect us to accept things so obscure and improbable to the imagination is too much!' Surely it is, if he *does* expect us to accept them; surely it was his especial business, in that case, to make them probable to the imagination by his skill in the telling, which (we may add) none, if he had chosen, could have done better. But Heracles, instead of relating what has happened, or explaining why he should not relate it, gives a reply which is not so mysterious as unintelligible. 'How didst thou bring her from beneath to this light?' 'By fighting the power with whom the matter lay[1].' But who is this *power* or *deity*? Admetus guesses *Death*, and the interpretation is coldly accepted. But what has become of Heracles' tongue, which before the enterprise was so eloquent and assured?

> I will go lie in wait for Death, black-stoled
> King of the corpses! I shall find him, sure,
> Drinking, beside the tomb, o' the sacrifice; . . . .

and so on. Why cannot he speak so now, and what does he mean?

Strange in itself is the reticence of Heracles, and stranger the acquiescence of the rest.

> 'A bout with Death! Where didst thou close with him?'
> 'At the tomb. I lay in wait, rushed out, and gripped.'

---

[1] μάχην ξυνάψας δαιμόνων τῷ κυρίῳ, the certain reading. The variant κοιράνῳ is a mere guess made (like οἰκεῖος in v. 811) to get rid of a difficulty. The guesser probably meant his δαιμόνων τῷ κοιράνῳ to signify *the lord of spirits*, which measures his competence to emend Euripides. Modern scholars, while hazarding this version, do not omit (see Paley) to point out that it will not pass: δαιμόνων κοιράνῳ would mean, if any one, *Zeus*; and δαιμόνων τῷ κοιράνῳ is not good Euripidean Greek for anything here admissible.

And no one has anything more to ask! Admetus indeed, by noticing at this moment the silence of Alcestis, suggests the thought that she perhaps may explain. But no; she is not to speak till the day after to-morrow; and this for a mystic reason which, stated baldly and in such a connexion, produces an effect like that of burlesque. In expounding the play it is now regular at this point to bid the reader observe (with Elmsley) that, if there was a religious reason why Alcestis should not speak, there was also a practical reason; inasmuch as, if she had, the play, which by means of changing masks could now be performed with two main actors capable of elocution, would in this scene have required three. And up to a certain point we must go with this observation. Undoubtedly the way in which her silence and the cause of it are treated by Euripides, the abruptness with which the subject is raised and dropped, and especially the coolness with which the mysterious precept is given and received, just as if it were some trivial apothecary's prescription about diet or exercise, are exactly calculated to prompt, in minds acquainted with the history of Athenian drama, the reflexion of Elmsley. But the inference is that the author intended to prompt it, or in other words, to give to the situation a touch of awkwardness and absurdity; for that his embarrassment was involuntary we really cannot believe. Long before the production of the *Alcestis*, and all through the career of Euripides, three-part scenes had been in regular use. Even if we suppose, what is sufficiently improbable, that all the three other plays which the author, as we know, exhibited with this, consisted wholly of two-part scenes, the *Alcestis* itself would show that he had no difficulty in obtaining such 'extras' as he wanted. He does not hesitate, because two actors are already on the stage, to introduce the effective but needless part of the orphan child[1], a part surely much harder to fill than it would have been to procure some one capable of delivering a verse or two, all that would here be needed or admissible, in the character of Alcestis. In the conditions of Greek performance it would have been possible, if necessary,

[1] *v.* 393.

to 'double' the parts of the son and the mother. But really it is not conceivable that there should be any difficulty about the matter. Besides, if difficulty there were, why exhibit it? Alcestis, after the disclosure, has scarcely time to speak before the play is over. Twenty ways, better theatrically than that selected, could have been taken to explain her silence, the best and obvious way being to let those who might notice it explain it for themselves. But Euripides chose here to do what he has done elsewhere, notably, as will be remembered, in his *Electra*; he satirises, in a manner all the more telling from its decorous gravity, the practice of his elders. In the religious tragedy of Aeschylus, silent personages played a great part. We know that their silence, though sometimes effective, was not always voluntary, but imposed by the narrow limitations of the cast[1]; and we also know, through Aristophanes, that the topic was, as it naturally would be, a favourite butt for the witticisms of the 'modern' and opposite school[2]. Such a sly shaft Euripides here discharges; and that he thinks the occasion suitable is proof by itself that he neither feels nor invites respect for the momentous doctrine which nevertheless this finale pretends to set forth. It is even something more than likely that he aims at a particular scene or passage, which we should recognize if, as in the case of the *Choephori* and Euripidean *Electra*, it had been spared to us by time. But however this be, the spirit and tone of his reference are (to my mind) manifest; and they are incompatible with the belief that he 'means seriously with' the supposed resurrection.

And for further confirmation be it observed that the sarcasm has yet another edge. Alcestis, says Heracles, must not yet speak because 'she will not have discharged her ceremonial obligations to the nether gods until the day after to-morrow.' Now obligations of this sort, contracted by the passage from death to life, are so seldom incurred within the limits of our human experience, that they are not much known or thought of. But the contrary passage from life to death is the commonest thing in the world, and no rules

---

[1] *e.g.* in the *Prometheus*.   [2] *Frogs*, 911.

more familiar than those which relate to it. It is interesting therefore to learn, on the respectable authority of a demi-god, that there is between the two cases so close a resemblance. When a man comes from the nether world to the upper, there is, it seems, a certain interval of transition, during which the claim of the nether powers is not entirely extinguished, but requires to be satisfied by proper observances. Just so, as we all know, when he goes the other way : the transition, in point of form, is not completed in a moment or in an hour. There is a time when he is, as it were, between the worlds, with us and yet with us no more, the time between our first perception of his death and the moment when we part with his body. By universal custom this interval should have a certain extension, and should be observed with careful ceremonies ; nor could it be cut short without our feeling, for grave, manifest, and imperative reasons, that the rights of the *upper* gods were being infringed. And the analogy extends even to the length of prescription. On the third day from that of his resurrection inclusive, but not before, a man may be surrendered altogether to this life. Exactly the same minimum, verbally the same, is fixed by Plato in the contrary case[1], and commends itself by our common experience. Most remarkable of all, both in the nether world and in the upper, the reciprocal obligation was denoted by the same Greek word, *hagnismos*, which was applied, it appears, as it was familiarly among the living to the formalities of a funeral, so among the ghosts to those of a resurrection. In short the precept of Heracles is plainly so shaped as to rebuke (and to punish) the wrong lately committed by Admetus against ordinances less shadowy, if not more important, than those of Pluto and Persephoné : and that he means it so, he shows by following it up with a final caution about 'hospitality,' another piety which the king has also neglected through the entangling consequences of his trespass against the dead. But in the midst of these witticisms, what are we to think of the miracle ?

And so the heroes part, with adieux the briefest possible.

---

[1] See the *Laws*, as above cited.

Admetus in dismissing himself and the rest is equally brief, and exhibits in his proclamation of festivities the same disinclination to particularity about the cause of them, which we have already observed in Heracles. It is a 'good hap,' and he himself is 'fortunate, as he will not deny.' A handsome concession, but who wants it, and why should it be supposed that he has anything to 'deny'? Lastly we are left with the Chorus, whose behaviour is an appropriate climax. Which now will they give us, we naturally ask, of the many reflexions that must be suggested to them, in the light of their previous utterances, by the resurrection of Alcestis? They had expressed a hope that in some way or other Admetus would be further rewarded for his piety towards the gods, and particularly towards Apollo. Here is a miracle which more than fulfils their anticipation; and though they do not know, as we do having heard the prologue, that the Pythian deity had himself foreseen and foretold the precise event, Apollo, whom neither Heracles nor Admetus has found time to mention, will now perhaps come in for the tribute of a stanza. Whoever may be 'compelled to haste,' the Chorus have leisure enough, for the play is still short. Or again there is the casuistry of hospitality, on which in the first instance they show so loyal a disposition to give up their own opinion for that of their master. Now that every one, as it would seem, agrees in their original view, it would not be unbecoming if they were to re-adopt it. But among the many topics on which we should like to hear them, there is one on which surely they are bound to be full and explicit. Within the last five minutes, if in the general hurry we rightly apprehend what has happened, the Chorus must have changed their belief on the most vital of problems, on nothing less than the whole nature and condition of humanity. At the very moment before Heracles enters with his prize, the poet has put in their mouths a creed which by its solemnity (it is perhaps the only passage in the play to which this word can well be applied) and by its strong personal emphasis arrests the attention of every reader[1]. 'For my part, after searching

[1] *v.* 962 ff.

deep and long, I find that *nothing*, no charm, no spell, no prayer, can prevail against that *Necessity*, that fixed *Order* of things, by which our world from lowest to highest is bound. Of this invincible order I see one fresh example in him who here helplessly mourns for his wife, helplessly, *for no weeping will raise up them that have perished.* Even the noblest perish in death. Even of an Alcestis there remains only the love of her and the praise of her virtues.' To such effect —with every mark of sincerity and earnestness—Euripides has just before addressed the audience by the voice of the Chorus. And now therefore, if this very Alcestis, who could not possibly rise, has actually risen before the eyes of the Chorus and ours, if the irreversible order of things has in its most impressive manifestation been signally reversed, if in short it has been proved (as all, if they saw such a thing happen, would understand and confess) that the bond of 'Necessity' does not bind, but itself is breakable by superior and, as we say, miraculous power,—what has become of that creed? Was it put forward only that the contrasted sequel might the more conspicuously exhibit its falsity? Has the poet refuted himself, and are his spokesmen convinced? This is the question to which, when the chief actors are gone, we are still awaiting an answer. Heracles is curt and evasive; Alcestis must not yet speak; Admetus says nothing to the purpose. No one—if the reader doubts this, I will ask him to glance again over the dialogue—has yet said the one thing, so simple and so essential to be said, 'This woman was dead and is alive again.' The Chorus only are left, and what have they to say? 'How often' say the Chorus 'things end otherwise than was expected! So does this story.' And away they go.

Now what is the meaning of all this? What is the purpose of this lame, impotent, and abrupt conclusion? How does it serve to harmonize the discordant elements of the drama and fix for us the impression which we are intended to carry away? How does it explain the author's motives in treating a story which, except in the single point of the heroine's character, he handles, as it would seem, only to injure it? By common consent the true answer to this question is that the finale does not satisfy any such demand, but is on the contrary altogether unsatisfactory. Even the Byzantine critics, who were not easily surprised, were surprised and displeased at the conclusion of the *Alcestis* : 'the conclusion of the play' says the second and most substantial of the three Greek introductory notes 'is too comic[1].' If a modern poet, a Browning let us say, should take the *Alcestis* in hand to remodel it freely and bring it more into accord with the author's assumed intentions, one thing which he would certainly do, besides such transformations of the *dramatis personae* as Balaustion makes in the case of Heracles, would be to re-write the finale completely, making Heracles say not 'little' but truly 'enough,' as Balaustion would fain have done had she dared, and generally elevating and expanding the treatment to the measure of the ostensible occasion. Why did not Euripides? This—if we shrink from the answer 'because he was a botcher, and did not know what he was about'—is the question which we are left to consider. Let us assume that Euripides was a man of sense, and that his purpose was as serious as he would seem to imply by the choice of his subject and by the sober, persuasive realism of his portraiture ; and let us gravely ask ourselves what that purpose can have been.

It is sometimes a helpful and, with proper caution, a legitimate way of judging the transactions of other times, to put a parallel case, real or fictitious, arising in our own times and among those circumstances to which we are accustomed. Remembering carefully that Euripides addressed an audience of whom a considerable portion regarded the resurrection of Alcestis as sacred truth, and all of whom, except open rebels against the religion of the state, were in the habit of assisting

---

[1] This remark or some other to the like effect has been apparently understood by the writer of the third note (ἡ σκηνὴ...ἐχόμενα) to mean that a tragedy ought not to end happily, on which ground, he says, 'both the *Orestes* and the *Alcestis* are ejected from the list of tragedies.' The words of the second writer do not imply this proposition ; and it would not be fair to put it upon him. In 'ending happily' the two plays mentioned do not differ from many 'tragedies' both of Euripides and his brother dramatists. Reasonable grounds might be given for associating the two, but what they are, this writer did not know.

at rites implying this belief or other beliefs warranted by the
same authority—carefully remembering this, let us ask what
we ourselves should think, if we read a newly-published
historical fiction in which a general outline, resembling *mutatis mutandis* that which Euripides gives to the death, burial,
and resurrection of Alcestis, were given to the death, burial,
and resurrection of Lazurus. Read first—I am anxious to
convince the reader that in my opinion this is no matter for
levity—read first the eleventh chapter of the *Gospel according
to St John*; and then suppose a story in which it should be
represented that, *for reasons special to the case and traceable,
according to the novelist, in the Bible itself,* Lazarus was really
conveyed to the tomb within an hour of his death, and was
restored in the course of the day. Or read the fourth chapter
of the *Second Book of Kings*; and then suppose a version of
the story in which Gehazi, on reaching the home of the
Shunammite, found that the child had revived immediately
after the mother's departure, and Elisha, instead of actually
restoring him in the way described, merely announced his intention to do so, an intention forestalled by the recovery.
Then go back to the *Alcestis*, and consider whether, if the
characters are ill-matched with the miraculous hypothesis
ostensibly propounded in the conclusion, *the facts* of the story
are not equally ill-devised to sustain this hypothesis; and
whether it is not fair, reasonable, and necessary to suppose
the author aware of this; and then whether—seeing that
everything in the drama from the 77th verse to the 1135th,
characters and facts alike, is repugnant to the theological
interpretation given ostensibly in the prologue and conclusion,
so that, to save the author's reputation for sense, we must
suppose him not serious either with the mass of his work or
with the fringes—whether we ought not to set 1059 verses
above 104, and look for serious meaning in the 1059, and for
signs of a presumable mockery in the 104.

'The resurrection of Alcestis' is represented by Euripides
as it could be only by a man *who did not believe that it was a
resurrection, and wished to convey this to others.* Suppose that,
when Admetus asks 'How did you bring her from below to

this light?', Heracles instead of meeting the question, as
Euripides makes him do, with a reply which is no reply,
evasive and unintelligible, had answered frankly 'How did I
do it? I went to the monument, and after waiting a fair
while till my head was cool, I went in. As soon as I saw
your wife I was sure she was alive, and I had not been there
long before she came to. When she felt fit to move, I cloaked
her (for I thought you deserved a trick) and we walked back.
There is no mystery about it. What I cannot understand is
why she was carried there with such haste as it seems she
was, and how you could fancy that she was dead.' If
Heracles had so replied, who, unless it were Admetus, could
have felt any astonishment, and how could Admetus himself
have disputed the simplicity of the explanation? The facts,
as given by Euripides, are these. The death of a certain
woman has been predicted for a certain day. She and her
family are convinced that on that day she will certainly die.
This expectation (be it observed) is grounded solely on the
prophecy[1]. Up to the morning of the day itself, and even on
that morning, she is so far from showing signs of danger,
that those who see her can even speak of her 'unchanged
complexion.' Nevertheless, acting upon the absolute certainty
of her approaching end, she rises at dawn, bathes, robes herself elaborately as for burial, and goes the round of the
palace in which she is queen, paying her devotion 'at every
altar which it contains.' She then takes a long and passionate
farewell of her chamber, then of her children, and then of all
the household (a royal household) 'down to the very meanest.'
From this time in fact till her 'death' she is occupied incessantly in adieux. She lies in her husband's arms, expecting
the end, surrounded by the whole weeping assembly, servants
and children, and still, so long as she can, repeating her farewells. Her case is treated from the first and throughout as
hopeless. No attempt is made to sustain her, either by herself
or the rest, except 'beseeching her not to depart.' In such
scenes the hours go by until she has become very weak; with
more adieux she becomes weaker; and at last it is plain that

---

[1] See the narrative beginning at *v.* 158.

she is sinking. Carried into the air, she rallies sufficiently for yet one prolonged farewell, after which she sinks again, sinks rapidly, and becomes unconscious. Being already prepared for burial, except for the addition of certain ornaments, which are also ready, the body, just as it lies, is carried to a neighbouring monument, laid there and left. Later in the day the woman is brought back from the tomb to her house.

Where is the miracle? There is no one now, and assuredly there was no one at Athens in the days of Protagoras, who *assuming these facts* would dream of a miraculous explanation, instead of the obvious explanation that the woman and her friends were mistaken, that she was not in such danger as she and they too credulously supposed, that she wanted nothing but a little rest from their killing importunities, and would have revived, not in a tomb but in her house, if the 'survivors' had given her time to do so. And in fact this is the conviction of all the *dramatis personae* in Euripides, of Heracles, Admetus, and the Chorus alike; only (as in the theatre of Dionysus one cannot exactly say so) instead of the natural and proper conclusion, the conclusion which might be expected from the course of the story, we have the miraculous explanation appended in a form transparently unreal. From the moment when it is understood that Alcestis has certainly come back, from the moment of the question 'How was the thing accomplished?' the actors *cease to act in character*; they cease to be conceivable as persons in the situation supposed, and show neither opinion nor emotion, except a general agreement to wind up the business as quickly as possible, joined in the case of Heracles with a strong disposition to sneer. 'The gods' as the author says with typical irony 'have found the way to *an ending unexpected*, instead of that *for which we looked*[1].' Such is the resurrection as related by

---

[1] I was mistaken when (in my first edition of the *Medea*, 1881) I said that this famous conclusion was 'quite inappropriate' to that play. It is quite appropriate; it calls attention to the contrast between the realism of the drama as a whole and the purely conventional 'supernaturalism' of the *dénouement*. The 'dragon-chariot' of Medea is entirely out of keeping with the tone and spirit of the work, a mere theatrical concession, and the 'tag' signifies this. The other examples are all interesting and similar, but cannot be discussed here.

Euripides, and such is the aspect in which alone the scheme, tone, and cast of the play are intelligible as a whole. But to make the matter fully comprehensible, I must ask the reader's patience for a larger historical survey.

The *Alcestis* in its general character, and in the relation between outward pretence and inward suggestion, is by no means exceptional among the works of the poet. Most of them show something of the same character, and one example at least, the *Ion*, corresponds to the type almost as perfectly as the *Alcestis*. It could not now possibly exist, at least in Western Europe, for many reasons and some highly satisfactory, nor perhaps could ever have been fully developed in any society except just at Athens in the fifth century before Christ. But there and then the conditions were such as to produce this type inevitably, a type of dramatic work whose meaning lies entirely in *innuendo*. The purpose of the *Alcestis* as a whole, and that which alone connects into a whole its otherwise inharmonious and repugnant elements, is neither to solemnize the legend, as would have been the purpose of Aeschylus, nor to embellish it, as might have been the purpose of Sophocles, but to *criticize* it, to expose it as fundamentally untrue and immoral, before an audience who were well acquainted with the general opinions of the author, well aware that from the circumstances of the case *innuendo* was the only way in which those opinions could be dramatically expressed, well accustomed to apprehend them in this form, and predisposed by mental and moral temper not merely to be content with such a mode of expression, but to regard it as the best possible condition for intellectual art and intellectual pleasure.

At Athens in the age of Euripides the relations of the drama, and of tragedy in particular, to other functions of society were so different from those in our experience, indeed so contrary to our experience, that although the facts are familiar, it is not easy to bear them always effectively in mind. In our own country particularly the theatre is not, rarely has been, and never has been since many generations, of general importance as an organ of public opinion or public

instruction. Such are our habits and traditions that even
now, when liberty of expression in almost all forms is established as a panacea and has perhaps produced some disease,
a drama which was designed to set forth and recommend
a particular opinion on some topic agitating the public mind
at the moment, would probably not be popular ; and whether
it were likely to be popular or not, it would not obtain a
licence. And in particular with regard to one class of subject,
the most widely and deeply interesting of all, there is and
long has been in England a rule, sanctioned by sentiment as
much as by law, that it may be discussed everywhere and
almost without limit, except on the stage, from which it is
rigidly excluded : and this is the subject of religion. Nor
do these restrictions excite impatience even in the most
determined agitators. When methods of publication more
efficient in the present conditions of life than a play could
be, though it were performed by order of Parliament at the
public expense in every theatre of London, are open to any
man whose opinions and style are intrinsically capable of
attracting attention ; and when religion, orthodox and unorthodox, is propagated without restraint in ways devised
by itself for its own ends ; it is not very likely that any one
would offer to the Lyceum a *Marriage in Cana* or *Jairus'
Daughter*, even if there were a chance that it would be
accepted. But it is notorious, although easily forgotten in
practice, that in Athens at the time of which we are speaking
the conditions, positive and negative, were exactly the reverse
of these. Drama was essentially the vehicle, not of pleasure,
though this was part of its purpose and one of its necessary
instruments, but of instruction and controversy on the most
exciting themes of the day. Comedy dealt mainly with
politics, tragedy always directly or indirectly with religion,
and with morals as related to religion. When Aristophanes
in the *Frogs* presents the personages of Aeschylus and
Euripides, each defending himself as an artist and assailing
the other, he assumes as a matter of course that the rivals
must be judged as public preachers, as aiming deliberately
at the spread of certain opinions and the production of a

certain character in their auditors. Upon this comparison he throws all the weight of the discussion, and gives to other matters, such matters as we should call *literary*, a treatment altogether subordinate and scarcely serious. In the fore-front of the argument he places a pair of contrasted prayers, both tragedians coming forward as representatives of religion, of two opposed religions. Aeschylus, representing the class of which he had in fact been the greatest prophet, the class who desired to deepen and spiritualize the legendary tradi-tions without breaking with them, prays in sacramental form to Demeter of Eleusis 'who feedest my soul,' and asks to be found worthy of her mysteries. Euripides, rejecting the gods of tradition for 'a mintage of his own,' asks of 'Air and the turn of the Tongue, Intelligence and the nostril of Per-ception' to make him 'a true critic of every subject presented to his sense'; nor does this petition deviate beyond the reasonable limits of professed parody from some which the tragedian himself finds occasion to put in the mouth of his characters. The creed of Euripides was that of nascent philosophy, science, and rationalism ; between which and the worship of the popular gods there was a war to which modern religious controversies offer no parallel. It was not merely that the current legends assumed as possible and true things which science rejected as incredible ; but the whole character of pagan tradition, loose, fluctuating, unsystematic, varying between city and city, shrine and shrine, and ready even to accommodate itself by arbitrary modifications to different moods of the same mind, was fundamentally incompatible with regular and consistent *theory* of any kind. The religious creeds of modern Europe are themselves to a large extent made up of science and philosophy. If they come into collision with 'science' in a more limited sense, this is not because their supporters do not hold as strongly as their opponents the necessity of system and regularity in thought. But the religion or rather the religious atmosphere of paganism was not a creed at all, nor able to take any such form without self-destruction. The duty preached by the philosophers, and by Euripides as a public teacher known to be in sympathy

with philosophers, was the duty of thinking on system, of
not adopting, without evidence or investigation, contradictory
hypotheses on different days of the month or at different
stages of a journey ; a duty which, as was seen with ever
increasing clearness, would if pursued make it impossible to
use at all such conceptions as 'Apollo,' or 'Artemis,' or
'Demeter,' and reduce even 'Zeus' to the position of an
inconvenient and misleading name.

That these were the views of Euripides, and that he
desired to impress them upon others, would have been
manifest to his fellow-citizens, if they had had no evidence
but what he himself put forth. And in such a community
as that of Athens, where the doings even of people inconspicuous and unimportant were better known than London
knows her 'celebrities,' where it was worth the while of a
comedian to bring up before the assembled state such little
personal jests as now would scarcely catch in a parish-
meeting, much that was not meant for publication must
nevertheless have been widely known about any man who
had won his way to the privilege, confined by necessity to
few, of being an exhibitor in the great dramatic festival. As
to Euripides, that it was the purpose and effect of his plays
to destroy the old religious beliefs, is repeatedly taken by
Aristophanes for notorious. To dwell upon the evidence
is unnecessary, as if not quite undisputed it is not really open
to reasonable dispute ; and the whole subject has recently
been re-stated, with knowledge and skill upon which I at
least cannot improve, in the second chapter of *Euripide et
l'esprit de son théâtre*[1] by Professor Paul Decharme, the best
treatise on the poet with which I am acquainted. There is
scarcely one of the extant plays which would not prove
him a determined enemy of the popular theology ; and even
in the unintelligent and uncritical summaries which are all
that remain to us of ancient biography respecting him, one
of the few traits which has an air of genuine history is,
that he was drawn to the stage only or mainly because it

---

[1] Paris, Garnier Frères.

provided him with armour as well as weapons for this contest [1].

It might be matter for surprise, if without making allowance for differences of condition we estimated the proceedings of distant ages upon the principles of our own, that such an author should have taken or have been permitted to take such a way of publication; that the plays of Euripides, abounding in sarcasms upon the traditional gods, should have been selected against powerful competitors for performance in a place dedicated to traditional religion. If we wanted to find any sort of parallel in our own life, it must be by supposing that some eminent Positivist or Agnostic were appointed for one Sunday in every month, upon certain terms of reticence and discretion, to preach the sermon in Westminster Abbey. But this or something like it could actually be enforced by public opinion, if the pulpit at Westminster were as uniquely important among the means of intellectual influence as was the stage of Dionysus at Athens, and if religious parties in their shades of distinction were so related as they were then. The Athenians under Pericles, though passionately intelligent and curious, were not in general collectors of books. It is not till the last quarter of the fifth century, not that is to say till the career of Euripides was drawing to a close, that we find in the rapid growth of prose literature the sign of a public accustomed to the amusement of solitary reading [2]. As for the echoing repetition by which in these days a new thought upon any subject of pressing interest is rapidly bandied about in volume, article, and paragraph, nothing of the sort, it is needless to say, had been dreamed of. Nor was the stage available as a daily expedient; for theatrical

---

[1] ἐπὶ τραγῳδίαν δὲ ἐτράπη τὸν Ἀναξαγόραν ἰδὼν ὑποστάντα κινδύνους δι᾽ ἅπερ εἰσῆξε δόγματα. Suidas, *Euripides*. The remark is meaningless except on the assumption that in tragedy he could express the opinions of Anaxagoras with more security.

[2] The earliest Greek author who, so far as I know, can be proved to have been familiarly *read in private* by ordinary persons is Euripides himself (*Frogs* 52), where *reading to oneself* (ἀναγιγνώσκειν πρὸς ἑαυτόν) marks the exceptional practice, as we now speak of ' reading *aloud*.'

exhibitions were commonly confined to the rare and solemn performance of the regular festivals. Under these circumstances the colossal advertisement obtained by exhibiting at these festivals before the assembled folk was an overpowering advantage in circulation. Everything goes to show that next to that ancient epic literature which the city of Athens had in the preceding century taken under her particular patronage, that 'Homer' which was recited on holidays and taught in the schools, no literature was half so well or so widely known as the favourite bits from the dramatists. It was not therefore likely to be tolerated, that out of respect for a local and temporal association between tragedy and the traditional theology, which was only a historic accident, due in great part to the personal inclinations of one creative genius, this unique advantage should be appropriated entirely by a section of the community, the sincere supporters of traditional theology, who throughout the century, in spite of their legal superiority, were continually losing ground. Although tragedy had been founded or re-founded by Aeschylus, yet a generation of whom (we have it from the Aeschylean Aristophanes) only a small minority were Aeschyleans would scarcely condemn themselves for this reason to hear nothing but Aeschylism from the orchestra which he had magnified ; and this especially when, by another historic accident, it happened that the man who of all living Athenians was perhaps the most richly endowed with the talents required for dramatic composition had espoused the contrary opinions with the zeal of a missionary.

For more reasons than one it was not in comedy, as comedy was practised at Athens in that age, that the new spirit, the spirit of philosophical criticism, could effectively make itself heard. To our habitual feelings it is somewhat odd to see Aristophanes, while in the very act of exhibiting in postures of farce or harlequinade the patron-god of the sacred theatre, idol and leader of the deepest and tenderest mysteries, turn round to vilify the innovators who dared to depreciate the accepted deities in comparison with their own inventions. But it is constantly assumed by the comedian, that no confusion was possible between his attitude in this relation and that of such a man as Euripides; it is assumed that his own ridicule was in the popular sense religious, and that of Euripides in the like sense irreligious, the two forms not merely different but antagonistic. Nor is it difficult to appreciate the distinction. In the first place the whole cast of comedy, its extravagance of imagination, was a sufficient safeguard against a severe interpretation of anything which the author might advance by way of helping a jest. The spectator would no more be embarrassed in his religious exercises by having seen a *Dionysus* take a flogging in competition with a slave upon the toughness of their respective skins, than he would be embarrassed in his politics by having seen the birds conspire to build a city in the air. But this licence of imagination would in itself have rendered the comic stage an unsuitable instrument for serious attack upon beliefs transcending common experience. No form of art could be further removed from Aristophanic comedy than the realistic cast of Euripides' tragedy. As he is made to say in the *Frogs*[1], doubtless because he did habitually say so in conversation, his whole aim is to put his audience 'among the things which we handle and live with,' in the world as it visibly is; and this, as he goes on to note, for the purpose of enabling them to *criticize* what is said and done there. The departing spectator took with him the pictures presented by the poet as things which could no more be supposed away than the streets through which he went home, and among these realities were the reflexions, grave or gay in form but alike serious in meaning, which were made in the drama, as on convenient occasions they were made in actual society, upon the current theology. But the difference goes even deeper than this. Taken with the proviso, which Aristophanes is careful to repeat, that in practice you will do well to worship according to the wont of your city, parish, and family, it was positively good for Zeus and Apollo to be supposed indulgent as to the way in which they were depicted, and lax in general as to intellectual belief. The local

[1] *v.* 959.

varieties of cult and legend could stand together on no
other supposition. To make a jest for the moment of the
almighty father and his offspring was an excellent means to
keep men in that flaccid, wavering habit of mind by which
Zeus *this*, Apollo *that*, and Artemis *the other*, could be
accepted according to the ritual of the place or shrine where
the worshipper happened to be.   It was another thing to
indict these personages in the name of *intelligence*, and with
constant incitements to clarify your thoughts and arrange
your propositions.

   Thus the conditions of the time and his own talents
combined to obtain for Euripides the permission to speak
from the stage of tragedy, and to speak there in his own
sense.   But it did not therefore follow that he could speak
there without disguise, nor that he would choose to do so, if
he could.   As things stood in Athens, a certain disguise or
semblance of disguise was desirable alike for safety and for
effect.   It was necessary that the veil should be transparent
for all who cared to look through it ; and this it was sure
to be from the nature of the case.   Take the *Alcestis* as an
example.   The legend commemorates a miracle wrought on
behalf of a man specially beloved and favoured by the
Pythian Apollo.   Now there cannot have been a man in
Athens interested in literature, not any one to whom the
tragic festival was more than an amusement for the eye, who
was unaware that Euripides laughed at the miracles of legend
and regarded the pretensions of Delphi with scorn.   It is
possible indeed, or probable, that when the *Alcestis* was
exhibited[1], he had not yet delivered himself on the stage so
frankly as he does in some of the extant plays.   He had
perhaps not yet denounced the Pythian deity as the accom-
plice and instigator of murders, which he does in the *Electra*,
the *Orestes*, and the *Andromache*, or as a lying, shuffling,
cheating ravisher, which he does in the *Ion*.   Probably he
became bolder as the new speculations spread wider and
were more widely avowed.   But we have remains enough
of his work at all periods to see that its tendency had been

---

[1] B.C. 438.

the same throughout; nor to his fellow-citizens, as we have already said, was the stage the only or the most authentic source of information about him. Now when it was announced that this man intended to present in the theatre the story of Alcestis, what did the Athenians expect? Suppose a parallel case among ourselves. It must needs be inexactly parallel, but we can make the resemblance sufficient. Suppose that once a year that part of the inhabitants of London which frequents the clubs and reads the magazines, were accustomed to assemble for the purpose of witnessing plays in which the stories of the Bible were presented after the manner of *Samson Agonistes*, with variations according to the taste of the composer, but in the same general spirit of acceptation and reverence. And suppose it then given out that the management had decided to exhibit a play entitled (let us say) *The Herdsmen of Gadara* or *The Shunammite*, and written by *Professor T.... H....* What sort of a piece would the audience anticipate, and what motive could they attribute to the author? It was a thing incredible in itself that Euripides intended to send his Athenian hearers with devotion warmed and faith exalted to the next celebration of those Apolline rites in which, as he tells us[1], this miraculous legend was a familiar theme. It was certain beforehand that his object must be precisely the contrary; and the only question open would be, what means he would find of conveying his known sentiments, and how far he would venture to go. His methods of attack are many. It would not for example have been easy to deal with the legend of Alcestis after the fashion of the *Heraclidae*, in which, though the chief personages are all of them 'gods,' that is to say objects of existing cults, the story, which is in effect a satire on the barbarity of ancient religion and ancient manners, is rigorously stripped of every supernatural incident except one. This incident is reported by a speaker who pointedly distinguishes it from the rest of his narrative as 'hearsay' and not guaranteed by his own observation[2]! There is this way, and there are many others. What way the poet would take

---

[1] *Alc.* 445—452.   [2] *Heraclidae*, 847 ff.

in his *Alcestis* could not be known ; but the point from which
he started was known and given, unless it were to be imagined
that he had suddenly changed his mind, an imagination which,
as we shall see hereafter, a few lines of the actual commence-
ment would be enough to correct.

The use of disguise was therefore artistically safe ; safe,
that is, to be penetrated by any one who chose to give himself
that satisfaction. But it was also, in a very different sense,
safe and essential to safety for the person of the author. It
is a common incident in the development of society that
between effectual prohibition and formal permission there
intervenes a stage, in which an act legally forbidden and
punishable is nevertheless protected by the predominance
of favourable opinion, and practicable therefore, so long as
adverse opinion is propitiated by a show of deference ; when
(in simpler terms) you may do the thing, provided only
that you make a decent pretence of not doing it. Every
one must have observed and be observing examples of this
phenomenon ; and it is wonderful to see how long the pretence may be used and even imposed, when it has become
so thin that only a historical explanation will account for
its existence. The whole character of Euripidean drama
fits in with the history of the time to show that to this
point had come, in the time of Pericles, Cleon, and Alci-
biades, the public expression of dissent from that moribund
theology upon which the established cults reposed. 'Impiety'
was at Athens a legal crime, and there was more than one
way of visiting it with penalties practically unlimited except
by the discretion of the adjudicating body. As to definition
of the offence, Athenian law was throughout, as would be
thought by the heirs of Roman jurisprudence, in this respect
objectionably lax ; and indeed this particular offence does
in fact belong to that most important class which, whatever
the law may say, will in any society where 'the masses'
have weight, refuse to be limited otherwise than by the
circumstances of the case. Libel and slander for instance,
among ourselves, notwithstanding disquisition and decision,
might still be defined without much practical error to be

such offensive speech or writing as a jury will *in the circumstances* find to be criminal or (as the case may be) will
visit with damages. 'Impiety' at Athens stood in the
same position, or to speak more properly, hung in the same
suspension. There is abundant evidence that the law could
be set in motion, and that fine, banishment, even death might
be incurred for offences against religion—if a jury could be
found so disposed. Once at least, as we know[1], Euripides
was the object of such proceedings; and it is a fair supposition, in the meagreness and fragmentary state of our
information, that the instance was not unique. It is certain
that his life must have been passed in much anxiety, and
probable that neither the privacy and almost concealment
in which, contrary to the habits of the place and people,
his proceedings other than theatrical were carried on, nor
his retirement at an advanced age from the land where he
must have hoped to repose, was altogether voluntary. There
is scarcely one of his plays in which an adversary might not
find passages sufficient, without any forcing, to support a
sentence of irreligion,—if only the court would consent to
say so. But on the other hand we can easily account for
his long career of impunity and success. For what would
have been the use of taking the *Alcestis* (let us say) into
court? That the publication of the play was an act of
'impiety' is as certain as that many sheep-stealers and
clippers of the coin who were acquitted in England when
the law on these subjects was out of adjustment with public
opinion, were nevertheless guilty of the charges, and that
the juries knew it. But how could an accuser expect a
conviction? An Athenian jury was a body of five hundred
men, brought together by proceedings carefully designed to
make it reflect as far as might be, without any modification,
the feelings of that general assembly, which it was supposed
for the nonce to represent. In such a jury there would
have been doubtless a certain number of persons, earnestly
devoted to the traditional worships, who thought it scandalous that such a writer as Euripides should 'obtain a chorus'

[1] Aristotle, *Rhet.* iii. 15.

and be allowed to exhibit ; and some also who, without going as far as this, thought him impertinent, mischievous, and deserving a snub. Aristophanes for example would have been in this latter class ; but he would have been influenced by mixed motives, and his vote, I should imagine, could not have been counted on when it came to the point. But if these classes had formed a majority among the citizens, or anything near a majority, the plays of Euripides would never have been selected for the national festival. Who made the majority ? A few no doubt, who thought it scandalous that Euripides, speaking 'reason' and 'common sense,' should be obliged to any measures of caution ; not a few worthy people who took no interest either in literature or speculation and knew nothing about the matter ; and a large mass, larger probably than all the rest put together, who knew all about the matter, who took their religion, so far as practical observance went, in the acquiescent way in which the majority is everywhere inclined, and had no desire to break with it, but who, being Athenians and having Athenian wits, found in the works of Euripides, just as they were, the greatest intellectual enjoyment which they had known, and would have been alike unwilling either to prohibit him altogether or to dispense with his delightful artifices. In such a jury the willing votes were impotent, and how were the unwilling to be forced ? The *Alcestis* impious ! Why so ? The reluctant had only to take the plausible objection—and they would be saved the trouble of raising it by the worthy people who knew nothing about the matter—that it lay with the accuser to make out his case. A man is not to be punished upon an ambiguous construction ! The defence could put up plenty of witnesses, not only dishonest witnesses, quieting their consciences with such reasonings about the necessity of the case and the iniquity of the inquisition itself as have always been found available in similar circumstances, but simple and honest witnesses, ready to swear that they saw no harm in the piece, but found it fairly edifying. I shall be surprised if such witnesses do not come forward on the present occasion, gravely assuring me that Euripides meant no such malice as I say, and lamenting, as they have done before, that I should insist on understanding him, instead of dismissing him as a dullard.

It is a highly significant fact, that one of the chief accusations, indeed almost the only accusation grounded on solid considerations of morality, which is alleged by Aristophanes against Euripides in such a way that we can suppose it seriously meant, is that his influence tended to impair the obligation of veracity, even in the most solemn and binding form. It is advanced with singular emphasis in the *Frogs*, where Dionysus, having to choose between Aeschylus and Euripides, and choosing at last Aeschylus in spite of a promise to the contrary, as Euripides asserts, flings in the face of the disappointed claimant his own famous saying from the *Hippolytus, The tongue hath sworn but the mind remains unbound*[1]. It has often been remarked, and could not escape an Athenian of average intelligence, to say nothing of Aristophanes, that this saying, taken with the facts to which Euripides has applied it, cannot with fairness or sense be cited in favour of perjury. This being so, Aristophanes may claim from us the equity of supposing that he had other reasons, not grounded upon the *Hippolytus*, for converting the verse into a general reproach against its author ; and for my own part I find no difficulty in believing it. The constant practice of dexterous ambiguity, and the habit of witnessing such dexterity with enjoyment, would not lose their tendency to weaken the springs of truth merely because the temptations, the justifications even, were strong, and the pleasure not only innocent in itself, but deserving to be classed for its intellectual quality among the highest of which humanity is capable. An Athenian notorious as an admirer of Euripides must frequently have had occasion to consider, not only in the law-courts but in various social relations, just how far he might go safely, or with a safe conscience, in pretending a convenient ignorance. It is likely

---

[1] *Hipp.* 612, see Paley's note. This verse played a conspicuous part in the accusation of 'impiety' above mentioned, though Aristotle does not say, as is sometimes said, that the accusation was founded on it. Probably the indictment took a much wider range ; the verse itself would come in most naturally in the impeachment of evidence.

enough that the enemies of such men would call them habitual liars, and not unlikely that they did something to deserve the appellation. Where in such cases the blame should rest, or how it should be distributed between those who practise deception and those who do their utmost to make it attractive or inevitable, is a problem which may be left to the student of politics and ethics, who will be frequently forced to consider it.

But to say the truth, in the particular case of Euripides, though the forms of concealment must have had their use and at times their necessity, we are not bound to suppose that practical security was the sole or the chief reason for maintaining them. From the Athenian point of view (and no man of candour, whatever his personal tastes, ought to have any difficulty in comprehending that point of view) Euripides as an artist had motive enough without the pressure of danger for 'keeping up the game,' so to speak, when once it was fairly started. It enabled him to gratify, as he was by nature endowed almost beyond human limits with the talents required for gratifying, what if not the strongest passion was at all events the most characteristic passion of his race and age. The love of the Athenians for *esprit*, for *wit* in the old and proper sense of the word, that is to say, the delicate and subtle manipulation of words and meanings, was their most remarkable gift for good and for evil, the national glory and the national vice. Irony, innuendo, insinuation, the whole class of mental and linguistic faculties which lie on the side of lying, were ingrained in them and in all that they produced. Their very language, their favourite tropes, are of this colour ; 'Attic understatement' figures even in the grammars. No people would have perceived more clearly, as no people perhaps is less adapted to perceive than we English are, the element of necessary truth contained in the Frenchman's epigram that 'language is given us to conceal our thoughts,' or could more clearly distinguish between the duty of saying what you mean and the equally important but not always compatible duty of saying what you mean to say. In season and out of season they practised their favourite art. They carried it to the bench of justice and to the seats of political debate. The philosophical observer of their assemblies has recorded in vivid and well-known terms the intense apprehension and preternatural quickness of the audience, their eagerness 'to applaud a subtlety before it was out, to catch the sense before it was spoken[1].' It may easily be imagined with what enthusiastic delight a people who could not be kept from indulging this temper even where, as many were wise enough to see, it was fraught, at least in its excess, with danger to their interests, would have turned in their hours of relaxation to such art as that of Euripides, to literary works of which it is the very basis and well-understood condition, that there is to be no blurting ; that the author, happily for the pleasure of intelligent and cultivated persons, must not be *plain* if he would, and would not if he might ; that the simpler and clearer he seems, the closer you have to watch him, sure that at last his truest and gravest meaning will be found in a corner, or round a corner, so that (thank the gods!) it is worth a man's while to look for it. Every man who can read the language of Swift and of Mr George Meredith, may qualify himself to understand this point of view, if he thinks it worth study. It is true that, comparatively speaking, there is not very much in our literature which will help him, whereas among French authors of the first rank there are few indeed who will not.

There is perhaps no one among the great writers of Athens who does not prove himself on occasion a master in the art of hinting. Aeschylus, a man sincere if ever man was, was so exercised in ambiguity that scarcely a modern comes near him, and wields it, as in the person of Clytemnestra, literally like a fiend. The irony of Sophocles, of Plato, of Demosthenes and many others is famous. The simplicity of Lysias, Athenian by breeding though not by birth, is not simple by any means. The reticences of Thucydides are often not less suggestive than his remarks. In every mind of Athenian texture some threads of the national quality are woven in. But in Euripides it was the base of the fabric. He had a

---

[1] The imaginary Cleon in Thucydides iii. 38.

mind in which a set of secondary faculties, extraordinary in
number and singly not contemptible in quality, eloquence and
pathos, the gift of fancy and the gift of song, were subject, as
perhaps they never were in any other, to an unsurpassed and,
it may be, unsurpassable wit. It so happened that the
circumstances of the time supplied to him in perfection the
conditions essential for the exercise of this colossal wit, grand
and grave solemnities, where it was his accepted part to find
language for truths or, to speak more modestly and humanly,
for a part of truth, which there and then was admissible only
under reserve. To overcome difficulties of expression, to put
a thought better and more effectively than your hearers could
expect in the given conditions, is the essence of wit. Euripides
was so placed that he must speak wittily, if he was to speak
his mind at all. As it happened that he had wit enough for
anything, and that his countrymen had wit enough for him,
nothing could have suited him better. It is the boast of the
Aristophanic Euripides, as it doubtless was of the real man,
that the effect of his writings was to apply an incessant
stimulus to the intelligence, to keep perception alert, 'habitually suspecting malice and everywhere seeing beyond[1].' The
Aristophanic Aeschylus subscribes to the boast as a reproach ;
' That is just what I say.' Whether we approve with the one
or condemn with the other, or more wisely decline to be
partizans in a needless quarrel, it is in the spirit which Aristophanes by both voices declares to be Euripidean that we
must approach the works of Euripides, if even in such limited
measure as is now possible we expect to interpret them truly.

And it is worth the trouble. To any one with a taste for
esprit the *Alcestis* alone offers reward enough for the effort
of realizing and fixing in his mind the presupposed relations
between author and audience. It is not merely in single
passages or expressions, in particular hits, that we are de-
lighted, although the play bristles with them, and the student
at each successive reading may go on finding them as long as
he has the inclination. More admirable than any such stroke,
more astonishing as an exhibition of intellectual skill, is the

---

[1] *Frogs*, 958 : κἀχ' ὑποτοπεῖσθαι, περινοεῖν ἅπαντα.

adaptation of the whole structure to its purpose, its exquisite poise and delicate preponderance. Without the use of a single plain blasphemy, without giving one single proof of 'impiety' at which an indulgent conformist could not comfortably wink or which a confessed unbeliever could not speciously disallow, the author contrives in scene after scene, each in itself a brilliant piece of portraiture, to impress with accumulating emphasis his own conception of the story, until we arrive at a catastrophe 'too deep' for any emotion except the pure intellectual thrill of thought uniting with thought, just only the joy of understanding. As to the touches of detail, it would require a complete commentary to bring out even those which with our manifestly inadequate means can now be detected; nor am I sure that it would be a service to the reader, who ought not to lose the pleasure of observation. One or two only of the most obvious shall here be noticed. None is perhaps more simply neat than the doubly double-edged reply of Admetus to Heracles, when questioned as to the identity of the woman for whom he is in mourning[1]. The parodies of Aristophanes apprise us that it became famous, as well it might. 'It cannot sure' says Heracles 'be your wife who is gone.' 'Of her' replies the husband, who placed as he is dares not confess his belief, and like a well-bred man prefers evasion to lying so long as he sees his way, 'of her I may speak in a double sense.' 'Do you mean,' says the other with pardonable bluntness, 'that she is dead or that she is alive?' '*She is...alive, and yet she is not: I feel it keenly*' is the equivocator's answer, explained, under further pressure, to mean that even a living person is *as good as dead*, when she lies under *an inevitable sentence of death*. The dramatic merit of these quibbles, as an exhibition of character and as points in the scene, makes but a small part of the pleasure derived by the accustomed auditor, who has long before this been assured, as he might indeed have guessed before the play began, that Alcestis is no more dead than she is likely to die, and now perceives that Admetus in his embarrassment has been forced to say so in so many words.

[1] *v.* 521.

But Euripides can do much better than a turn like this, of which, as Aristophanes not unjustly implies, the type is too formal for frequency. Such are for ears that need pricking, and are employed sparingly. Far above these, and touching surely the high-water mark of ingenuity, is the passage already signalized, in which a maid-servant relates to the Chorus the proceedings of Alcestis upon the 'fatal' morning[1]. Here we have first to notice the skill with which this important narrative is introduced. In the mechanism of the piece, as conceived by the author, the cardinal fact is the precipitation of the funeral. As soon as we know that Alcestis will be buried without delay, whenever her husband believes her dead, we have the key to the situation, and are ready to appreciate the treatment. Now it is just before the narrative of the maid-servant begins that this intention on the part of Admetus, hinted in the opening dialogue of the Chorus, is fully disclosed; 'There is, I suppose, no hope of saving her life.—No; it is the day of fate, irresistible.—Then... with regard to her person...they are doing, are they not... what is required?—*The adornment, yes, it is ready, to be buried by her husband along with her.*' Here, when the reader has received his cue and fixed his attention, at a word of admiration from the Chorus the maid-servant breaks out into a full description of what has passed. Now the facts which she relates have two distinct bearings, both in the conception of Euripides equally important, though only one side is applicable to the primitive and miraculous legend. First they exhibit the patience and resolution of the victim, whose self-sacrifice remains of course as complete and heroic upon the Euripidean hypothesis as upon the other. But secondly this narrative makes equally plain, to minds not wholly pre-possessed with the conviction that 'Apollo' cannot err, nor his devotees conceivably be deluded, the fact that, except the prophecy, there is not the smallest reason to fear for Alcestis on this day rather than another; that humanly speaking her life cannot possibly be in danger; and that if, as is clear enough, she is already suffering cruelly, if her strength is

[1] *vv.* 152 ff.

failing and threatens a grave collapse, this is simply because
from the night onwards she herself with her family and household, in the simplicity of their faith, have been doing their
utmost, as they are doing still and will persist in doing so
long as she remains conscious, to torture beyond human
endurance a delicate frame already shaken by expectation.
Who but a fanatic could imagine a woman to be approaching
inevitable death, to be already beyond the reach of aid, when
not only, as we are told, is her appearance unaltered, but she
is able without assistance to perambulate a palace, and to go
through a prolonged series of fatiguing devotions and harrow-
ing farewells? Who but a fanatic could see the work of a
special providence, could see anything but the regularity of
self-revenging nature, when these exercises, continued without
remission till the effect is produced, lead from weakness to
exhaustion, and finally to hallucination, fainting, coma, and all
the appearance of death? *Astonishment* the rational auditor
will undoubtedly feel, when he is told of the preparations for
this predicted and foreseen decease, a double astonishment,
both of admiration for the courage with which such horrors
are borne, and of anger, like that of Lucretius, against the
superstition which prompts them :—

> What kind of creature should the woman prove
> That has surpassed Alkestis?—surelier shown
> Preference for her husband to herself
> Than by determining to die for him?
> But so much all our city knows indeed :
> Hear what she did indoors—and *wonder* then[1].

There are some minds, and the literature of Athens in the
classical age unites in proving that then and there such minds
were a prevalent type, to which no art of language, no art of
any sort, could give pleasure more intense in its kind than
they will derive from the triumphant duplicity of this single
word. There is no better point in *The Egotist*.

One more touch only of this fashion I will ask leave to
point out, because I find it myself so signally delightful. If
the visitors to whom the maid-servant addresses her story had
been capable of reasoning, of calculation, of reflecting (like

---

[1] *vv.* 153—157, Browning's version.

honest Heracles[1]) that to weep for a bare prediction, as things
go in this world, is somewhat premature, if they had not in
short been the slaves of oracular dictum, their simple course
would have been to rescue the lady at once from the bigots
who are abetting her suicide, to scatter the servants, amuse
the children, silence the 'imploring' husband, and tell the
queen herself, that if she will only think it possible to live, if
she will only take food and keep quiet, 'the fatal day' will
bring no further harm whatever, and to-morrow she will find
herself, as she was this morning, perfectly well. Instead of
this these 'particular friends' of Admetus, being on this side
blind as himself, begin desperately to pray, 'O Zeus, deliver
us! O Paean, help us! No hope but in heaven!' and so on.
Great indeed must be the relief and thankfulness of the
judicious spectator, when after a few minutes of this folly
they innocently exclaim, *Is not this enough to make a man cut
his throat, yes, more than enough to make a man hang himself?
His dear, his dearest wife will perish within this day, and he
will see her die!*[2]

It is not however in any such gems of cleverness, thick-
set and brilliant as they are, that the power of the piece is
mainly placed. It is in the design of the whole, by which the
fabulous legend is so skilfully translated into facts of 'this
common life in which we live,' that minds prepared could not
escape the reflexion 'Thus indeed, or in some such way, the
thing may have taken place, and the story may have arisen!'
As for the preparation of mind, it was given by the notoriety
of the author's aims and sentiments, re-inforced for the
occasion by the subtle and characteristic travesty which
serves as a prologue. Of this we have hitherto not spoken,
or had occasion to speak, since the play proper stands independent of it in plot, persons, and otherwise, pursuing its
course exactly as if no such conversation as the prologue
presents had taken place, nor any such personages as the two
'deities,' between whom that conversation is held, had ever
existed. The speakers are Apollo and Death. Apollo in
the opening speech informs us that he has been revisiting the

---

[1] *v.* 526.　　　　　[2] *vv.* 213—232.

house of Admetus; Death in his closing speech, informs us that he is about to cut from the head of Alcestis, with the sword which he holds, the 'hair of consecration,' and thus devote her to the underworld. But when in the sequel we are reintroduced to the familiar world, when the departed 'gods' are replaced by men and women such as we know, these human beings are found not to be aware either that Apollo has just been among them, or that Death, in the shape at least of a gentleman with a sword, is among them now, nor are the deities any longer visible to us. The supernatural personages are neither mixed with the others on the same plane of action, nor indicated as moving on a line of their own which intersects, as it were, the line of humanity at certain points, so that perception is then mutual between the two classes of being. The divine action of the prologue and the human action of the play take place in spheres mutually exclusive; so that, if instead of the existing preface, we were supplied with a paper stating that such and such is 'the legend of Alcestis, as taught at Delphi and in places of religion generally,' we should be placed, so far as the sequel is concerned, precisely where the dramatic introduction does actually leave us. To the purpose of Euripides as an 'atheist' this separation is of course not universally necessary. It was open to him, and he has taken this line elsewhere, as in the *Hippolytus* and the *Madness of Heracles*, to exhibit scenes in which, for the sake of argument, he supposes and presents interaction between man and the creatures of anthropomorphic fancy, saying the while to his audience, by all sorts of signs and whispers, 'Such are the creatures which they would have us believe in, which they would have us adore. What kind of a figure do you think they make?' But when the object of the dramatist is to present a 'sacred' story in a version from which the gods are left out, it is desirable to draw the line more sharply between what is proposed for belief and what is proposed for disbelief. Such is the method pursued by Euripides practically in the *Ion*, the *Orestes*, and elsewhere, but nowhere perhaps so perfectly and with so firm a demarcation as in the *Alcestis*.

It is in reading the prologue to this play, more than in any other part of it, that we may be moved to feel surprise at the prevalent misunderstanding of the poet's intention. In general neither the existence nor the duration of this misunderstanding is matter for wonder; for the explanation is ready. The modern expositors (and the same applies to those Christian scholars of the 'Lower Empire' who composed the chief part and transmitted the whole of the Greek *scholia* and *hypotheses*) approach the *Alcestis* and other works of Euripides with a fixed prepossession, one of those habitual assumptions which rule the mind all the more absolutely because never stated in words, that *the story which the poet handles is by every one known for a fable*. It is always hard to suppose effectively, in such a way, I mean, that our thoughts are controlled by the supposition as they would be controlled by the reality, the contrary of constant experience. Nothing is easier than to make such a supposition in words, nothing more difficult than to make it effectively. Now it is a constant experience, fortified by the European literature of twenty centuries at least, that those who speak of Zeus, Apollo, and the like recognize these personages for imaginary types, accepted material of art, in relation to which the question of literal truth or falsehood is idle and irrelevant. Less than two hundred years after the death of Euripides the use of the Greek legends after this fashion was brought into general vogue by the accomplished Hellenists of Alexandria; from that time to this it has never entirely ceased; and on the whole we may say with substantial correctness that it has flourished vigorously in proportion to the general vigour of literature. It results that every lover and student of literature imbibes this habit of mind inevitably as the air which he breathes. Of contrary experience the amount is infinitesimal, too small to affect appreciably the habitual tone of our feelings. Of writers who now have readers or, speaking broadly with reference to the world as a whole, have ever had readers enough to affect the balance, how many are there in whose productions it is an active and indispensable factor that they believed, really, heartily, passionately believed, in the

theology of Delphi? I can think of only two, Pindar and
Aeschylus. The epic poets, it is true, were no Alexandrians,
neither was Sophocles. But it is possible without serious
loss, or at least without loss perceived, to read both Homer
and Sophocles in a purely Alexandrian spirit; it is not only
possible but habitually done. At any rate, let the list of
believers be enlarged to the utmost, what is it, when set
against the host of persuasive tongues, from Theocritus down
to the poets of yesterday, who have helped to engrain in our
minds, as a presumption of thought like the laws of arith-
metic, that 'Apollo' is a beautiful and convenient fiction,
universally accepted and universally disbelieved? Now it is
plain that wherever and whenever this view, this 'Alexandrian'
view, prevailed, it would be absurd and inconceivable that a
story should be composed with the purpose of leading the
reader to desist from regarding a given Apolline legend as
literally and historically true; it would be to butt the air. In
the Augustan age of Roman literature, for instance, in the
circle of Maecenas, such an attitude would have been ridiculous and incomprehensible, inasmuch as, notwithstanding
the symbolic splendours of the Palatine temple, the educated
classes of the Empire were scarcely more in danger of mental
injury from this quarter than Pope or Keats. But in the
fifth century before Christ—and let it be understood that this
is a proposition not one whit the less hard to believe effectively, because it is formally a truism—in the fifth century
before Christ the Alexandrian type of mind did not yet
exist. No one, or only a negligible quantity of persons, in
the days of Euripides, regarded a legend about Heracles from
the point of view which has ruled, with various subordinate
modifications, in almost every European society where literature of high value and influence has been created. In the
society addressed by Euripides when he started on his
career, to have realized the difference between a legend and
a historical fact was the latest and highest effort of intelligence, and to increase the number of persons capable of this
effort was a noble enterprise, an invaluable service. And to
make 'tragedy' serve this purpose was a feat especially

useful and especially attractive, because the art of Aeschylus
was the most powerful intellectual weapon which had been
employed on the other side. The very purpose of Aeschylean
drama is, as Aristophanes puts it[1], to make gods and heroes
think, speak, and look 'as they naturally would,' in other
words, to aid people, just conscious of a difficulty about the
matter, in continuing to feel that the Heracles who raised
Alcestis was a person as real and well certified as Darius, and
the ghost of Darius a thing which, in suitable circumstances,
you might as naturally expect to see as the living Darius
himself. When things were so, it was neither useless nor
tasteless to compose a drama with the contrary purpose,
with the purpose of diffusing the conviction, or at least the
suspicion, that the exploits of Heracles, whatever they were,
did *not* include the raising of the dead, and that the appearance
of Darius after death *ought not* to be as readily supposed as
the construction of the bridge over the Hellespont. But that
things were so in the time of Euripides is one of those facts
which, according to the true distinction of the philosopher,
'we know but do not believe.' It is not hard to ignore a
proposition, however manifest, which we cannot really take
into our minds without first hypothetically annihilating and
'thinking away' the intellectual atmosphere which has been
inhaled by ourselves and our predecessors for a hundred
generations.

Accordingly it is not in general surprising that modern
readers should have failed to find, or even to seek, the clue to
such a piece as the *Alcestis*. It is true that without the clue
we have been unable, as we loudly proclaim, to make sense of
it. Nevertheless the author's point of departure lies so remote
from our habits, and he on the other hand was necessarily so
far from anticipating such readers as us, that there is little
wonder if we remain blind to signals, which he must have
thought almost too grossly legible for the intended effect.
But the prologue is really too much. Almost every one
stumbles over it (as witness the annotations); and we can
scarcely believe that even Balaustion, though Browning does

[1] *Frogs*, 1060.

not betray her, sat through it without a smile. Among the
devices of Euripides for discrediting the inhabitants of
Olympus, none were more effective or better understood,
than that of painting them in his own colours; 'by representing the gods he persuades the men that they do not
exist[1]'; and of this the best example extant is the prologue
to the *Alcestis*. His Death and Apollo, considered as superhuman creatures, as deities, are self-refuting. The question
whether Alcestis shall die, or whether Death shall take
instead of her one of the old people, is discussed between
them exactly as two well-bred landlords, neighbours in the
country and living on bad terms, might discuss a question of
encroachment or ancient lights. Both are men of cultivated
intelligence, quick of apprehension and tenacious of their
point. Both in short are pure Athenians, and neither of them
has about him a scrap of such divinity as could seem divine
to other men as well educated as themselves. What was the
tone, the bearing, the style which could pass for Olympian in
the city of Pericles, we may see in the Athena of Aeschylus,
or in the Athena of Sophocles, or even (for Euripides himself could echo this tone when it suited his purpose) in the
Artemis who takes part in the closing scene of his *Hippolytus*,
or in the Dionysus of his *Bacchae*. In the Apollo of the
Aeschylean *Eumenides*, and in the Furies themselves, there
is majesty and terror ; nor even when they dispute do they
cease to be terrible and majestic. But look at this[2]:

Apollo.	Go take her !—for I doubt persuading thee...
Death.	To kill the doomed one? What my function else ?
Apollo.	No ! Rather to despatch the true mature.
Death.	Truly I take thy meaning, see thy drift.
Apollo.	Is there a way then she may reach old age ?
Death.	No way ! I glad me in my honours too !
Apollo.	But young or old, thou tak'st one life, no more !
Death.	Younger they die, greater my praise redounds !
Apollo.	If she die old,—the sumptuous funeral !
Death.	Thou layest down a law the rich would like.

[1] Aristoph. *Thesm.* 450.
[2] Browning's version : Mr Way's will equally serve the purpose.

A very legitimate translation, though wanting a little, as it needs must want, of the facility which is the signet of Euripides. But who is awed? Who feels any thrill of fear, any movement of respect? Who can fancy that he is listening to the King of Terrors, or that there is any affinity between this punctilious usurer and the demon described by Balaustion?

> Like some dread heapy blackness, ruffled wing,
> Convulsed and cowering head that is all eye,
> Which proves a ruined eagle who, too blind
> Swooping in quest o' the quarry, fawn or kid,
> Descried deep down the chasm 'twixt rock and rock,
> Has wedged and mortised, into either wall
> O' the mountain, the pent earthquake of his power.

Thus to the eye of Browning appeared the god of death confronted by the superior god of life; so, or in some such figure, Aeschylus would have seen him; and if Euripides suggested any such picture, then indeed we should have known that we were bidden to be grave and humble, as men should be in the presence of that which is greater than they. As it is we are commanded and compelled by Euripides to smile as he smiles himself. But no man could smile, or encourage his audience to smile, over a debate on such a theme and between such interlocutors, if he proposed in real earnest or in earnest imagination to relate how a human being was raised from the dead.

Doubtless there were many in the theatre, yokels, boys, visitors from Acarnania, and the like, who listened to the quips of Apollo without a suspicion that the faith of the poet was not as naïve as their own; doubtless there were many, as there are in all theatres, who did not *hear*, with the true literary sense, at all, and could have given no closer account of the scene than that it was 'the usual sort of thing.' But the class to whom Euripides wanted to speak, the growing class whom study made quick of thought, must have been assured by the prologue, if they were not already assured by the title, that the poet proposed to treat the legend of Alcestis in the only way which could be expected of him, as a groundless fiction; that he thought of Apollo and Apolline miracles

as he always had, and would express himself to the attentive
in the fashion permitted and approved. Nor were they kept
long waiting for a sufficient signal. The god has not spoken
a score of verses before he is provided with words, which
never could have been put in his mouth by an intelligent
writer, unless with the purpose of provoking an infidel sneer.
The touch is so characteristic that though not important it
deserves particular notice. Having related how leave was
obtained for Admetus to redeem himself from fate, if he
could find a substitute within the limits prescribed, Apollo
continues thus :

> But *trying all in turn, the friendly list,*
> Why he found no one, none who loved so much,
> Nor father, nor the aged mother's self
> That bore him, no, not any save his wife
> Willing to die instead of him.

In the words which are emphasized Browning has repro-
duced closely the colour of the original, which he sees to be
laughable and has even derided himself[1]. Browning (it must
be remembered) frankly gives up Admetus, fortifying himself
with the 'half-deity' which he has discovered or rather created
in Heracles. But I appeal to the reader's impartial consideration. Is not this notion of Admetus *seeking* a substitute,
and *going the round* to find one, just the very thing which
you, as an intelligent man, if you had accepted the legend,
either as an inspired truth or as an inspiring fiction, and
desired to present it sympathetically, would *not* on any
account allow yourself to entertain or suggest ? Of course it
is possible, it is even almost inevitable, if we come to think of
it, that, given the supposed circumstances, something of the
kind should occur. This it is which gives 'the atheist' his
opportunity, the kind of opportunity which none would be
quicker to see and use than the sharp-witted Euripides. But
a believer in the legend, or one who desired to evoke an
imaginary belief, would *not* see it, would resolutely refuse to

---

[1] p. 78,　When King Admetos went his rounds, poor soul,
　　　　　　A-begging somebody to be so brave
　　　　　　As die for one afraid to die himself.

see it, if his glance fell that way. An Admetus ridiculous
kills the legend; and to see him *begging* is to see him, if only
for that moment, ridiculous. If Euripides perceived this,
then he began his play *with the intention of killing the legend*.
If he did not perceive it, then he was a man inconceivably
dull. Such are the alternatives presented to us at the outset
of the piece, and repeated in every scene.

Altogether, with what the Athenian audience knew beforehand about the author, what they or many of them probably
knew beforehand about the play itself, with the suggestions
conveyed by the spoken parts, and other suggestions, corro-
borating the spoken, in which the dramatist, being also stage-
manager, would naturally instruct the persons (friends of his,
such as Cephisophon) by whom the play was performed—
altogether it may be assumed that even at the festival most
people, if intellectually qualified to understand or care for his
meaning, were not left in doubt of it. But for those who
were, there was still abundant opportunity. The effect produced by a play at the stage-performance (and in the case of
Euripides more especially) was neither the whole nor the chief
part of what the author might hope to achieve. As was said
before, we know that Euripides at least was widely read, and
this at a time when habitual reading was a new force. And
what was even more important in a society so constituted as
Athens, we know by direct testimony, and it is manifest from
the nature of Athenians, that plays which received what we
have ventured to call the 'advertisement' of the Dionysia,
were copiously talked about. Here again we are perhaps
liable not perfectly to realize a condition of things so different
from our own. For a play of these days, the stage-effect is
not only the first thing but almost the last. Our reading
body is so scattered, so disparate, so distracted, and it has so
many ways of obtaining imaginative amusement without the
intervention of the theatre, that even with the help of printed
criticism a dramatist would not be well-advised in counting
upon any sustained and harmonious impression from the
interchange of ideas among the members of his fluctuating audiences. But the audience of Euripides *was always*

assembled. All the year round the few thousand men and few
score women—'one among many, not alien from the muse[1]'
—who made Euripides' world, were going in and out of the
same narrow streets and markets, gardens and colonnades,
courts and quays, sitting-rooms and supper-rooms, crossing
and conversing incessantly. And whenever the group in
contact for the instant had a mind to talk literature, which,
it is plain, they often did, no topic was so obvious, so surely
dominant as the plays of the Dionysia, positively the only
writings, except the school Homer, with which this people of
talkers were generally familiar. It is this state of things, this
unique opportunity of mutual comment and elucidation,
which alone, to my mind, makes intelligible the existence of
such works as those of the Attic tragedians. Speaking for
myself, I cannot imagine a man, much less a people, who
without such help could appreciate their subtle, compressed,
and elaborate art ; and it is certain that in those times such
help, if obtained at all, was obtained not by way of reading
but by way of talk.

With regard to Euripides in particular we have express
evidence to show how strong was the stimulus applied by his
writings to literary and critical conversation as a means of
mutual teaching ; with what eager zest, all the stronger
doubtless for the flavour of 'impiety' and rebellion, the
younger men especially scrutinized and analysed his 'lessons
in chatter,' and spent in measuring his phrases 'with rule and
square' the hours when, as people past learning would remark with a snarl, 'they ought to have been in the gymnasium.'
Nor should we omit to notice, what even our unfriendly
witness has the fairness to add, that these circles then proved
themselves—as where such exist they do still—the most
efficient of intellectual schools, shaping sometimes, out of
the rudest material which that extraordinary sea-port could
furnish, debaters so sure and so ready that, to the horror
of men bred in a different discipline, they were not unwilling
to 'answer an official speaker[2]'! While thinkers of graver
complexion and more catholic taste, men upon whose minds

---

[1] *Medea,* 1084.   [2] Aristoph. *Frogs,* 954 ff., 1069 ff.

had dawned the notion of what is now called 'liberal scholarship,' were forming parties, such as those ascribed to Socrates
by the writer of his memoirs[1], for the study of 'the *old* wits,'
it was over the productions of the day, and of that author
above all who most exactly answered to the taste of the day,
that the mass of ambitious youths enchanted themselves in
the exchange of notions. Aided by the lively picture of
Aristophanes we may even now ourselves be present for a
moment in such a circle, while copies (as we may suppose) of
the master's latest deliverance, imperfect probably and pieced
out with recollections, are passing from hand to hand, and
the excited disputants are displaying their ingenuity in ex-
tracting the moral lesson from the intricacies of the dialogue.
We may hear their queries and challenges, 'What is the
meaning of this?...And pray where is that?...Now who took
this?' and so on. We may hear also the growl of the
impatient senior—Aristophanes himself had probably played
the part on occasion—mocking the enquirers with such a
parody as the comedian puts into the mouth of Dionysus :
" *Where is that?   Who took that?* Where's that kettle?
Who took that fish? It is like a housekeeper scolding in
the pantry!" And we may also witness the self-com-
placency of the young person who felt able to declare that
he 'saw through the whole thing in an instant,' so well had
he profited by the schooling of the great improver, who
'had brought into his art the practice of reasoning and
reflexion[2].'

It is impossible to overestimate the significance of these
facile and perpetual discussions, if we would understand the
method of Euripidean art. As truly as a song is written to be
sung, the plays of Euripides were written to be talked about,
and only in this stage of their working were expected to produce their final and complete effect. Of course this is not to
say that the broad theatrical impression of them conveyed by
the public (and only important) performance was not highly

---

[1] Xen. *Mem.* i. 6. 14.
[2] Aristoph. *Frogs*, 971—991 : λογισμὸν ἐνθεὶς τῇ τέχνῃ καὶ σκέψιν ὥστ᾽ ἤδη
νοεῖν ἄπαντα καὶ διειδέναι.

valued by the poet and carefully studied. This it must have been, not merely for its own sake, but for its influence in increasing or diminishing the vogue of the piece as matter of criticism. But not any one, however acute and practised, could carry away from one performance, much less from a performance under the conditions of the Athenian theatre, an exhaustive comprehension of such a play as the *Alcestis* ; nor, I am convinced, did any one hope to do so. On the contrary it would have been to Euripidean circles a disappointment, if when they came to compare notes on a new piece, it had seemed that there was *nothing in particular to find out*. They would have said simply that the master was getting dull. It was by conversation that the sympathetic auditors, who each in his measure and fashion had understood, combined their items into a whole; and it was by conversation that fresh sympathisers were gained, fresh understandings prepared, and the 'latest opinions' preached with far more effect and attraction, Athenians being what they were, than if it had been permissible to proclaim them openly in the orchestra.

To hear even the author himself, though he was not very accessible or affable, cannot have been, in the conditions of Athenian life, an ambition beyond the reach of determined seekers. How he talked (not gracefully, but to the purpose) of his own works and aims, we know well enough, at least in outline and general tone, from the caricatures of the great satirist, produced in circumstances which, apart from the intrinsic proofs of serious meaning, guarantee them not wholly unfounded[1]. "And pray," we may fancy him saying to a visitor who had reproached him with the evil tendency of his works and had pressed him to make atonement to religion

---

[1] Especially the *Frogs*. It should be noted that there is a broad difference, in point of utility as biographical evidence, between such a portrait as the Euripides of the *Frogs*, and such a portrait as the Socrates of the *Clouds*. It is possible that *twenty years before Socrates' death* not many persons were as yet seriously interested in him. The *Frogs* was produced immediately after Euripides had closed a long career of theatrical fame in pathetic circumstances and amid public mourning. Under these conditions a baseless misrepresentation would have been suicidal.

by dramatizing the legend of Alcestis and treating it with
that solemnity, mystery, and grandeur 'natural to gods and
heroes' which would have been bestowed on the subject by
Aeschylus:—" And pray, sir, what is the use of such tragedy
as you invite me to imitate? The function of the dramatist,
commissioned and subsidized by his fellow-citizens, is to
improve his fellow-citizens, to be of use in his generation?
What good would Athens get, what good did she ever get,
from an Aeschylean *Alcestis*? The duty, as I understand
you, of a poet in dealing with that sacred theme would be to
wrap it up in a cloud of vague, impalpable, inapprehensible
verbiage, to set it in an atmosphere as remote as possible
from familiar experience,—in short by all available means *to
prevent the mind from getting at it*. I have said and shall
always say that if this be true tragedy, tragedy is the art of
'gulling,' the art of 'keeping men stupid[1].' The resurrection
of Alcestis is one of those tempting, fascinating, enervating
falsehoods, by help of which the impostors of our oracle-
mongering sanctuaries are still enabled, notwithstanding the
struggles of intelligence, to cross the counsels of statesmen
and embarrass the enquiries of philosophers. So long as men
are banished, fined, imprisoned, and even murdered in the
name of doctrines which have no other foundation than this
fable and other such, so long as the leaders of thought among
us, the men in whom lies the sole chance of making human
life a little more tolerable than it is, are silenced and perse-
cuted because Apollo must not be impeached, the only purpose
which a man of feeling could have in touching this fiction at
all—is *to expose it*.

"And indeed, if Delphi were powerless, if such men as
Pericles and Anaxagoras were no longer in danger, I should
still think it unworthy of rational beings to assemble, with
pomp and circumstance proper to the realities of political life,
for the purpose of doing honour to an *event*, which no one
can realize without absurdity. How can we expect, while
the city continues to put such lessons before her youth, to

---

[1] *Frogs*, 909. Aristophanes proceeds, as his business was, to disarm the
epigram by an illustration which obviously does not support it.

build in them that critical intelligence which is the instrument of sound learning? What wonder if they are so careless of truth and falsehood that, as you may have heard said by a distinguished person, here in Athens itself gross errors are universally current with regard to the capital facts of our history not a hundred years since[1]? Is this childishness to continue for ever?

"Why should I believe the resurrection of Alcestis? Why do you? You would not believe it, if it were said to have happened yesterday in the next deme. In such a case you would act upon the sane conviction that the *necessity* and law of the world forbid us to expect such a thing. This conviction is even expressed, rudely but justly, in some of your sacred stories. Those who first related that Asclepius, for raising men from the dead, was slain by the thunderbolt of Zeus, did actually mean to say in their fashion, that the laws of this world *are inviolable*. That is a fairy-tale indeed, but a fairy-tale of wise men; and if I should deal with the subject (as you suggest), I shall take care to set it in contrast with the legend of Alcestis, which is a fairy-tale of fools[2]. Why do you believe it? If you want to try it, take it out of that Aeschylean haze where 'nothing is clear,' and put it, as they twit me for repeating so often, 'among the things we handle and can test.' What would you say if it were a story of yesterday? That the facts were not properly ascertained. That the buried person, if buried she was, had been entombed before she was dead. Why not say so in this case? The legend, as you know, does not even allege that the death of Alcestis was carefully ascertained; for it grew up in minds not capable of entertaining the question of evidence. The Pythians, if you asked them, would doubtless now reply that the death was ascertained, would say very likely that the body was actually burnt. But I have just as much right to

---

[1] Thuc. 6. 54.

[2] *vv.* 3—4, 122—129. From the first passage in particular it is clear that the two legends were in origin hostile, the product of what in later stages of civilisation would be called a religious controversy, or at least that Euripides thought so. The prologues of Euripides are full of such lights, for us unhappily obscured.

say that it was buried, and this prematurely. Nay, I have much more right; for I will show you—I have had thoughts on the subject, and you shall see an *Alcestis* before long—that from the very circumstances of the situation, as you yourselves present it, we should conclude that the funeral of Alcestis would be performed by Admetus with the utmost possible haste. But how was it, you may ask me, that her 'apparent' death came to occur so conveniently on the very day which Apollo (that is to say, the Pythians) had fixed beforehand for her actual death? That also is no great mystery. Wait and see. Suppose for the moment that it did so occur; the rise and spread of the miraculous version requires no further explanation. Delphi, not to be convicted of error, would take care of that, and would find, as still she does, an easy credence from the cowardice of mortality, even if by the persons actually engaged in the transaction no hint for a miracle had been given.

"But again, what right have you to assume that, supposing the facts were really and manifestly normal, nothing can have passed, which might serve in minds predisposed as a hint for the supernatural explanation? I could show you the contrary, and that out of the mouth of your own prophets. Who was it that achieved the resurrection, that 'brought Alcestis back and wrested her out of the hands of death'? It was Heracles. Well, what sort of a person, according to you who believe in him, was Heracles? Does a single festival pass in which some pious comedian does not show us a legend depicting this same Heracles drunk? I know very well that, when the pious spectators are next invited to worship Heracles as a divine redeemer, the drunken Heracles of those other legends is quietly put out of sight and forgotten. But with what right? The man, if he existed, was the same man. Both accounts of him have the same, if any, sort of evidence. Proceed then, if you want us to act upon this history in the dearest concerns of life, to behave as if history it were; compare and combine your information; put your drinking Heracles into your story of Alcestis—since he was drunk so often, perhaps it was then a wet day with him—and see how he looks. If I refuse, as I do, to believe that Heracles did actually wrestle with Death, that is partly because I am perfectly ready to suppose, from your own account of him, that *he may have said he would.* From the one statement to the other is a small step for the activity of rumour : but it is a step nevertheless.

" I have myself heard the admirable Cratinus, *in a certain mood,* announce his intention of swallowing the moon. I can even imagine (for the mood, you know, recurs) that he might say so at the very moment before the moon disappeared in a cloud. I should not myself believe that he had done it, not even if it had been predicted at Delphi that the moon would be swallowed on that particular night. It seems as if there must be some people who would.

" As for the other marvellous elements in your legend, such as the residence of Apollo with Admetus in the character of a herdsman and his wonderful feats there, you must excuse me from considering them, till we have ascertained the resurrection. It is implied even by the Delphian story, that of what was done in Pherae ' by Apollo ' there never was, properly speaking, any evidence at all. We are told that Admetus was vastly enriched as a reward for his kind treatment of this serf. The moral is excellent ; I have no wish to detract one jot from the service rendered by Pytho, in days when she was before the world and not behind it, in preaching such humanities; it is our duty still to preach them, as I hope I do, by other and better ways. But the moral implies, and every one of course understands, that when the lord showed this kindness the serf was not known for a god. It would be absurd to praise a man's ' virtue ' because he treated with consideration a personage who, however depressed for the moment, was known to be immortal and only a little less than almighty. Limited therefore to the facts, and stripped of imaginative inferences, the assertion is (and I can believe the whole of it), that the wonderful prosperity of King Admetus was attributed to the gratitude of the deity. He was in the habit of treating his servants generously; and he was assured, by the usual intermediary agency, that one of his servants

had been in truth Apollo. And therefore if it is said, for
example, that this herdsman by playing the pipe would bring
the wild beasts out of the forest, this means (we must suppose)
that, being Apollo, he doubtless did so—when no one was
looking. Doubtless he did, if he was Apollo ; and a very
pretty song it would make. I can hear the melody of it, and
echo it too, not worse perhaps than another :—

> And the spotted lynxes for joy of thy singing
> Mixed with thy flocks ; and from Othrys' dell
> Trooped tawny lions : the witchery-winging
> Notes brought dancing around thy shell,
> Phoebus, the dappled fawn from the shadow
> Of the tall-tressed pines tripping forth to the meadow,
> Beating time to the chime of the rapture-ringing
> Music, with light feet tranced by its spell[1].

Your Apollo is beautiful enough ; and when you cease to
command men, on pain of forfeiting friends, fortune, country,
to believe in his existence, to believe him lord of life and of
death, none will be happier than I to grace him with the best
colours that I can lay on. For the present, if I exhibit his
person at all, it will not be as piping to fawns, nor to Admetus
either. I shall show him—well, you will see how, but so at
any rate 'as he ought to be shown,' so long as there are
defenders of his existence. Prove me first some act of his
deity which can at least be supposed, on the face of the
allegations, to have been submitted successfully to the test of
human sense. Prove me the resuscitation of Alcestis ; and
then I will give you a chorus of as many lions and lynxes as
you please.

"So much for the truth of the tale which you would have
me, responsible as I am for the public opportunities bestowed
on me, recommend by art to the acceptance of my fellow-
citizens. And then for its morality—But mind you, so long
as the question of truth is open, I do not allow that there is
any separate question of the morality. As things are now,
the first and paramount interest of morality is to be rid of
such an incubus as Apollo. But waiving this, as to the

---

[1] *Alc.* 579—587 ; Mr Way's translation.

morality of your legend, I deny that it is a good morality.
These ancient stories, to which by the conditions of our
theatre we tragedians are at present practically restricted,
are some of them graceful growths, but all of them rooted in
bad times, and rank of the soil. The devotion of Alcestis!
Assuredly the heroic unselfishness of woman is a beautiful
thing ; and I warrant you that, the gods helping me, Alcestis
shall take no injury from my hands. But what of Admetus
as a husband ? That is an aspect of the matter upon which
our hymnists and our congregations are little disposed to
dwell ; and they find no difficulty in ignoring it. It belongs
to the skimble-skamble thinking which aids and is aided by
faith in these monstrosities never to see anything steadily,
never to see anything *whole*, but only such parts as please.
And your heroic tragedy is beloved for flattering this habit.
But there are flatterers enough ; and for my part, I intend to
give you much more of Admetus than of Alcestis. He is
much better for you. You are accustomed to rest with complacency on the picture of the self-sacrificing woman as the
ideal of wives. For herself she deserves such admiration,
but for men and for society, no ! I should like to make you
feel, and I mean to try, what a blind, barbarous, self-defeating
selfishness is at the bottom of all this rapture about the
devotion of woman. You will say that the women join in it.
But what sort of women ? What are the women bred by our
system of semi-humanity, but the most dangerous of our
slaves[1]? Prohibited by your generosity from acquiring intelligence except at the cost of respect, the poor creatures are
so dull that they cannot even distinguish a friend from an
enemy. Your magnanimous satirists have no difficulty in

---

[1] Compare Aristotle, *Poetic*, 15. 1 'Even a woman may be good, and also a
slave ; though the woman may be said to be an inferior being, and the slave is
absolutely bad.' It is pleasant to fancy the smile with which Euripides would
have read this sentence. Of all the ancient moralists he is alone, or alone with
Plato, in showing an *adequate* notion of that radical disease, an imperfect ideal
of woman, of which, more than of anything else, ancient civilisation perished.
The gross and undoubtedly deliberate misrepresentation of this matter by
Aristophanes is the part of his polemic which is least easily forgiven. Indeed
it is the only part which in the ancient world seems to have done any mischief.

directing the almost unanimous resentment of the sex against whoever dares to see and show what mischief to themselves and to us results from their ill-governed virtue not less than from their ungoverned vice. I pity Alcestis, and I pity her husband. What would she make of him? What *does* she make of him? Wait and see.

" But this after all, grave though it be, is in our present position a minor point. So long as the spring of right action is clogged and corroded by the habit of believing without cause, so long as the art which in spite of murmur and menace I am still permitted to practise, is persistently employed by others so as to foment this habit, so long will the contrary purpose be still the main purpose with me. You know that for the majority of our nation the main interest, and the only real interest, of the story in question lies in the alleged resurrection, accepted as a fact, and associated with certain dependent beliefs and hopes which I need not now particularize. We are forbidden, you know, to *reveal the mysteries*. What would be the effect upon mankind, in what way good and how far, of receiving (if we suppose it possible, as it may be for all I know) real proof of such an event, it is not for me to consider. I cannot see so much. What I see very well is the wide-spread, infinite harm of putting fancy for knowledge (to speak like Socrates), or rather of living by choice in a twilight of the mind where fancy and knowledge are indiscernible. That *necessity* can never be overruled, uniformity never contradicted, the dead (for example) never raised to life, I do not say, and you will not hear me say from the stage. What you will hear—if you do me the honour of attention—is that *in tradition, enquire as I may, I find no reason for supposing or expecting such a contradiction*[1]. That I shall say, as solemnly as I am able, and I shall not retract it. If divinity is seen in *achieving the unexpected*, then wait and see it! *Divinity*—I have said it before, and may say it again—*has more shapes than one*[2]; and to this kind of miracle, to *achieving the unexpected*, the gods I worship may not be found unequal."

[1] *Alc.* 962—972. [2] *Alc.* 1159—1163, the ' Euripidean tag.'

by the choice of personages for his prologue and by the tenor of their conversation. Death, assuming the attitude of an independent and uncontrollable power, declares his intention to take and keep the mortal who is his lawful property. Apollo, though he condescends to parley, and to recognize a customary claim on the part of his opponent, concludes nevertheless with a forecast which is in truth a fiat, by declaring that if Death persists, Alcestis shall be taken out of his hands. This miracle is the thing which we are to see performed. The return of Alcestis from death to life is the central point of the legend and the central theme of the play as propounded by Euripides himself; the rest is circumstance and detail. That the persons in whose interest the saving power is to be put forth are virtuous and deserving persons, is a part and a natural part of the religious conception. By the Apollo of the prologue their story is exhibited just so far as is needed to explain how he and Death come to be opposed, and why this particular mortal is to be rescued. But the opposition itself, the rescue itself, the divine and not the human element in the action, is the gist of the matter, as appears both by the character of the persons who are selected to propound the subject, and by the proportion of topics in the preliminary scene of exposition.

Nor could any other view of the story be taken, so long as the religious legend was the object of a vital belief. The question whether and where there exists in the universe a power which can do what Apollo promises in the opening of this play, whether such a thing has, to the knowledge of mankind, been actually done, is one by the side of which every other has been, is, and always must be insignificant. To every human being, that power which he thinks capable of dealing in the last resort with human life, is God. On his conception of that power depends, directly or indirectly, all that he can think. In the days of Euripides the defenders of the old religion maintained with regard to this question exactly what is assumed in the prologue, that this power resided in certain beings who had many organs of communication with man, but one organ of incomparable importance, the oracle of the Pythian Apollo : and upon this foundation reposed a vast structure of social, civil, and national usage just then beginning perceptibly to totter. The modern reader is able to forget the resurrection of Alcestis, and to occupy himself with her heroism, or her husband's ' hospitality,' or what not, only because he neither believes, nor thinks it believable, that she was really raised. But while this was believable, what else in her story could be comparatively significant, or could the interest be centred anywhere but in this stupendous fact ? There could in those days be but two tolerable ways of treating the story. One would have been that of Aeschylus, faithfully and earnestly to support the resurrection as true. The other is that of Euripides, with equal zeal and earnestness to exhibit the resurrection as false. But on the resurrection, on the divine deliverance, as a piece of history asserted or denied, attention must be fixed ; and the actual form of Euripides' prologue should merely confirm us in attributing to him the only conception of his subject which he could entertain without insulting his audience.

And if it is morally possible for us to ignore or overlook the true theme of the piece as propounded by the author, and to substitute for it some choice of our own, it is not possible for us to miss the discovery that the author and we are for some reason strangely at war. All readers make this discovery and proclaim it in their various ways. The construction and the cast become ' careless,' ' mistaken,' ' intolerable,' in short inexplicable. The false resurrection, or in other words the premature burial, is the centre upon which the scenes converge. Their common point and purpose is to shew how it came to pass that Alcestis was entombed before she was dead, and how out of this fact might arise the belief in her resuscitation. When we have put this out of sight and taken something else for the essence of the matter, we find ourselves with the greater part of the drama left, so to speak, upon our hands, irrelevant, even noxious. The commentaries written from such a point of view amount in the sum to a demonstration that not one scene is shaped and handled as it ought to have been for the end supposed. I say 'not one,' because even the death-scene itself, the only one in which the fault is not *ex hypothesi* obvious, a common-place of criticism, even this has not escaped objections *ex hypothesi* perfectly just. It has often been said, and on the current assumption truly, that it was a technical error in the dramatist to make Alcestis actually die upon the stage. Undoubtedly it was an error, an error extraordinary in a practised composer, if he meant the audience to suppose her dead. Playwrights and play-goers know that an acted death, even when the supposed cause of it is clear and present to the imagination, as a wound, or poison, or extreme old age, is a difficult business, apt to fall flat and to miss persuasion. How much more must this be the case with a death such as that of Alcestis in the circumstances presented by Euripides, a sort of miraculous death, which has not, so far as we are informed, any cause whatever known to common experience. In narrative, as distinct from drama, such an event, by the aid of transcendental causes skilfully suggested, might be made to carry persuasion ; the passing of Oedipus in Sophocles may serve for an instance, and others will easily be recollected. But to put it in action, the whole process down to the last expiring breath, and ' expose it to the incorruptible witness of the eye,' was to court a failure, to offend gratuitously against rules enforced by experience long before they were formulated by the Roman critic and his authorities. And observe that Euripides, while making (as is supposed) this inordinate demand on our fancy, refuses to help us. When Sophocles presents, in narrative not in action, the mysterious departure of Oedipus, he provides incidents appropriately suggesting the intervention of supernatural power, which are perceived by the witnesses present and transmitted to us. The impatient voice which reminds the old man that his hour has come, is heard, as the story affirms, not only by him but by all[1]. But the death of Alcestis in Euripides, though at least as wonderful as that of Oedipus, though caused by nothing more tangible than 'destiny,' is nevertheless accompanied by no such supernatural manifestation, by nothing adapted to overcome the revolt of sense and reason against

[1] *Oed. Col.* 1624.

the impossible thing performed.   Except in being causeless, her death is an ordinary death.   No one present betrays any unusual sensation, nor indeed does the patient herself; for if at one time she hears 'Charon call' and sees 'winged Hades beckon,' such fancies are not wonderful in a woman who, if she were not by this time light-headed, must be made of iron, and no confirmation whatever is obtained from the other personages on the stage.   Indeed these visions, such as they are, are so placed by the poet in the scene[1]—as if of malice prepense—that they are useless for the purpose of aiding belief; for Alcestis, when she sees them, is certainly *not* at the point of death.   It is after this that, without any remonstrance on the part of Charon and Hades, she makes a farewell speech, long, lucid, and sustained, and again after this that still without further summons she 'dies.'   Her situation and language are exceedingly pathetic ; but so far as stage-effect is concerned, no tiro could do worse than the master here has done, if he meant the audience to suppose Alcestis dead.   But since, according to the intention of Euripides, Alcestis does not die, there was naturally no harm, but advantage on the contrary, in so presenting her 'death' that, according to all theatrical experience, the audience were likely to disbelieve it.

In fact the real danger in this scene, from the Euripidean point of view, lay on the opposite side.   Euripides has seen it, and has met it by a device of admirable simplicity and cleverness.   The question for him was not 'How shall Alcestis appear to be dying?' but rather this : 'Since Alcestis is not dying, and in the circumstances could not be dying, how shall it seem natural that Admetus and his friends should suppose her dead?   His friends may without improbability be made to act upon his belief.   But how account for the belief of Admetus?   Certainly he must not essay any restoration, nor even apply such simple tests as are used in every death-chamber as a matter of course.   He must be convinced abruptly, instantly, without reason or rational delay.   How shall I justify this?'   To a certain extent, a very considerable

[1] *Alc.* 252—262.

extent, the behaviour of Admetus at the moment of his wife's supposed death, his neglect of every natural effort and precaution, preposterous as it is, is accounted for by his fanatical trust in prophecy and his absorbing preoccupation with the funeral. He is so certain that his wife will die, and die to-day, he is so anxious to have her buried as soon as ever she is dead, that it is not very surprising if he has neither inclination nor leisure to ascertain the fact of her death. Still there might have been some difficulty, some technical difficulty at least, in turning the corner, in giving the premature conviction a lodgement, so to speak, in his mind. All such difficulty is cleared away, the passage made perfectly natural, and at the same time an element added to the pathos, by the happy thought, hazardous perhaps in the Greek theatre but absolutely justified to a reader, of introducing the little boy Eumelus. When Alcestis with a last 'Farewell!' sinks into the final swoon, and before there is time for the husband and friends to say or do anything beyond one horrified exclamation, this child, the elder of the two and old enough to comprehend the notion of death, breaks into a piteous outcry :—

Look—look on her eyelids, her hands drooping nerveless! O hear me, O hear me!
It is I—I beseech thee, my mother! thine own little own little bird!
It is I—O, I cast me upon thee—thy lips are so near me, so near me
Unto mine am I pressing them, mother! I plead for a word—but a word!

During the minute or two for which this childish lamentation is prolonged Admetus scarcely speaks; and when he does again speak in a collected manner...it is to urge the performance of the funeral[1]. Thus the child and his terrors are the true source from which the rest, prepared as they are by their prejudices, receive the conviction that all is really over. It is of course impossible that the child should know anything of the matter one way or the other; what he notes for marks of death (they appear in the foregoing quotation) are manifestly

[1] *vv.* 390—424. See Mr Way. Browning paraphrases here and makes the scene unrecognizable.

not marks of death, and could not have on any but a childish
imagination the effect which they have upon his. But the
spoken word is never without a certain weight. Admetus and
the visitors being predisposed as they are, the child's belief
and his loud expression of it just give to their belief the
opportunity of settling into assurance, just bridge the interval
in which they might otherwise have entertained a question,
and transport them, the husband especially, with a natural
precipitation from the 'death' to the sequel.

To return however from this digression upon a detail—the
death-scene as a whole, like the other scenes, plays up to the
general purpose of the work; and it does so, as speaking
broadly they all do, by virtue of those very qualities which
current criticism, starting from wrong premisses, notes for
defects. Indeed it would not be bad counsel to the reader
who would arrive at Euripides that, whatever notes of censure
he finds in his commentary, he should take them upside
down. It is at any rate valid for some plays, the *Alcestis*
conspicuously being one. For example, the drunkenness of
Heracles is treated by common consent as the most unsuitable,
incongruous, and insignificant element in the composition.
It is precisely the master-stroke, and occupies for that reason
its cardinal place in the work. There is cleverness, much
cleverness, in the device which, through the presumable
character of Admetus, deduces from the legendary data the
precipitation of the funeral. But this invention, the basis of
the play, is comparatively easy. Beyond this lay the greater
difficulty, which yet had to be solved before the design could
be completely executed, how, given that the resurrection was
to be false, and Heracles to do no more than bring back
from the tomb a person who had never been dead, the story
should yet be presented so as to give a natural starting-point
for a miraculous translation in process of rumour and fable.
The solution of this problem by the honest rodomontade of
the too convivial hero, in its felicitous adaptation to every
requirement of the case, and in the skill with which the
necessary delineation has been carried out, is in my judgement
a feat of pure wit, which is in its kind, like the devotion of

Alcestis, not even conceivably surpassable. 'He that would better it, what should he do?' we may ask in the language of the handmaiden.

So also with the remainder of the work. The altercation between Admetus and Pheres with its scorn-provoking egoisms, the concluding scene with its low pitch of sentiment and final abruptness, are not to be forced out of their nature, or explained as divergences from a theme which requires a different treatment, as the author would have felt, if he had had full command of his faculties. Once for all, let us not flatter ourselves that we can take the lead of Euripides, and show him how he might have improved this and that, if he had only known what he was doing. His clever countrymen thought him their cleverest; the works we possess are a selection of his best; and if anywhere we suspect him of dulness, we should quietly mark that place for something which probably we do not understand. In this way, though it is beyond hope that we should ever follow him with the perfect appreciation which he expected from his contemporaries, we may at least arrive at the power of enjoying not merely bits of the *Alcestis*, nor the *Alcestis* in bits, but the whole as a whole, for the flawless masterpiece of wit which in truth it is[1].

Not that Euripides, any more than another, must needs be pleasing to every mind which comprehends him. On the contrary, of his art, as of all kinds of art, it may be said that there are minds, many minds, which would the less find pleasure in him, the better they understood. Their natural food lies elsewhere, and it were waste of time to detain them from it by argument. If for instance any one should say—in our age of hurry and preoccupation with practical needs, it is a possible objection, although the countrymen and contemporaries of Mr George Meredith should know better—that

---

[1] It is by no means to be assumed as an axiom that even Aristotle could not be mistaken in details. Is it not notorious that Voltaire sometimes misunderstood and misrepresented Corneille, and Aristotle Plato? The history of criticism is full of proved errors much less likely than an occasional error on the part of an encyclopaedic philosopher about a poet of a widely different age.

the deliberate use of the clear-obscure, the habit of indirectness and hinting, is an artistic defect, because it embarrasses the percipient, it can be of no use to answer that this is the very essence of 'the spiritual,' *Anglicè* wit. The mental product for which, unless we will invent another name, this name ought to be kept, cannot be had except on this con- dition : and this is so strictly true, that unless the necessary bar to facility and openness is found ready-made in some external circumstances of prohibition—Euripides luckily found it ready-made—the would-be wit must first put up such a bar, for the purpose of leaping it. The leap is the art. But you could not explain this, except to those who might fairly resent the explanation. You could only refer the objector, if he would pursue the subject, to the works of 'spiritual' men.

One point however in this connexion it may be well to note. It touches the other Attic dramatists to some extent, but none so nearly as Euripides. In the case of drama the practice of indirect, slight expression, and the correlative habits of patience and alertness bred in those who as audience or readers are accustomed to find pleasure in such work, have a certain value in relation to the art in general, quite apart from their particular and necessary connexion with the faculty of wit. In drama, hampered as it always must be by intrinsic limitations, full expression often means unnatural expression. It means that in order to make things a little easier for the spectator or reader, the *dramatis personae* have been made to say right out what in real life they would at most have hinted, and to hint in words what in real life they would suggest, if at all, in some other way. By convention, that is to say by the common agreement of artist and audience to save trouble, such things are tolerated ; but they are not admired. In such situations, the more trouble the audience is ready to take, the more natural, and so far the better, can be made the imitation. In this respect the Athenian stage, and that of Euripides especially, is greatly superior even to the best modern work ; nor is it likely that the superiority will be reversed. An illustration is supplied

by the *Alcestis*. In arranging to bury the heroine hastily
and by stealth, Admetus and his friends are doing a thing
which natural sentiment detests. They are in fact for the
time in the position of conspirators. They have a secret.
Now every one knows and has laughed at the conventional
'secret' and 'conspirator' of the ordinary stage, and the shifts
to which the unlucky dramatist is reduced by the necessity of
reminding the audience perpetually, through the mouths of
the *dramatis personae*, of something which must on no account
be mentioned. The 'dissembling' and 'disguising,' the absurd
ostentation of mystery, has been ridiculed till parody is tired.
But the practice persists nevertheless, and will persist; for
the simple reason that if on the stage people with an unpleasant thought between them were made to talk as they
really would, the slower half of the audience would miss
the point, would not see that something 'was up.' Now
Euripides in such a case as this had the advantage that, so
far from being expected to make himself everywhere and
instantly intelligible to the whole of a theatrical crowd upon
the first hearing, he neither might be nor wished to be. He
is therefore able to deal with such a situation in a natural
way. He is not bound, as a modern dramatist would be,
to keep Admetus, his slaves, and his friends, for ever *talking*
about what is to be done. Things of this sort are not talked
about in the doing, but simply *done*, with as little talking
as possibly may be. So it is with the burial of Alcestis.
When the Chorus are first told that she is actually sinking,
they say, in language obscured by a certain shame, 'Then
doubtless you are doing about her...*what is required.*' They
are understood, as people in such circumstances do understand one another in reality, but on the stage do not. 'Yes,
the vesture to be buried with her is ready[1].' And with that
the subject is dropped. So again after the supposed death
Admetus bids the visitors 'wait a while for the burial,' which,
having come for the purpose, they naturally do without
a word. This, and a few hints exchanged by the Chorus
in their opening conversation, is all the talking that passes

[1] *vv.* 148—149.

on the subject, being about as much as in reality might pass. The artistic gain is double ; first, the imitation of life is felt to be truly like it, and not merely passed as a likeness by reluctant convention ; secondly, in catching the point, there is exercise for fixed attention and a quick mind, which exercise is part of the intended pleasure

Hence to understand Euripides fully was even for his contemporaries and for the most sympathetic among them, as Aristophanes gives us to know, a task for patience and some mutual help. He wrote for a people of slave-masters a people with leisure, newly-awakened to the literary chase and eager for hunting-ground. As for us, we cannot expect to be always ' in at the death,' or always even to find. But if we do not find, or do not care to beat the wood, we should abstain from crying that there is no game. Among the complaints which criticism, in the vein of Schlegel, has alleged against the conduct of this play, none is more startling (though the point in question is not of great magnitude) than that of ' inconsistency' as to the disposition of the corpse. According to Euripides (as all are agreed and without possibility of doubt) the body of Alcestis is *buried* or rather *entombed*. She is not *burnt*, but laid just as she died in the place where she is left. The expostulation of Admetus[1] ' Why was I not permitted to fling myself down into her grave, there to rest with her at last ? ' accords with other indications on all hands to settle the point completely. " How careless then," cry detractors[2], "how careless is the author to say, not once only but twice, that it is the intention of Admetus to consume the body by fire ? "

> This corpse even now, with all things meet, my servants
> Bear on their shoulders to *the tomb and pyre*[3].

And again,

> Let us, for we must bear the present ill,
> Pass on, to lay our dead *upon the pyre*[3].

' *In* the pyre' not ' upon the pyre' are the exact words, and in the idiom of Euripidean dialogue—with an older poet

---

[1] *v.* 897.   [2] Munk, and many others.   [3] *vv.* 608, 740.   Way.

it might be otherwise—the prepositions are not indifferent. But any way there is *the pyre*. How very careless! Yes indeed, how grossly, incredibly careless, if careless at all. A man sits down to write the story of a miraculous resurrection; and he leaves it a point unfixed, a matter so little considered that he contradicts himself about it unawares, what was done with the body between death and revival, even whether or no it was completely destroyed. They were going to burn it. But did they? Well, it seems not; no, certainly not. But you may make and take it just as you like. He had not thought of it. Then what was he thinking of, where was his mind, what attention can he have bestowed on his subject? The point is critical, central, vital, the heart of the story which he has undertaken to tell. And observe that if these references to *the pyre* are oversights, they have not the excuse of being inconspicuous. One of them is thrust into prominence, placed in the composition so that a dramatist could scarcely help pausing upon it. The verse *Let us be going, that in the pyre we may place the dead* is an *exit-verse*; after saying this, Admetus heading the procession quits the scene. Cues of exit have always a catch for the ear; all dramatists study them, using and turning them with more or less happy device. But Euripides had not thought of it.

But indeed he had. If instead of supposing him careless we will suppose ourselves ill-informed, we may learn something, something not without interest in itself, and illuminating for the play. The references to the entombment of Alcestis are quite simple, consistent, and adapted to the author's intention; only they presume us acquainted with practices which in fact are foreign to us. The intention of Admetus is indeed, as he says, to lay his dead *in a pyre*; she is actually laid *in a pyre*; and if she had not risen, she would have been burnt *in* it. But nevertheless the first thing done with her body, and as things turn out the only thing actually done, is to *bury* or *entomb* it. The place to which she is carried, as it is described to Heracles[1], is a 'stone-built' monument,

---

[1] *v.* 836.

of sufficient size and dignity to catch the eye of a person
going out of the town in that direction. It is there called
simply a *tomb*; but when Admetus refers to it in the first
of the passages above quoted, it is described more exactly
as 'both grave and pyre'; 'my servants,' he says, 'are ready
to bear the corpse to grave-and-pyre[1]'—if we may venture
clumsily to figure by hyphens a connexion for which, as it
happens, we have not in use any neat verbal equivalent.
We should note that *grave* comes first, a proof that what
Admetus has in his mind is not the burning first and then
the interment of the ashes; for the grammarians' exploded
figure of *hysteron proteron* or 'cart-before-horse' must be left,
at least so far as Euripides is concerned, in the grammars.
If he had meant 'to pyre and to grave,' he would have said
so. The sort of *pyra*[2] which he has in view is a *grave-pyre*,
in which, as he says, not *on* which, the corpse would be
placed. It is a mortuary kiln, a chamber in the royal tomb,
opening from the floor of it. Here the body would be laid;
here that of Alcestis was laid and left by the performers
of the funeral. Afterwards—at night we should probably
suppose, since one object of the whole arrangement was to
achieve a sanitary purpose without insulting the majesty
of the dead or affronting the eyes of the living—fire would
be put to the fuel with which the chamber had been provided, and the chamber closed. This method of sepulture,
combining burial and burning in one, is known elsewhere;
and though it was not the common practice of the Greeks
in historical times or probably at any time, it certainly had
been used by them, and for all we know may have long
continued in use, *for persons or families of great dignity.*
The form of the royal sepulchre at Pherae, as conceived
by Euripides, and the custom of it, precisely resemble in
essentials those of the so-called 'Tomb of Agamemnon'
discovered by Schliemann at Mycenae, where the splendidly
attired and jewelled corpses " were sunk in graves under the

----

[1] ἐς τάφον τε καὶ πυράν.

[2] *Pyra*, it should be remembered, does not properly mean *pile*, but *fire-place.*

earth, which were large enough to receive them, had they
not been filled up round the bottom with rudely built walls
or pieces of stone, so as to reduce the area, but to create
perhaps some ventilation for *the fire which had partly consumed the bodies when they were found*[1]." Just in this condition,
jewellery, charred relics, and all, would be found the corpse
of one interred after the fashion implied in the *Alcestis*. It
is not impossible that among the magnates of Thessaly, who
had customs of their own, such a use may have come down
even into the fifth century. This however we need not
suppose. It would be enough that it was a method practised
in that unknown time when the legend first took shape.
Once fixed in the story, the circumstances of the interment
would be preserved with the rest in tradition. For they are
material to the religious purpose. It was not without reason
that the scene of this resurrection was laid among a family
whose custom it was to make a fire in the grave. It prevented
an obvious suspicion. For assuming, as believers of course
did assume, that between the death and the rising again
a satisfactory time had elapsed, the custom would put beyond
question the miraculous character of the revival ; while
nevertheless, to the unschooled instinctive imagination, the
reconstitution of the person would seem more comprehensible,
more believable therefore, under the circumstances, than if
the body had been visibly, totally destroyed by burning in
the open air. But when the ' atheist ' had rationalized the
story by putting the resurrection within an hour or two of
the death, the peculiar method of interment became to him
equally serviceable. If according to the consecrated version
Alcestis had been inhumed in a coffin, or burnt after the
common Greek fashion in the presence of the mourners, then

---

[1] Mahaffy (after Schliemann), *Rambles and Studies in Greece*, p. 411.
Compare the tomb-pyre of Capaneus (Eur. *Suppl.* 1058), which however appears
to be in an open place under a rock, and the 'fiery rock-chamber' of the
Iphigenia in Taurica (626). The last example is peculiarly interesting in connexion with Mycenae, because the express purpose with which the sepulture
is described is to console a certain '*Argive*,' who is in fact the son of
Agamemnon, for the loss of the rites which he would have received at home
(*vv.* 627—631).

either way the hypothesis must have been altered, before she could be made presently to wake up and walk home. "But you know," we may hear Euripides whisper, "you know it was not so. We all know that Admetus merely laid his wife in an open tomb-chamber, where she would be burnt or partially burnt...afterwards no doubt, if she stayed there (let us say) till next morning. But if, as after all seems more likely, she *rose again* in the course of the day on which she *died*, why, then you see how providentially the Pheraean method of sepulture was adapted to the requirements of a resurrection!"

It may be worth notice that, in addressing Alcestis herself on her death-bed, Admetus declares that he will join her hereafter, and will have himself laid, when he comes to die, 'side by side with her in the same cedar[1].' If this means, as is generally supposed and seems most probable, that she is to be buried in a cedar *coffin*, then the promise is not justified by the facts. As appears from what comes after, and indeed from what comes before, such a burial is neither executed nor planned, and is practically incompatible with the prompt and surreptitious obsequies, which Admetus has really projected. That he should belie his intentions at this moment is nevertheless quite natural, nor need he be accused of deliberate falsehood. He is in no state for deliberation. If it is not strictly true that Alcestis is to be buried in a coffin, neither is it strictly true that Admetus, if he could, would have 'descended to Hades' in search of her, 'passing Charon and Cerberus undismayed.' The whole of this speech, excellently interpreted by Browning, is mere extravagance, prompted partly by the husband's genuine grief, partly by his uneasy conscience ; and the 'cedar coffin' comes well in with the rest.

But we must go back to those verses which Euripides so carelessly wrote without thinking, for we have not yet done with them. We have not yet done half of what, as Aristophanes assures us, Euripides expected and got from contemporary students. We have not applied to the lines

[1] *v.* 365.

any subtleties of the ‘foot-rule,’ we have not ‘measured them as it were with a square[1].’ But let us do it for once, since we were meant to do it; it may perhaps repay us. Let us first recall the situation. Pheres has flung his last taunt and retired. Admetus, having hurled after him a final curse, returns, with our peccant couplet, to the business of the moment. His words, if we may discard elegance for the sake of as near an approach as may be to exactness, will run thus : "For our part—since what is before the feet must be borne though evil—let us be going, that in the burning-place we may put the corpse[2]." Now if these sentences are to be taken as hasty scribbling, and searched for blunders, we may find one surely worse, or at least more conspicuous, than the pyre. I mean the strangely unhappy expression ‘the evil that is before the feet must be borne.’ The phrase is proverbial in cast, and equivalent nearly in our idiom to ‘we must take things as they come.’ But a phrase, because proverbial, is not to be used in all circumstances indiscriminately, not in literature at least. Applied as it is here to the business of carrying a corpse, which the *bearers*[3] have put down and are now to take up again, the expression ‘what is before the feet must be borne’ is no better than a pun. It is of course impossible to suppose Admetus conscious of such a bearing. He has a right, if we may say so, to blunder unawares. But the author has not; and the charitable presumption is (especially at the close of a scene in which the prince has been made to expose himself so freely) that the author, who does not love him, is playing him false. Reasonably therefore we may look for the like, when he continues with ‘let us go, that in the burning-place we may put the corpse.’ Now the reader will remember that this sentence, running in this order, is the finale of a scene,

---

[1] *Frogs*, 956.

[2] *vv.* 739—740 ἡμεῖς δέ—τοὐν ποσὶν γὰρ οἰστέον κακόν—
   στείχωμεν, ὡς ἂν ἐν πυρᾷ θῶμεν νεκρόν.

The ἐν in ἐν ποσίν, literally *at* or *among*, is an archaism surviving as such do in a byword.

[3] φέρουσιν ἄρδην, *v.* 608.

an *exit-cue*. Turning over the play, or any other play of
Euripides, we may satisfy ourselves that he was artist enough
to know the importance of climax at such a point[1]. But the
sentence before us, ' let us be going that in the burning-place
we may put the corpse,' is so shaped that it cannot be made
climactic or saved from a weak, trailing effect, unless you put,
as the pathos of the situation naturally suggests, a stress on
the close of it ; otherwise it ought to have stopped at ' let us
be going.' To lay the dead in her resting-place is all that
can be done for her *being dead* : a like point has already been
made in the indignant protest ' Go ; leave me free to bury
this my dead[2].' Moreover the poet has taken other pre-
cautions to secure this emphasis. The last word (*nekron*,
' the corpse') stands twice at the end of verse and sentence
within a few lines before[3], so that it has got upon the ear,
as it were ; and that this is no accident may be seen by
comparing the conclusion of a previous scene[4], where another
key-word or key-note is treated in the same way. But if,
obeying these directions of the author, you do accent the
close, you may get a shock ; for the Greek word, ambiguous
in a way which I am unable to reproduce, signifies equally
' *the* corpse' and ' *a* corpse.' Take it in the second way, ' let
us be going, that in the burning-place we may put...a corpse';
and note that by a delicate variation in the form of the
final clause[5] it is hinted that the object in view may possibly
not be attained. What then does it suggest? Plainly that
if they do not go, if after the time already wasted by the
interruptions of Heracles and Pheres they allow any further
delays, the ' corpse,' before they lay it in its resting-place,
may be no corpse. Which is precisely the state of the
case.

This couplet written carelessly ! The man who got it
made after an hour of experiments might feel that he had done

---

[1] See e.g. *Alc.* 434, 567, 733, 860. It is the same with the conclusion of a
tirade.

[2] *v.* 729.   [3] *vv.* 724, 729.   [4] ξένος in *vv.* 550, 558, 559, 567.

[5] By the insertion of ἄν,—ὡς ἄν...θῶμεν instead of ὡς θῶμεν. The possibility
which Admetus himself has in view is that of further interruption.

a full hour's work. We may say, if we like, that it is a waste
of time, and that for our part we have neither taste nor
leisure for the 'squaring' and 'measuring' of phrases which
he expected. Only let us remember that Euripides wrote
expressly for those who had such leisure, and faculties also
and facilities ten times as great as ours for this particular
study. It is for us to follow him as far as we choose, and
when we will not or cannot, to go away.

ION

" Hermes thus, Cyllenian, Argeiphontes
Spake with a wink in his eye."

Homeric Hymn.

IF modern criticism has not been occupied as much with
the inconsistencies, confusions, and errors chargeable (according to current assumptions) upon the author of the *Ion*,
as with the like faults when exhibited (*ex hypothesi*) in the
Alcestis, this is not the fault of Euripides. The case of the
Ion is neither better nor worse. Both plays exhibit (always
ex hypothesi) the same crying incongruity between promise
and execution, the same inexplicable carelessness of development, the same futility in the termination, in short the
same marks of 'the botcher.' If the *Ion* has encountered
comparatively little censure, that is because it has been
comparatively neglected, and in fact, like the majority of
Euripides' extant works, has been studied mostly, by those
who have studied it at all, as a piece of instructive Greek,
a collection of references. From this fate, from being relegated to the school-room and the lecture-room, the *Alcestis*
has been saved, as we said, by the character of the heroine,
which appealing directly to universal feelings has kept alive
interest enough in the whole work, not erudite interest but
naïve emotional interest, to provoke denunciation of its supposed offences. The attractiveness of the youthful devotee
who gives his name to the *Ion*, though none would dispute
it, depends more than that of the unselfish wife upon historical
imagination ; and he is marred, as a mere object for affection,

by traits of opposite tendency. To the ordinary world of readers, outside of Hellenistic circles, he and his legend seem to be altogether unknown; and as for the play of Euripides, notwithstanding the fact that a few years ago it was (for certain practical reasons) selected against others of Euripides for performance in Cambridge, my belief is (and I do not speak without enquiry) that except for purposes of erudition it is seldom opened. Like the mass of Euripides, 'it does not count.'

And if the commentaries current, or current till recently[1], upon its plot and purpose were really the last word on the subject, I could only say that in my opinion the general neglect is justified. It is in vain that attention is directed to the undoubted beauties of many several parts, to the charm of an isolated picture, the passion in a particular monologue, the smartness of a certain conversation or sweetness of a separate ode. It is not such bribes as these which will buy approval for a play from the world which 'judges undisturbed,' and least of all for an Attic play. It is the grasp of an organic conception which makes the work of art, and especially it is this quality which more than anything else constitutes the power of the Attic theatre, of the *Orestea*, the *Oedipus Tyrannus*, or the *Hippolytus*, and which therefore is expected from a play claiming admission to such company. The plain reader will insist on the plain question " What is the dramatist driving at, and what is it all about? What general notion had he of his subject, and what is the view of it to which he would lead us ? " But in the case of the *Ion*, as in the case of the *Alcestis*, these questions, if we are to answer them on the prevailing hypothesis, bring us inevitably to the conclusion, apprehended even before we justify it by minute analysis, that the dramatist did not know what he was about ; and we go away, not to return ; or if we return, it is only to dip in remembered places and pick out a pleasing

---

[1] It is with great pleasure that I acknowledge the countenance given by Mr M. A. Bayfield, when reprinting his edition of the play, to the general view of its purpose which I propounded in 1890, when I translated the play in verse.

bit. We see that, given the hypothesis, Euripides must have lacked precisely that power which the art of his country has taught us to consider supreme; and we speak of him, with Jowett, as 'no true Greek.'

I have already, when making in 1890 the translation noticed below, discussed the plot of the *Ion*, and have offered an explanation of its peculiarities. It will not however be unprofitable to resume the subject in this connexion; for the *Ion* is no isolated phenomenon, and cannot properly be seen in total separation from other works of the poet. With the *Alcestis* in particular, notwithstanding a broad difference of colour, it has in scheme a close resemblance, a resemblance so close as to show, what is amply confirmed by other works, that Euripides came to use almost conventionally and as an established form certain methods of dealing with the peculiar relation between him and his theatre of exhibition, between the sentiments which he desired to express and the form imposed by accident.

Both plays, the *Ion* and the *Alcestis*, offer at first sight exactly the same problem. Not that in the *Ion* we are disturbed by 'comic elements'; but, to repeat the distinction of the previous essay, it is not really because they are 'comedy' that the characters and scenes of the *Alcestis* have provoked so much objection. They would have been accepted with content under any name, if they had appeared *consistent* and *relevant*. Irrelevancy and self-contradiction are the supposed faults which offend in the *Alcestis*; irrelevancy and self-contradiction appear equally *prima facie* to mark the arrangement of the *Ion*. Part for part the plays may be parallel and the like repugnancy revealed in their corresponding elements.

The *Ion*, like the *Alcestis*, purports to set forth a certain story proving the power of the Pythian Apollo. As in the *Alcestis*, so here, the facts are stated and the divine intentions announced in a preface, which, though taking the more usual form of a monologue (not a dialogue, as in the *Alcestis*), resembles it in the essential point that it is spoken by a deity, who thereupon disappears entirely from the action. The deity is in this case Hermes, who appears before the oracular temple of Apollo at Delphi. He informs us that 'in Athens many years before, Creusa, a daughter of the noble house of Erechtheus, became by Apollo's violence the mother of a boy, whom she brought forth secretly and left in a cradle, with certain tokens upon him, at a certain cave on the Athenian Acropolis. Thence by Apollo's command Hermes conveyed the cradle and child to the temple at Delphi and left them on the steps. The prophetess of Apollo, the Pythia, found him and brought him up. He is now adult and is still in the service of the temple. Creusa the mother has since married a well-born soldier of fortune, the Aeolid Xuthus. They have no children, and are coming to-day to consult Apollo on this matter.' What follows I will give in the original form, preferring Mr Way's translation to my own, as I shall throughout where I find it substantially faithful, by way of a guard against prepossession.

> Now Loxias[1] guides their fate
> To this, nor hath forgotten, as might seem.
> He shall give Xuthus, when he entereth,
> His own child, saying to him, " Lo, thy son,"
> That the lad, coming home, made known may be
> Unto Kreusa, Loxias' deed abide
> Unknown, and so the child may have his right.
> And Ion shall he cause him to be called
> Through Greece, the founder of an Asian realm.
> Now to yon hollow bay-embowered I go
> To watch how destiny dealeth with the lad.

Nothing, as the reader sees, can be plainer than this declaration. Apollo, having foreknowledge of the future and guiding for his own purposes the fates of men, has arranged a destiny for his child, unacknowledged hitherto, in which all the parties concerned, and Apollo himself among them, will find their account. Xuthus is to become father of the boy Ion in his own opinion and that of the world. At Athens his true parentage is to be revealed to Creusa, and to Creusa only,

[1] Prophet-name of Apollo.

' Apollo's deed' thus remaining a secret between himself and her, while her son, as the putative offspring of her human husband, succeeds by her consent to her vacant heritage, and every one lives happy ever after. Hermes, as a good brother to Apollo, has been useful in the matter before, and has come to see and enjoy the realisation of this forethought. Precisely as in the *Alcestis*, the thing that we are to witness is a triumph of Apollo, in this case the sure dexterity, so different from the blundering of mortals who cannot see before them, with which he will achieve a foregone conclusion.

One small point of difference we notice, which may or may not prove significant. The Apollo of the *Alcestis*, though his tone is far from Olympian, is as a man not open to censure. He has, so far as appears, a fair record and a clear conscience. We can hardly say as much for the Apollo of the *Ion*, who, even in the sympathetic representation of his brother, appears as intending for good reasons to keep a veil over an incident in his past. However since his skill in doing this is to be a point in his success and every one in the end is to be left secure of happiness, the blemish is not distressing; if he has done what humanly speaking must be called an injury, he has both the will and the power to repair it.

Now let us turn from the opening of the play to the end, and see where Apollo is left. Neither of him, nor of Hermes, nor of any divine personage have we seen anything in the interval, nor have they been reported as taking part personally in the proceedings that have occurred. Through a series of complications the question of Ion's parentage has arrived at what seems to Ion himself a hopeless entanglement, when the goddess Athena presents herself to pronounce a decision. Her speech, so much of it as is relevant, shall be taken again from the version of Mr Way, though here I shall have to note a small divergence. She speaks, it should be said, in the presence of Ion, Creusa, a train of maid-servants (the Chorus) who accompany Creusa, and a crowd of Delphians,

armed men and others, who have been drawn to the spot by
the events of the drama[1].

> Fly not; no foe am I that ye should flee,
> But as in Athens, so here, gracious-willed.
> I come from thy land—land that bears my name:
> I Pallas from Apollo speed in haste,
> Who deigned not to reveal him to your sight,
> Else must he chide you for things overpast,
> But sendeth me to tell to you his words:—
> Thee this queen bare, begotten of Apollo:
> He gives to whom he gave, not that they gat thee,
> But for thy bringing home to a princely house;
> But when the matter was laid bare and told,
> Fearing lest thou should of her plot be slain,
> And she of thee, saved thee by that device.
> Now the God would have kept the secret hid
> Until in Athens he revealed her thine,
> And thee the son of her and Phoebus born.

Here she diverts to other matters, interesting to the
Athenian populace but throwing no light on the conduct
of Apollo's plan, of which this is the last that we hear.
Where then is Apollo left, and what has become of the
far-sighted project, the skilful 'guidance of fate,' which was
promised to us in the prologue? In the first place it is
astonishing that the personal intervention of a deity should
be thus required. A knot to be cut! But this is a case in
which, if Apollo's credit as a prophet was to be preserved,
there ought not to have been any knot. Did Hermes expect
any? Look at his words and see whether it is conceivable. If
Apollo in a delicate matter intimately concerning himself, to
which he had long given particular attention, could not see
to the end of the passing day, where is his superiority over
the ordinary man? In the next place it is the common
feeling of readers, and surely the natural feeling, that if a
deity must appear, the non-appearance of Apollo himself has,

---

[1] For the guards and crowd see *vv.* 1260—1280 (with the notes and stage-
directions, *e.g.* Mr Way's). They are indispensable to the action and must be
supposed to remain till the end, as there is no opportunity (not to say warrant
in the text) for their departure. The Chorus of slaves has actually the final
voice.

for Apollo, a miserable effect. The place is his own temple ;
the affair is his own ; he himself (we were told) took the
management of it. If by the fault (of course) of others there
is something to put right, if faith is to be restored and dis-
content rebuked, Apollo surely is the intervener for whom
we look. That in the last resort he should send excuses
would be compromising for his dignity, even if the reason
alleged for his absence were satisfactory. But is it ? It
is so far from satisfactory, as worded by Euripides, that
Mr Way for example, who would spare Apollo, has to put
a gloss upon it :

> He *deigned* not to reveal him to your sight,
> *Else must he chide you* for things overpast.

This (with deference) is, as a mere translation, not legitimate.
*He did not think fit to come into your sight, lest blame for
former things should come between*—such are the words[1].
According to Mr Way, the blame meant is that which Apollo,
if he came, would unwillingly have to bestow on Ion and
Creusa for their conduct in the course of the day, not that
which he might himself incur for his conduct towards them in
the past. As an interpretation let this pass ; but it is an
interpretation, not a verbal equivalent. The words distinctly
extend to blame on either side ; nor is it strange that most
readers should have thought rather of Apollo's offences,
since the subject of complaint is defined as *former things* or
things of the past. Now the errors of Creusa and of Ion (so
far as he can be accused of any) have been committed within
the last hour ; the offences of Apollo, for which he has been
denounced in the play repeatedly both by Ion and by Creusa
in terms still applicable, began about fifteen years ago and
have continued since. Moreover it is not *prima facie* easy
to see why the desire not to express blame on his own part
need prevent him *from appearing* ; it lay with himself to say
or not say what he thought fit for the moment. On the
whole then it is difficult not to believe, as readers do in

---

[1] ὃς εἰς μὲν ὄψιν σφῷν μολεῖν οὐκ ἠξίου
μὴ τῶν πάροιθε μέμψις εἰς μέσον μόλῃ.

general believe, that Apollo's offences were in the view of the poet. And if they were not, the reason alleged should have been worded otherwise, not thus left open to misunderstanding on so important a point. In any case therefore Apollo's excuse for absence is in substance unsatisfactory, as well as unsatisfactory *per se*, because the occasion does not permit him to absent himself with dignity.

But we have not yet touched the heart of the matter. Take it as granted that Apollo may properly appear by deputy, and let us hear what his deputy has to say.

> Now the God would have kept the secret hid
> Until in Athens he revealed her thine,
> And thee the son of her and Phoebus born.

Precisely so ; we have not forgotten it ; we learnt all this about the intentions of Loxias from Hermes in the prologue, all this and in fact a little more ; for before the event the prophet-god, as represented by his brother, was just a shade more outspoken :—

> He shall give Xuthus, when he entereth,
> His own child, saying to him, " Lo, thy son,"
> That the lad, coming home, made known may be
> *Unto Kreusa*, Loxias' deed abide
> Unknown, and so the child may have his right.

But if Euripides really meant, as he pretends, to base his play on the assumption that Apollo was the supreme unerring prophet, what good is it, or rather how is it tolerable, that this plan of his should be recalled to us now ? It is just because we know it that the present situation of Apollo appears, from a religious point of view, so hopeless. For what has become of the plan ? It is visibly ruined, ruined already as far as he himself is concerned, and ruined prospectively in its other parts. His secret, which he proposed to communicate *afterwards to Creusa*, he has perforce to proclaim now to a crowd ; it is shouted literally upon the house-top ; and although the development of the fiasco is arrested by the abrupt and arbitrary termination of the play at this point, it is impossible not to see that all the pleasing arrangements, proposed for the happy family of Creusa, Xuthus, and Ion, have shared in the wreck. They all depend, as Hermes correctly assumes, on *the preservation of Apollo's secret*, which has not been preserved. Apollo by his deputy repeats them now[1], but what is the use of that, when we have just been taught that Apollo can neither foresee his own concerns nor protect his own interest?

I will not here discuss how far, in the few lines of dialogue which wind up the play, Euripides has represented the *dramatis personae* as accepting with content the declarations of Athena. The traditional cast of the parts has been altered (this is fact[2]) by modern critics, in order to strengthen this impression; and I would rather not enter on technical controversy. Let it be taken that the declarations pass without criticism from the stage, and that the form of religious submission is fully kept up. The essential point remains unaffected.

And that point is this. If Euripides did not see that, whatever his personages are made to say, his finale is in fact for Apollo a complete failure, and that the declarations of Athena, instead of supporting the ostensible and orthodox conclusion, are exactly calculated to forbid such a conclusion, his character as a serious writer, as an artist to be spoken of with Aeschylus and Sophocles, is absolutely indefensible. The ancient world was mistaken about him; Mr Swinburne and others are right when they depose him from his pretensions; he was a 'botcher'; and the *Ion*, let apologists plead as they will, together with the mass of his works, will be flung aside as they are now; 'they do not count.' This is no question of a small slip, such as may befall any man. It goes to the root of his power as a playwright. In the *Ion* he offers a plot where, as in the *Alcestis* but even more plainly, *there is no real dénouement*. When we are told by Athena that the foresight of Apollo has been justified, we are told what is palpably untrue; and since the pretended unity of the piece turns wholly upon this justification, either the author was a bungler, who has mis-spent by trying too high

---

[1] *v.* 1601.   [2] See my edition, *Introduction*, p. xviii.

a flight his little talent for songs and smart writing,—or else he meant something other than he pretends. It makes no difference, except to increase our suspicion, that Athena exhibits an illuminated scroll of Ion's future descendants, the Ionian race. To distract and amuse the theatre this might do very well, but it does not touch the case and conduct of Apollo, to which from first to last the author invites our attention. Once again let us repeat: Euripides either saw this, or he did not, with inferences as before.

It would be easy to show that these difficulties have been fully appreciated by the generality of readers; and if it be asked why expositors have clung to the view that in some way or other Euripides meant Apollo to be justified, the answer is that the alternative has been thought to lie between this conclusion and supposing that the play has no serious meaning at all. In fact the whole problem of the *Alcestis* recurs again in a slightly different shape. The story of the *Ion* is intensely, powerfully realistic, just as that of the *Alcestis* is realistic; that the *Alcestis* is largely comic in tone, the *Ion* almost wholly grave and tragic, makes in this respect no difference. Both are realistic; they have no touch of grotesque; it is impossible to believe that the poet is intentionally playing with his theme, and offering to our imagination things which are not realisable and are not even to be supposed real. As in the *Alcestis* therefore, so here, the religious solution—in the one case that Apollo could raise the dead, in the other case that Apollo could foresee the future—has been taken for Euripidean in spite of all embarrassments, as being the only doctrine on the subject which could be of practical moment. Here, in this last assumption, is the fallacy in both cases. In the age of Euripides, and in relation to his audience, there were in each case *two* doctrines, and not only one, of practical moment, *two* doctrines worthy to be recommended by serious art, one that Apollo could raise the dead and could foresee the future, the other, at that time equally and more than equally requiring serious argument, *that Apollo could not, because Apollo did not exist but was a fiction, originated in times of ignorance and perpetuated by fraud.* Exactly as in the *Alcestis,* so in the *Ion,* Euripides has had before him the problem, how to say this in a theatre devoted to the religion of which Apollo was the corner-stone; and in both cases the problem is dealt with essentially in the same way. A religious hypothesis is propounded by a god, and we are given to understand that the coming story will illustrate this hypothesis. The story which follows does not in the least illustrate the hypothesis, but on the contrary clashes with it more and more unmistakably. And finally, when we have been sufficiently mystified or instructed (according to our knowledge of the author and his ways), the original religious explanation, now seen as completely incredible and inapplicable to the facts, is repeated with transparent irony,—and we are sent off to consider and enquire. In the *Ion,* which is a much bolder piece of work than the *Alcestis,* as it is probably much later, the false conclusion has the advantage of being uttered, like the false prologue, by a divine personage. It is not too much to say that on the Euripidean stage whatever is said by a divinity is to be regarded, in general, as *ipso facto* discredited. It is in all cases objectionable from the author's point of view, and almost always a lie. 'By representing the deities he persuaded men that they did not exist.' The real meaning of the *Ion* is contained wholly in that elaborate realistic story in action, which lies between the exit of Hermes with his falsehoods and the entrance of Athena to repeat the same falsehoods. Their theory is that the Delphian oracle is in communication with an unerring deity who foresees the future. The facts of the story in action are irreconcilable with this theory. The alternative theory, which was rapidly gaining ground in the age of Euripides, and which he in particular was universally known to maintain, was that the Delphians were not in communication with any deity, but that their oracle was a fraud. Just as in the case of the *Alcestis* the action and colour of the story, otherwise inconsequent and inharmonious, become natural the moment you regard them under the rationalistic assumption that *Alcestis was not really dead,* so in the *Ion* the action and tone of the story, monstrously repugnant to the conception that the oracular business is carried on by a being fit for worship and endowed with divine intelligence, become simple at every stage, so soon as you apply to them the obvious rationalistic assumption that *the oracle is carried on by cheats*. That Hermes and Athena do not say so, but offer an explanation of the facts which finds room for such personages as themselves, is a matter of course, and makes no difference. It is not to 'Hermes' that you would apply to be told whether 'Apollo' exists. In the 'atheistic' language of Euripides, language which in the latter part of his career must have been understood by everyone except the wilfully deaf, a preliminary exposition 'by Hermes' means simply a view of the coming story which in sentiment, or morality, or fact, or all together, is false, contemptible, and not to be accepted. As in the *Alcestis*, so in the *Ion*, the truth begins to be told, or rather shown, when the 'god' is dismissed and the men come on. What this truth exactly is, we could not expect to be told in plain words from the orchestra. The tragic theatre belonged to 'Hermes,' 'Apollo,' 'Athena,' and their like, who will merely repeat their manifest falsehoods. But we can find the truth for ourselves if we please; or at Athens, if we did not see our way or care for the trouble, we should have met people who knew all about it, and had known ever since the play was begun, the first time we fell into a literary chat in the Ceramicus. I shall show in a subsequent essay that centuries after the death of Euripides, and when all such knowledge was crumbling into the gulf, the principles of Euripidean exposition were still perfectly comprehended by instructed and sympathetic persons such as Lucian.

To lighten a statement in which, as it is not new except in form, I wish to be brief, I shall say little here on the moral character of Apollo as exhibited in the *Ion*, and the absurdity of Euripides' delineation, if he means to recommend him as an object of worship. That the supposed behaviour of Apollo to Creusa is that of a cowardly, selfish ruffian, and that nothing which he now can do, no future happiness which he can give her (even if there were the least reason to expect that she will get it) will affect the brutality of his original outrage and the

cruelty of his fifteen years' silence about the fate of her child,
—all this is pointed out again and again in the plainest and
most biting terms which the author can find[1]. And if we
suppose him to presume reverence for Apollo as the ground
of his play, this raises over again all the regular, hopeless
difficulties, and leads to the regular conclusion that the author
is a 'botcher.' But to our immediate purpose the moral
character of Apollo is not directly relevant; for what we
propose to show is that according to the story the oracle is
a fraud and its god *non-existent*. Now the question of his
existence is not, strictly speaking, affected by his moral
character. It is theoretically possible to take Euripides as
holding, and meaning to recommend by his play, the view
that there really was a person of superhuman intelligence,
who knowing both past and future did veritably make reve-
lations through the Delphian prophetess, and also further
that this superhuman person had a moral character deserving
hatred and contempt, that he was in short a 'devil.' There
is no logical inconsistency or impossibility in such a view.
It has been actually maintained by many Christians. I do
not think indeed that those who are acquainted with the
condition of Greek thought and controversy in the fifth
century before Christ will hold it probable that Euripides
meant this. Such a view was not then in the field; whereas
the belief that the oracles were fraudulent human tricks was
not only in the field but gaining. Nor, as could easily be
shown, does such a view suit with the rationalistic and vaguely
monotheistic tendency of Euripides' speculations in general.
However it is a conceivable view; and therefore we will here
pass over the attacks on Apollo's moral character, and examine
the story strictly upon the question, whether there spoke by
the Pythia at Delphi a person of superhuman intelligence.

The facts exhibited are as follows:

At the temple of Delphi lives a youth just come to man-
hood, who has been ever since his birth a slave in the service
of the oracle and has become a minister of importance. It is
a day of public consultation, and the young servant is seen

---

[1] *vv*, 357—8, 436 ff., 859 ff. and *passim*.

before the temple, engaged with others in preparing the place. Presently, preceded by female attendants, there arrives a lady from Athens, Creusa of the house of Erechtheus. From her conversation with the ministrant we learn on the one hand that he is a foundling, brought up by the Pythian prophetess and ignorant of his parentage, on the other hand that Creusa desires to consult Apollo 'for a friend of hers,' who many years ago, having been forcibly outraged by the god, concealed the truth and exposed her offspring, which disappeared and has never since been heard of. The lad replies that if the story be true (which he neither admits nor denies) to consult Apollo on the subject is impossible; he must wish to keep his secret. Hereupon arrives Xuthus, the husband of Creusa, who was travelling in her company but had stayed for an incidental purpose on the way. The pair have no children after many years of marriage, and the professed purpose of their visit is to consult the prophetess respecting a remedy. The enquiry is to be made by the husband, who proceeds into the temple, while the rest excepting the attendants of Creusa withdraw. (*Sc.* i.)

Presently the young ministrant, who has been occupied with duties elsewhere, returns to ask whether the consultation of Xuthus is at an end. At this moment he is heard coming out. As soon as he appears he falls upon the astonished lad and attempts to embrace him as his son. He explains his conduct by repeating the declaration of the prophetess.

Ion. What was this, the word of Phoebus?
Xuthus.   That the man who met my face—
Ion. Met thee—met thee?
Xuthus.   As I came out of Apollo's holy place—
Ion. Ay, and what should be his fate?
Xuthus.   My true-begotten son is this.
Ion. Born thy son or given of others?
Xuthus.   Given—and born from me he is[1].

After some resistance the lad, convinced that the oracle, in which he has implicit confidence, has made this declaration, consents to investigate; and it soon appears that so far as

[1] *vv.* 534—537, Way.

the fact is concerned there is no cause for suspicion.   Xuthus,
at the time which the lad's age would presuppose, had visited
Delphi to take part in the feast of Bacchus performed at night
by the women of Delphi upon Parnassus.   It was accompanied
upon that occasion by the usual disorders, and accounts completely for the present discovery that he is the father of a
Delphian foundling.   The question thus set at rest, Xuthus
resolves to pay his thanks, as seems proper, by a birth-sacrifice
upon the mountain-top, and directs his son (on whom, because
he *came to meet him coming*, he bestows the name of *Ion*, that
is to say *Comer*) to give a farewell banquet to the Delphians.
He must remove to Athens, for the present as a pretended
visitor.   Later on Creusa may be informed and pacified; for
the present she must be kept in the dark; and her attendants
are severely cautioned to that effect.   (*Sc.* ii.)

But their sympathies are entirely with their mistress.
They are transported with indignation at the injustice which
is to be done and at the proposed invasion of Athenian rights.
As for the alleged oracle, it appears to them tainted with
fraud, treacherous, and altogether suspicious.   And when
Creusa returns, with an old man-slave to whom she is much
attached, they disclose to her all that has happened.   Amid
general indignation the old 'tutor' urges his mistress, for
revenge and safety, to murder her husband and his son.   But
Creusa for the moment is absorbed in her own feelings, and
in uncontrollable passion breaks out against Apollo.   Pouring
her invectives into the temple, she relates now as of herself
the horrible story which she had formerly attributed to a
pretended 'friend,' the violence of the god, the birth, and all
the sequel, and repeats the same account more calmly under
the questions of her guardian.   He renews the suggestion of
murder, and it is agreed that he shall poison Ion at the
approaching banquet.   Creusa now produces a gold chain
or bracelet which she wears upon her arm.   It had been
(she says) the necklace given by the goddess Athena to
Erichthonius the first ancestor of her house, when an infant,
and in two little pyxes attached to it are contained two drops
of blood from the Gorgon whom Athena slew.   One drop is

an elixir, the other a deadly poison. She gives him the jewel, and directs him to put the poison in Ion's cup. She herself returns to her lodging. (*Sc.* iii.)

Between this and the next scene the banquet has taken place. A servant of Creusa, searching for her, narrates to the handmaidens the failure and detection of the plot. One of the sacred doves, by tasting of Ion's libation, revealed the poison before he drank. The old slave has been arrested and tortured into confession. The Delphian judges have condemned Creusa to be flung from the cliffs. Ion and the populace are seeking her. Creusa enters in flight, and takes refuge at the great altar before the temple, closely followed by her pursuers. After a fierce altercation, Ion seems to be on the point of dragging her from sanctuary, when the Pythian prophetess enters bearing a cradle, and commands him to forbear. The cradle, she says, is that in which the lad, when a new-born babe, had been found by her on the temple-steps: within it are tokens then found upon him, which may enable him to discover his mother. She retires; and Ion unwraps the cradle. Instantly Creusa pronounces it to be the cradle in which she herself exposed her baby at Athens, and claims Ion as her child. On his demand, she undertakes to prove her statement by describing the contents, which she does and is pronounced to be right. She and Ion embrace with rapture.

But presently Ion refers to Xuthus as his father, which forces from Creusa a confession that this is not the fact. He was born before her marriage. Ion is horrified, and even more (upon reflexion) by the addition that his true father was Apollo. He urges Creusa to retract this charge against the God, and points out that it cannot be true; because the oracle, which cannot without 'confusion of soul' be supposed capable of falsehood, has declared him the son of Xuthus.

Ion.   How gave he then his own son to another
            And called me Xuthus' son—begotten son?
Creusa. Nay, not begotten; but his gift art thou
            Sprung from himself—as friend to friend should give
            His own son that his house might have an heir.

Ion.	Is the God true? or naught his prophecies?
	Mother, my soul it troubleth: well it may.
Creusa.	Hear now what cometh to my mind, my son.
	Of kindness Loxias giveth thee a place
	In a proud house: hadst thou been called his son,
	Thou hadst had none inheritance thereof,
	Nor a sire's name:—how couldst thou, when myself
	Still hid his rape, yes, by thy secret death?
	Thee for thy good to another sire he gives.
Ion.	Nay, not thus lightly on the quest I press.
	I will ask Phoebus, entering his fane,
	"Am I of Loxias or a mortal sire[1]?"

Here Athena appears; she pronounces, in the words before quoted, in favour of Creusa, whose story she confirms as deputy of Apollo; and the play ends with the appearance (more or less perfect is no matter) of religious submission to her divine authority.   The question then is this: was this story *really* composed in the spirit of religious submission, that is, to illustrate the proposition that *the Pythian oracle reveals truth dictated by Apollo*?   This was the belief of orthodox Greeks in the time of Euripides, and must be assumed as the basis of submission to such an authority as 'Athena.' But is it the lesson of the facts?

Now I earnestly beg the reader—I have to contend with much respectable prejudice, and may be excused for insistence —to ask himself seriously, what sort of a man Euripides can have been, if he composed this story to illustrate that proposition.   Would the reader himself, would any writer whom he happens to respect, dream of so framing a story with that object?   Does it not palpably contradict the proposition, and is not this pointed out, as plainly as words can do it, in the dilemma propounded by Ion?   In the story one statement, and only one, is made by the oracle, namely that *Ion is the natural son of Xuthus*.   Either that statement is true or it is false.   If it is false, the oracle does not reveal truth.   If it is true, the oracles are not dictated by Apollo, for Apollo, by his deputy Athena, confirms the incompatible story of Creusa Is any doubt admissible whether the statement was made by

---

[1] *vv.* 1532—1548, Way.

the prophetess? It is reported by Xuthus immediately after he has heard it, he rejects emphatically the possibility of mistake, nor (which is conclusive) is mis-report suggested by Athena. Were the words ambiguous? This, according to the notions of believers in oracles, might be a defence. But were they ambiguous? Not in the least according to Xuthus, who purports to quote them and holds to his report under questioning; nor (which again is conclusive) is any ambiguity in the wording suggested by Athena[1]. Neither from Athena

---

[1] I have given above (p. 151) Mr Way's translation of Xuthus' report, which is substantially faithful, but perhaps does not fully bring out its emphasis and precision. Here is the original, and another version.

ΞΟ.　　　　　πατὴρ σός εἰμι καὶ σὺ παῖς ἐμός.
ΙΩ.　τίς λέγει τάδ ;
ΞΟ.　　　　　　ὅς σ' ἔθρεψεν ὄντα Λοξίας ἐμόν.
ΙΩ.　μαρτυρεῖς σαυτῷ.
ΞΟ.　　　　　τὰ τοῦ θεοῦ γ' ἐκμαθὼν χρηστήρια.
ΙΩ.　ἐσφάλης αἴνιγμ' ἀκούσας.
ΞΟ.　　　　　　οὐκ ἄρ' ὄρθ' ἀκούομεν;
ΙΩ.　ὁ δὲ λόγος τίς ἐστι Φοίβου;
ΞΟ.　　　　　　τὸν συναντήσαντά μοι—
ΙΩ.　τίνα συνάντησιν;
ΞΟ.　　　　　δόμων τῶνδ' ἐξιόντι τοῦ θεοῦ—
ΙΩ.　συμφορᾶς τίνος κυρῆσαι;
ΞΟ.　　　　　παῖδ' ἐμὸν πεφυκέναι.
ΙΩ.　σὸν γεγῶτ' ἢ δῶρον ἄλλως;
ΞΟ.　　　　　δῶρον, ὄντα δ' ἐξ ἐμοῦ.

　　　　　　　　　　　Xuth. I am thy sire;
Thou art my son. *Ion.* Who saith it? *Xuth.* Loxias,
Who reared thee, being mine. *Ion.* Thine own report
Attests it! *Xuth.* But I have his speech by heart!
Ion. His rede was dark and thou hast missed the sense.
Xuth. Not if mine ears hear truly. *Ion.* Give me then
The wording. *Xuth.* 'He that should encounter me...'
Ion. Encounter! How encounter? *Xuth.* 'As I came
Forth from the temple...' *Ion.* What should come to him
Of this encounter? *Xuth.* 'He should be my son.'
Ion. Son of thy loins or given thee? *Xuth.* 'Given indeed
Yet of my flesh.'

Creusa (*v.* 1534) and Athena (*v.* 1561) assure us that what 'Apollo' meant *to do* was merely to foist *his own* offspring upon the consultant. Be it so; but no attempt is made to show that the truth or alleged truth of the matter can by any ingenuity be reconciled with what the prophetess said. Nor can it, and without this the 'intentions of Apollo' are irrelevant to Ion's dilemma.

nor from any of the *dramatis personae* do we receive a hint that the oracle did not speak as Xuthus reports, or that it could be understood in any sense but the plain sense which he puts upon it. It must be taken therefore as a *datum* that words and sense were such as he says: consequently the dilemma of Ion is unsolved, and the story directly contradicts the proposition that *the oracle reveals truth at the dictation of Apollo.* Whatever is true, ' Athena ' and Athena's explanation are false, and as we have from the author no explanation but hers, we have in fact none at all.

Now in what way, short of an express statement in words, could the author more plainly intimate that his story is a problem, of which the solution is not given, than by arresting it at such a moment as this? So arrested, it simply *is* such a problem. Put the matter this way. If a play were discovered claiming the name, let us say, of Sophocles or Racine, and it were found to break off in such confusion; what would critics say? Assuredly that if any part of the work correctly represented the author, the finale did not; he must have left it incomplete; for the end was no end, and could not pass for such with a dramatist supposed intelligent. Why should not Euripides, whom the ancient world supposed intelligent, have the benefit of a like presumption? Here again the treatment is that of the *Alcestis*, only much bolder. The ostensible finale does not fit the story either in the article already here indicated or in many others, which I have pointed out elsewhere[1]; but this one is enough. Either the drama is nonsense or the comments of Athena are nonsense: between these alternatives Euripides forces us to choose. When the goddess appears we are apparently on the verge of some discovery, of which the one thing certain is, that it must be most unpleasant for the Pythian oracle. Athena...praises Apollo and magnifies Athens. From her we could expect nothing else; but...what are the facts?

If then readers are left to discover what hypothesis about the Pythian oracle the author did intend to illustrate, the circumstances of Euripides' time suggest, and suggested then,

[1] See my edition.

the hypothesis which we ought to try. There existed in that age two opinions, and only two, about the oracle, one, here inadmissible, that it spoke truth dictated by Apollo, and the other, proved in some cases and suspected in many more, that it was a fraud worked by ordinary human means. This hypothesis accords perfectly with the general opinions which Euripides was known to entertain and constantly betrays, and the obvious course of the reader, now as then, is to enquire whether it clears up the confusion in which we are left.

Referring the reader for details to my edition of the play, I will give here the result of this enquiry in brief.

A woman of Delphi (the Pythian prophetess) having 'found,' according to her own account, an infant in the temple, adopts and rears it. When the infant is grown up, there comes to the temple a visitor from Athens (Xuthus), who is told by the prophetess that he is the father of the foundling. He accepts the statement without demur, and confirms it as probable by his account of a former visit paid to Delphi at the time indicated. Putting 'divine authority' aside, what is the natural interpretation of this incident? That the statement is true, and that the woman, if not herself the mother (to which in the *Ion* many suggestions point, and against which there is nothing), must at any rate have known the mother and learnt the facts at the time. If instead of saying 'this young man is your son' she says, 'the young man, whom you will meet on leaving this temple, is your son,' the said young man being at that moment engaged in audible conversation with some women at the door, shall we change our inference? Or only add to it, that she chooses, or is compelled, to express herself indirectly, and that the enquirer, if he takes the communication for miraculous because of its form, is blinded by superstition and by his pleasure in the discovery?

So far then there is no occasion for 'Apollo.' He is a superfluous hypothesis. The revelation to Xuthus, like the resurrection of Alcestis, is a 'miracle' described by a rationalist, manifestly no miracle. The alleged accident is presumptively fraudulent, and (which is conclusive) Euripides suggests the presumption[1].

Next as to the story of Creusa, the villainous outrage, the secret birth, the exposure and disappearance of the babe. It is needless to prove that 'Apollo' is here a superfluous hypothesis. To intelligent piety he is even an impossible hypothesis. Even Pindar would have shuddered at such a story, and told it otherwise, or not at all[2]. What was Sophocles likely to think, or Socrates? Piety, to be intelligent, must prefer here the obvious explanation which omits 'Apollo' and presumes the criminal to have been some unknown man; and again (which is conclusive) *Euripides points this out*[3].

Thirdly, there is the production by the prophetess of the cradle and tokens. Here again (*and Euripides elaborately points it out*[4]) the Apolline hypothesis is manifestly incredible. The circumstances under which the evidence, 'concealed' for so many years, is now produced, are *prima facie* proof to common sense that the account given of it is 'a new story' devised at the moment to achieve the purpose which it does achieve[5], that is, to prevent the sacrilegious murder of Creusa by Ion and the populace. The 'Apollo' who, knowing all the alleged facts from the first and intending to make them known to Creusa, must have postponed this revelation by choice until just after she has attempted the murder of 'her son' and thereby come within an ace of perishing by his hand, is a personage *prima facie* absurd; and nothing is said by the author to diminish the weight of the objections which at the moment and elsewhere[6] he ostentatiously indicates. On the other hand, if the proceedings of the oracle are managed by ordinary human agents, all these objections vanish. The

---

[1] *vv.* 691—692.

[2] See *Pyth.* 9. 30 (49) ff. The gentle homily, in which Chiron (as preceptor of Apollo) enforces the duty of πειθώ, 'courting,' as opposed to the *voie de fait* suggested by the youth himself, is in fact a corrective, after Pindar's manner, upon the older and ruder stories imitated and satirised by Euripides.

[3] ἀνδρὸς ἀδικίαν αἰσχύνεται, *v.* 341.   See also *v.* 1523 ff.

[4] *vv.* 1339—1345.   [5] *v.* 1565.

[6] Contrast with this scene the anticipations of Hermes in the prologue and the perplexities of Ion in the conclusion.

reasons why the managers did not attempt before this to prove Ion the son of Creusa are *first*, that they knew he was not her son but was, as declared by themselves, a Delphian foundling, son of Xuthus and a woman of Delphi, and *secondly*, that before the confession 'shrieked' by Creusa 'into the ear of Apollo[1]' they did not know the fact in her past history which is the necessary basis of such an allegation. And the reason why they do attempt the proof now is the manifest reason, that they have in the circumstances no other way of preventing the sacrilegious murder. So far then 'Apollo' is still, upon the facts of the story, a superfluous and inapplicable hypothesis.

Lastly we come to the alleged 'proof' of the relation between Ion and Creusa, the only part of the story in which the rationalist hypothesis about the facts is not instantaneously preferable to the miraculous and orthodox. The proof is that Creusa, from her recollections of her own exposed infant, describes, without seeing them, the patterns of the objects, especially the customary baby-necklace and shawl, worn, as alleged, by Ion when found at Delphi, and describes them right.

Creusa.	See there the web I wove in girlhood's days.
Ion.	Its fashion? girls be ever weaving webs.
Creusa.	No perfect work, 'twas but a prentice hand.
Ion.	The pattern tell; thou shalt not trick me so.
Creusa.	A Gorgon in the mid-threads of a shawl.
Ion (aside).	O Zeus, what weird is this that dogs our steps!
Creusa.	'Tis fringed with serpents, with the Aegis fringe.
Ion.	Behold! This is the web: lo, here the oracle[2].
Creusa.	O work of girlhood's loom, so long unseen!
Ion.	Is there aught else?—or this thy one true shot?
Creusa.	Serpents, an old device, with golden jaws—
Ion.	Athena's gift, who biddeth deck babes so?
Creusa.	Moulded from Erichthonius' snakes of old.
Ion.	What use, what purpose tell me hath the jewel?

[1] *v.* 911.

[2] This line is not correctly rendered. In reality it proves, as I will presently show, that Ion *imagines* a resemblance between pattern and description, and is himself dissatisfied.

Creusa.   A necklace for the new-born babe, my child.
Ion.   Even these be here. The third I long to know.
Creusa.   A wreath of olive set I on thee then:
            Athena brought it first unto our rock.
            If this be here, it hath not lost its green
            But blooms yet, from the sacred olive sprung[1].

Now it is plain that as between the two hypotheses which we are balancing—that this evidence is genuine and that it is forged by the managers of the oracle, the decision must turn on the necklace. The pattern of the baby's shawl might, as Ion points out, be on Creusa's part a lucky guess. Equally then it may be a lucky guess on the part of the forgers, and it will be shown hereafter that the alleged resemblance is not satisfactory to Ion. It therefore proves nothing. The ' miraculous wreath' is on the wrong side for ' Apollo,' and proves, if anything, forgery. The real wreath of Creusa's babe ought to have been dust long ago, as Euripides points out. Creusa does not mention it till she is prompted by Ion; and from the eagerness to which he is wrought by her previous success it is no illegitimate inference that he lets her see it. The extravagant superstition by which she then accounts for its presence is such as, propounded by a known rationalist, could only prompt suspicion. *Prima facie* a *fresh* wreath is the hasty new-made production of a forger and fits in with other like circumstances about the cradle to which the author has previously directed our notice[2]. The decision therefore turns on the necklace, which (in one sense) could not be forged. For though the managers of the Delphian oracle not only might know, but could not be ignorant, that the baby-necklace of Creusa's infant would be of the famous pattern used for the purpose by her family (the topic of illustrious traditions with which Ion, for instance, shows himself well acquainted both here and in his first conversation with Creusa[3]), this knowledge would avail them nothing, unless such a necklace were in their hands. They could not on the spur of the moment make it. This is the proof and the only proof which is furnished for the

---

[1] *vv.* 1417—1436, Way.   [2] *vv.* 1391—1394.
[3] *v.* 265 ff.

theory of 'Apollo.' But it happens that according to the story told by Euripides the required necklace, the exact thing, has just been brought to the oracle; *and the author here points us to the fact.* The reader will observe that this dialogue of discovery is written, after the Attic fashion, with severe terseness and finish of form. Every speech on both sides takes us on a step and goes straight to the business of ascertaining the correspondence between the contents of the cradle and the recollections of Creusa: all the dialogue follows this purpose strictly—except one couplet:—

Ion.	Is there aught else?—or this thy one true shot?
Creusa.	Serpents, an old device, with golden jaws—
Ion.	*Athena's gift, who biddeth deck babes so?*
Creusa.	*Moulded[1] from Erichthonius' snakes of old.*
Ion.	What use, what purpose tell me hath the jewel?
Creusa.	A necklace for the new-born babe, my child.

Now what is the purpose in this connexion of the two lines marked? The fact that the necklaces used for infants of the house of Erichthonius were all copies of one original, is wholly irrelevant to the ostensible question in hand, whether Creusa can describe correctly the necklace which is in the cradle. So manifest is it that these two lines break the natural course of the enquiry, that some critics have proposed to recast the parts, and others have observed, with the accustomed sneer, that Euripides must have inserted the couplet 'to please the vanity of the Athenians[2].' Such is the candour with which he is commonly read! If Euripides in a most critical passage of his drama, a passage visibly constructed with scrupulous care, inserts one staring irrelevancy, the inference for those who would understand him is that the fact so scored is vitally important to his meaning. And so it is. Once observed, it instantly destroys the validity of the alleged evidence, by removing the one difficulty in the way of supposing it forged. For we have ourselves seen *the original necklace of Erichthonius,* and we know that it has just been in the hands of the Delphian authorities; it was worn by Creusa as a bracelet, given by her to the slave who was to poison Ion, and found upon him when

---

[1] *Copied, imitated,* is the exact word. [2] See Paley's note.

V. E. 11

the attempt failed[1]. All this is related in the play; and as
soon as we bring it into connexion with the evidence of the
cradle, *as the author by his reference directs us to do*, that
evidence is instantly seen as the forgery which, in every part
except the necklace, it would appear to be *prima facie*.
Throughout the play in fact the legends connected with this
bracelet are treated with an emphasis which receives no explanation in the ostensible *dénouement*, and would alone prove,
if the author is to be credited with ordinary judgement, that
they have some importance other than at first appears.   In
particular the history of the pattern and the fact that the
'bracelet' is really a baby's necklace, is so dragged in by way
of a conventional dialogue between Creusa and the old slave[2]
(a theatrical 'you also know' in the immemorial stage-fashion
ridiculed by Sheridan) that we are bound to find some outcome
of it in the sequel, or else to suppose Euripides unacquainted
with the rudiments of story-telling.

The real story then of the *Ion*, the story which becomes
perfectly clear when the prologue 'by Hermes' and the
epilogue 'by Athena' are dismissed as the absurdities that
they are, is simply this.—A certain lad, the bastard of an
Achaean adventurer by a woman of Delphi, was brought
up in the sanctuary there by the Pythian prophetess as a
slave and minister of the temple.   When he is adult his
father, who has in the meantime married a lady of Athens
but has no legitimate children, comes with his wife to consult
the prophetess on this misfortune.   The prophetess, to gratify
the father and to make the fortune of the son, reveals to the
father the connexion between the two.   This discovery is
accidentally betrayed to the wife, who besides the feelings
natural to her position has, or believes herself to have, an
especial cause for indignation against Apollo in the fact that
before her marriage she had been the victim of an outrage
which, as shame suggested and superstition allowed, she
attributed to the god.   Her child, the fruit of this outrage,
was exposed and in fact perished; but it was her secret hope
that at Delphi she might learn something of its fate.   Wrought

---

[1] *vv.* 985—1038, 1213—1216.   [2] *vv.* 999—1009. See also *vv.* 20—26.

to frenzy by her disappointment she proclaims her story, for the disgrace of the god, to all within hearing, among others especially to the prophetess and her coadjutors in the temple. To revenge her injuries she is tempted and persuaded to poison her husband's child. For this purpose she entrusts to her emissary *a jewel which she wears as a bracelet, though it is in fact a baby-necklace and the model of those which are always worn by infants of her ancient house.* The emissary is detected and the jewel seized. The youth, supported by the Delphian populace, furious at the 'sacrilege,' wrests from the authorities a sentence of death against her for the attempt, and finding her at the altar is about to violate the sanctuary by delivering her to the fanatical mob. As a desperate expedient for preventing this murder, the managers and particularly the prophetess hastily determine to make a pretended discovery that the lad is the lost child born at Athens and mentioned in the woman's confession. In the face of the previous affirmation by the oracle of the true fact, that he is the natural son of the husband and was born at Delphi, it is impossible for them to pass off this 'new story' by their mere authority. But the possession of *the baby-necklace* opens a possibility of offering an apparent proof. It is put, together with two other objects which they think suitable to support the fraud, into a cradle which, wrapped up in bandages 'miraculously fresh in appearance,' the prophetess carries out and delivers to the youth, directing him to 'find his mother' by the tokens within. The woman at the altar, the perishing fugitive, leaps, as might naturally be anticipated, at the obvious suggestion, and claims her son. Put to the test of describing the tokens, she succeeds of course triumphantly in the crucial point of the necklace, and in the mutual rapture of the recognition the fact that this is her sole success (we will return to this point hereafter) is disregarded, and the various contingent impossibilities of her story are swallowed without criticism. For the moment therefore the purpose of the fraud is achieved. But as soon as the lad learns that if he is, as he now supposes, the son of the lady, he cannot be, as the oracle declared, the son of the man who is now her husband, and that, according to her belief, he must have been begotten by the crime of his patron-god, he revolts in horror against the new allegations, and in the utmost distress of mind decides to unravel the imbroglio by a fresh enquiry at the oracle. Had this enquiry been made and followed up (and in real life that could not have been prevented), it must have resulted in one of those exposures, too ghastly even for ridicule, which occur from time to time in the history of Delphi and all places of like pretension. And such is the real termination of the tragic story, which, as in other cases, we can easily complete, although the 'sanctity' of the Athenian theatre did not allow of the exhibition, and therefore the action is abruptly arrested at the last moment by one of those Euripidean gods whom all the world knew to be nothing but theatrical shams. Of the power with which the story is handled this bald statement can of course give no idea. Not even in Euripides is there anything more terrible or more pathetic than are some of the scenes in this play, if we do not make them unintelligible by taking for part of the true narrative the lies of Hermes and Athena.

Thus the problem propounded at the close by Ion's unsolved dilemma offers no difficulty whatever, if we choose to take it up. I have stated the solution here summarily, and will ask leave to refer for details to my former work on the play. My object in restating the explanation in a somewhat different form is to exhibit the parallel in method between this case and the *Alcestis*. Both plays begin and end with a miraculous 'divine' interpretation of the facts exhibited in the story proper. In both it is manifest that, if we judge by the ordinary laws of reason and taste, there is between the story and the divine interpretation a startling repugnance. This is accounted for, or at least has been accounted for, together with masses of similar facts scattered over the poet's works, by the compendious assumption that he did not know his business, was in short a 'botcher,' and therefore we must be prepared to overlook in him inconsistencies and contradictions which would astonish us in a tiro; we must console ourselves as best we can for the perversity of his plays as plays by admiring the eloquence, passion, or grace of single scenes, single speeches, or single odes. And the natural consequence is that Euripides 'does not count.'

He will recover his rights, and we our due enjoyment, only when it is seen (as it was by Lucian) that his works, some of them wholly, almost all in some part, are in the nature of theatrical problems, a type produced by the unique circumstances of the time and place, which made the stage necessary to him as an organ of expression, and at the same time made it impossible that, speaking from the stage, he should express his known opinions otherwise than under formal reserve. The *Ion*, if accepted as an exposition of the religious hypothesis with which it formally concludes, is a tissue of contradictions and blunders. The 'god' whom it pretends to celebrate appears in it morally as a monster, intellectually as a fool. The incidents, if supposed to be guided or influenced by him, are left at the critical points without any intelligible explanation, and must be regarded, like the intoxication of Heracles in the *Alcestis*, as both fortuitous and offensive. The work as a whole, whatever the author may pretend in the finale, is *possible* (if he was a man of sense) only on the assumption that he meant to exhibit the Delphian Apollo as an impudent myth, and the oracle therefore as a fraud; just as the *Alcestis* is possible as a whole, only if the author did not believe in the alleged resurrection, and wished to exhibit it as not really miraculous. If on these suppositions the stories respectively are found intelligible, harmonious, and coherent, then, and only then, we can allow to the author the preliminary qualification for pretending to a seat beside Aeschylus and Sophocles. If he meant anything else, the Athenians were wrong, and the moderns right: Euripides, as an artist, ought not to count.

What is the logical result of attempting to unite the belief that Euripides composed the *Ion*, as the finale pretends, upon orthodox assumptions about the oracle and its deity, with the belief that he was a competent artist and a man of average intelligence, is well seen in the observations of the translator from whom I have been citing. It is one of the many aspects in which the posture of affairs just before the pretended *dénouement* is seen as hopeless of any issue agreeable to 'Apollo' or compatible with faith in his deity or existence, that Ion, educated as a votary of that faith, has been forced by the course of events to take the very step which he has himself, with crushing force, shown to be irreconcilable with his religion.

> I will ask Phoebus, entering his fane,
> "Am I of Loxias or a mortal sire?"

This is the same youth who, on the same morning, when it was proposed by Creusa that Phoebus should be consulted as to the fate of the child alleged to have been borne to the god by Creusa's 'friend,' received the proposal thus:—

> There's none will ask the God of this for thee.
> For, in his own halls were he villain proved,
> Vengeance on him who brought thee that response
> Would Phoebus justly wreak. Ah lady, go:
> We must not seek his shrine to flout the God.
> For lo, what height of folly should we reach
> If in the Gods' despite we wrest their will,
> By sacrifice of sheep on altars, or
> By flight of birds, to tell what they would veil.
> Could we of force wring aught from Gods full loth,
> Profitless blessings, lady, should we grasp;
> But what they give free-willed are boons indeed.

This is the same youth who, forced by Creusa's story of her 'friend' to meditate uncomfortably for a moment on the savage traits of traditional theology, traits which in the days of Euripides believers and quasi-believers were trying hard to put out of sight and to refine away without destroying the foundation, launches at the inconsequence of *immoral religion* this pointed weapon:—

> For wickedness in man the gods chastise.
> What justice then that ye, who set the law
> To mortal man, should sin against the law?
> If, if (to feign a thing impossible)
> For such like thefts upon humanity
> Thou, or Poseidon, or the King of Heaven
> Should be amerced, to quit the fines would leave
> Your temples empty. Ye, to have your will,

> Do thoughtless wrong: then just it is to blame
> Not imitative man, but them whose taste
> Instructs our admiration what to ape[1].

Such is the frankness with which repeatedly throughout the work, and without any set-off on the other side, the author exposes the undivine divinity of that god whom nevertheless (it appears) we are expected in the finale to accept as an ideal of goodness and wisdom. It is needless to say that 'Athena,' who tells us that 'Apollo has done all things well,' nevertheless neither proves nor attempts to prove that these reproaches are not applicable, that 'Apollo' has not been guilty of the act imputed, or that this act is not a crime, a detestable and contemptible crime. Now there are three ways open to criticism in dealing with this situation. One is that of modern tradition, to say that the passages in question and the lesson of the finale are in fact irreconcilable, and that the poet knew this, but nevertheless meant us to accept them both hypothetically for the purpose of his play. He really means us to draw an orthodox conclusion from infidel premises. As to the unity of his piece as a work of art, he did not care about it; he was not a serious artist, and provided he could say, somewhere and somehow, something that would please every one, including himself, how it all jumbled together and what was the upshot did not signify. Aeschylus composed *plays*, Sophocles *plays*, but Euripides strings of dialogues and songs stitched and botched together without pretence of principle. The second way is to suppose that the premisses and the conclusion being irreconcilable, and the author being a serious artist, he must intend us to reject the conclusion as ironical, and deduce his real meaning for ourselves from the facts and comments which he has submitted. The third and only other way is to say that the whole is reconcilable, and the story really supports the conclusion. As for example, when Ion 'pleads with Phoebus' upon the incongruity of such a crime as has been attributed to him with his character as a deity, this, we must think, 'well displays that *perfect love which casteth out fear*,'

---

[1] *v.* 440. My own translation; Mr Way accepts κακά for καλά in *v.* 450, which I think injurious.

as when Moses pleads with God not to diminish His glory by
slaying His people as one man[1]. We must hold, that is to
say, that in the end Phoebus is cleared, as Ion knew he would
be, and that, since (as it seems) he preserved the life of his
alleged child, he did nothing to complain of in the rape, nor
in hiding the child for years, while the mother ate her heart
in the misery of ignorance; or at any rate these blemishes,
if not already pardonable, will be so when (as he says and we
must blindly believe in spite of our senses and the warnings
of the author[2]) the child will be comfortably established at the
expense of nothing more wicked than a perpetual fraud.   Or
again when Apollo, as we saw, declines to present himself in
person before Ion, Creusa, and the Delphian assembly, 'lest
reproach for past matters should intervene,' we must hold it
impossible that this refers to reproaches against the god;
although we have been expressly told that to ask the god,
about the matter which he would be asked about if he now
appeared, would be to 'flout' him and to 'prove him villain
in his own halls.'   We must argue on the contrary that since
Ion shrank from 'flouting' Apollo by such a question, Apollo,
now that Ion has asked the question, cannot be deterred from
appearing to answer it by his dread of the reproaches of Ion.
"The interpretation which assumes that Apollo was afraid
lest *he* should be chidden by those whose lives he was crowning
with blessing, by two Greeks whose reverential awe made
them fear even to gaze on divinity, is little in harmony with
Ion's own words:—

> "For in his own halls were he villain proved,
>   Vengeance on him who brought thee that response
>   Would Phoebus justly wreak[3]."

Now this is courageous and logical.   This is to pursue to its
true conclusion the theory that the finale of the play is given
by Euripides for his real interpretation of the story, that it is
serious and not ironical.   This is the way, and the only way,
to treat the passage in question and all the play, if the current
exposition of it is to be reconciled with supposing that
Euripides was an artist.   He must have thought that the

---

[1] Mr Way on *v.* 436.   [2] *vv.* 585 ff.   [3] Mr Way on *v.* 1558.

reproaches of Ion were refutable, and that he has refuted them. To those who can believe this, I have no more to say. But the Euripides of Schlegel and Hermann, who knew that he had not refuted but proved these reproaches, and yet expected his readers, at the command forsooth of 'Athena,' to put down the play comfortably and dismiss all the questions which he has raised,—this Euripides was no artist, no man of intelligence, no man, to me at least, intelligible or conceivable at all. To say that 'Apollo' was a lying, blundering ruffian, was to say that Apollo, as imagined by Athenian orthodoxy in the time of Euripides, did not exist; and what then becomes of Athena?

But the truth is that the wild assumptions of Athena are not wanted to explain the facts of the story *and do not explain them.* The story of the play is no more consistent with the existence of Apollo than *Candide* is consistent with the existence of the saints, or the recent novel of M. Zola with the existence of 'Notre Dame de Lourdes.' Indeed in the spirit and even the matter of *Lourdes* there is much that is closely akin to the *Ion.* Like M. Zola, Euripides is exceedingly anxious to show that he has 'sympathy' with the objects of his attack, having sense and heart enough to see what many able satirists have to their own confusion neglected, that without 'sympathy' the blow will lose half its force. The charming picture of pious simplicity in the person of the lad Ion, a picture which (to judge by other evidence) the poet has rather over-painted, putting into it at least as much moral beauty as a cold justice to Delphi would have required, plays in the work a parallel part to M. Zola's pathetic biography of Bernadette; and as in *Lourdes* so in *Ion*, the idyll is used in the end as a weapon against the institution assailed. All the objects of the French realist's attack, the prodigious luxury, the fraud, the incessant systematic profit, even the demoralized populace, devotees in a fashion of the religion which brings wealth to their feet, all have their counterparts in the work of the Greek realist, although it is needless to say that there are deep and broad differences both in treatment and facts. If you have read *Lourdes*, or think fit to read it on my recommendation, and will consider what it might have been like, if the author's only efficient way of publication had been to shape it as a play, to be performed between *Athalie* and *Esther* in the nave of Notre Dame, you will have as near an analogy to the *Ion* as could be composed of modern elements. And on one point particularly the supposition, extravagant as it is, may even throw direct light.   In France at this moment[1] an attack on the miracles of the grotto will excite some sympathy, even among Frenchmen who regard the pilgrimages and the cures with indifference or even approval so far as religion only is concerned, because of the connexion or supposed connexion between Lourdes and reactionary politics. Much in the same way there were two sides, from an Athenian point of view, to Delphi, the religious and the political or diplomatic; and the political offences of Delphi against Athens have probably something to do not indeed with the hatred of Euripides, which seems to have been purely intellectual, that is to say religious, but with the licence which in the latter part of his career he was able to take.

In the case of the *Ion* it is improbable that the orthodox pretence of the prologue and finale really imposed at the time upon any one, or was meant to do it.   Apart from the fact that after a time the whole public must have taken the measure of a Euripidean 'god,' and the sort of 'truth' which might be expected from him, the bad character of Hermes in this article, even among the orthodox, would aid suspicion; and when it is added that the story which he tells in the prologue *contradicts the primitive belief of the Athenians* (who held Ion, the eponym of the Ionians, to be the son, as Euripides makes him, of Xuthus, and not, as 'Hermes' makes him, of Apollo[2]), there was enough

---

[1] July, 1894.

[2] As to the development of the legend see Miss Harrison, *Mythology and Mon. of Athens*, p. lxxxi.   To gratify Athenian pride Ion was converted from 'son of Xuthus' into 'son of Apollo,' which could of course be easily done without importing into the story any of the horrors engrafted on it by Euripides.   This version, though probably not at all ancient, attained so much vogue as to be cited by Plato (*Euthydemus* 302 C, D) as the received explanation of the title *Apollo Patrōos*.   Plato, as I understand him, sneers at it, implying that if Apollo was ancestor of the Athenians, he was not a god.

to put on the track any one who had interest in following it. Actual danger there cannot have been, when the *Ion* was acted, in attacking the god of Delphi; if there had been, the play could not possibly have 'got a chorus.' The pretence of concealment is here a mere conventional trick, kept up more for the humour of it and for a sort of politeness, than for real necessity.

At present the *Ion* is commonly read, when read for pleasure at all, in the same fashion as many other works of the poet, that is to say, the reader will go through with it once, and having discovered, as he inevitably does, that it ends in a quagmire out of which (according to the current theory) Euripides did not see his way and in fact there is no way, he bestows a *pshaw* or two on the bungler, and thenceforth, if he goes back to the work, only glances at a bit here and there, Ion's morning-hymn, or Creusa's confession, or the banquet. And so it always will be, so Euripides will always be read, or rather not read, until the truth is recognized that the story is contained solely in the action proper, without the prologue and finale, which are not the story but comments on the story by 'gods,' that is to say 'liars.' If we reject their gratuitous and inefficient epicycle of miracles, the phenomena explain themselves. I must not take space here even to work them out fully, much less to do justice to the directory points with which, like the *Alcestis*, the play abounds. For these the reader will naturally go to the text itself; some of them I have ventured to mark in my edition. But really no particular directions are wanted; nothing is wanted but attention. When the dramatist insists on informing us without apparent relevance that Creusa's bracelet, the instrument of the murder, is the chain of the infant Erichthonius, we must assume that we are to remember this and shall find it significant. When we are afterwards told, again with apparent irrelevance, that the necklace found in the cradle is 'copied from that of Erichthonius,' we must put two and two together. That is all the mystery. For clearness' sake, as this is the crucial question, we will run through the scene once more. That the evidence of the cradle is a forgery we should presume from the circumstances in which it is produced, and when we are shown that the woollen wrappings of the cradle are not rotten (which as Ion naïvely remarks they should be in course of nature) but *perfectly fresh*, doubt is no longer possible.   It is also evident that both Ion and Creusa, burning to discover she her child and he his mother, will be deceived with ease, and the only remaining interest is to see how the fraud is worked.   The objects wanted are the *spargana* or baby-things of an exposed infant belonging to the house of Erechtheus, that is to say its garment, shawl, or wrap, and above all its *chain* or *necklace*, the regular appurtenance and mark of a Greek baby.   The shawl is nothing.   Such likeness as its pattern has to Creusa's description is fairly accounted for by Ion as 'one stroke of luck'; and what is more important, a thing in itself decisive as to the intended bearing of the scene, *it is pointed out to us by him that the resemblance is slight and, if considered strictly, not satisfactory.* I dwell particularly on this because I had not remarked it when I annotated the play.

When Creusa has described her shawl, Ion produces one with these words: " Behold it !...Here *is* your weaving—*after the fashion in which we trace prophecy*[1]."   Now this expression has caused the greatest perplexity among expositors, and is in fact unintelligible, so long as we suppose that the alleged proof is sound, and the shawl really the shawl worked by Creusa.   Accordingly various devices have been tried, by punctuating, correcting, and twisting the words, to get out of them something consistent with the general sense assumed. But upon the true assumption, that the shawl is *not* really what is pretended, the words are perfectly clear.   What Ion means and says is that Creusa's description may be found in the shawl *as nearly as is commonly expected in divine, mysterious, and providential matters*; there is the same sort of resemblance as we habitually trace *between prophecy and fulfilment.*   It is to

---

[1] *v.* 1424   ἰδού·

τόδ᾽ ἐσθ᾽ ὕφασμα,—θέσφαθ᾽ ὡς εὑρίσκομεν.

See Paley's note.   In my edition I assumed, like my predecessors, that there is an error in the text.

be remembered that Ion, though a devout believer, is by no means an unintelligent, abject, or slavish believer. He shows throughout the play, together with a desire to worship, an equally creditable desire to obtain satisfaction for the reasonable scruples both of his heart and of his head. And he speaks here like himself. He is not, upon careful inspection, by any means satisfied, as a matter of judgement, that the work does answer the description. But resemblances certainly not stronger are accepted in matters divine, for example, when *an oracle* is in question. He is afraid of requiring too much. And so he goes on, somewhat disheartened as he shows by his captious tone, to the next question: " Is there anything more? Or is this your one stroke of luck?" This leads to the necklace, and apparently settles the matter. The touch is exquisite, as an exhibition of character, as a step in the process of conviction, and from every point of view. But it is altogether meaningless, unless the evidence is in reality unsatisfactory; and it was put in on purpose to emphasize the true intention of the scene. The pattern described by Creusa is 'a Gorgon in a border of snakes *represented imperfectly as they would be by a girl just learning to weave.*' We may presume that the 'samplers' of Greek girls, like modern samplers, obeyed the rigidly conservative laws of feminine education and varied very little: so that probably it would have been difficult to find any two in which you might not, with a good will, imagine as much resemblance as Ion admits, to wit, 'that sort of correspondence which we trace in matters divine.'

The shawl then is nothing. But the necklace (if only it were not 'copied from' that of Erichthonius) would be everything. It convinces Ion completely, as well it may. The prospect of finding a mother in so noble a house, and in a woman who at the first meeting had made so much impression on his feelings, entrances him with delight. He throws off all suspicion, becomes as eager for success as Creusa herself, and actually prompts her, contrary of course to the very principle of the test, with the fact that there is another object in the cradle and only one more. There ought not to have been

anything more; but the concoctors of the evidence, being
superstitious as well as fraudulent (the common combination),
supposed, according to a popular fancy, that the wreath which
the mother would or might put on her exposed infant as a
preparation for its death, being in this case made necessarily
of 'sacred' olive from the Athenian acropolis, would never
wither; so they put in a wreath of fresh olive; and Creusa,
when she sees it (for the pair are by this time almost in each
other's arms, and she has no need to guess), is at no loss for
an explanation. This third piece of 'evidence' is only important as showing, what is clearly agreeable to nature, that,
given the necklace, it was practically impossible for the fraud
to fail. Covered by that, any inconsistency, however gross,
would have been explained away by the willing dupes as
easily as the 'miraculously fresh wrappings' and the 'im-
perishable wreath.'

Thus the trick succeeds in its immediate purpose, and
Creusa is saved.   Nay, it might even have accomplished more
than this, and might have led Ion, as well as Creusa, to
acquiesce in the belief that he is not only her son but also
Apollo's, if it were not that Ion takes his religion seriously,
and has upon his shoulders the head of a man. This being
so, his further enquiries and final desperation are inevitable.
The course of the play from this point to Ion's determination
that the oracle shall be consulted again is marvellously impressive in its combination of humour with the profoundest
tragedy, tragedy infinitely deeper than the satisfaction or
disappointment of the boy or the woman, the never-ending
tragedy of faith.   When Athena appears, all is over; to put
up Athena is to confess that 'Apollo' is, as manifestly he is,
hopelessly beaten. What exactly would have happened in
real life it is not easy to guess, nor does it matter. Very
speedily the truth must have come out, and then, if any of
'the Gorgon's blood' was left, the best thing for the parties
concerned would have been to share it between them. But
their fates, pathetic as they are—the outbreak of Creusa's
secret, her accusation of the god and confession to her slave,
is in my judgement unrivalled in its kind—these individual

fates are not the main affair, but something immeasurably more significant, the honour or dishonour of Delphi. Before an audience whose fathers had lived and died, an audience of whom many hoped to meet death, by belief in the Pythian Apollo, the question *Is the god true, or naught his oracles?* was not one with which it was permissible to play for an hour without meaning something, one way *or the other*. Nor can the *Ion* appeal with success to any one, who does not see that this is the problem of it, and will not follow the problem out to the end foreshown, as if it were the dearest concern of his life. The experiment of presenting the *Ion* as a mere drama of incident, supposed to be cleared up by the pretended *dénouement*, and disengaged from its religious problem, to persons of ordinary judgement not interested in Greek as Greek, was tried, as I have mentioned, here at Cambridge in 1890. I need not though I was myself one of the experimenters hesitate to say (for I could call unimpeachable witnesses) that the experiment was instructive. As spectacles the various groups, thanks to the able archaeologists and managers by whom they were set for us, were beautiful enough. One or two scenes went well. But the audience was visibly disappointed. It was impossible to convince those who had seen the *Oedipus Tyrannus* and the *Eumenides* that the work, taken as a play completed, was on the same level, or worthy at all to be compared, with those of Aeschylus and Sophocles. The revolting nature of the subject, unredeemed (so far as was understood) by any serious purpose, provoked a merited disgust; nor was there need of an exact analysis to make people feel that somehow 'Athena' did not satisfy. The piece is not rounded off but chopped off, and there (if you leave it there) is the end of the matter. And in general, since it is impossible that the mass of a modern audience should appreciate or even understand Euripides' real situation and point of view, his works are unfit for our theatres. But that has nothing to do with their meaning, value, and interest.

There are some plays of Euripides (a very few) in which such a difficulty would not be materially felt. The *Medea* is one such. Unluckily there would be other difficulties almost insuperable in acting the *Medea* under academical conditions. Whether there is any play of Euripides which satisfies all the conditions is a doubtful question, and not perhaps, as the reader may think, very grave. An experiment is to be made[1], and probably will have been made before this essay appears, with the *Iphigenia in Taurica*. This, I think, gives as favourable a chance as could be found ; and I am led by the circumstances, as well as by the intrinsic interest of that drama, in its points of resemblance and not less in its points of contrast to those which we have been considering, to offer next some remarks not so much on the whole of it, as on some of its most characteristic features.

---

[1] Written in August, 1894. A note on the representation is added to the next essay.

IPHIGENIA

"Rome, unique objet de mon ressentiment."

WE have seen in the foregoing essays that with certain subordinate differences both the plays in question exhibit a common principle of construction which fits and corresponds to the peculiar position of the author, as a notorious rationalist compelled by the circumstances of the time to use for his organ of expression a stage appropriated by origin and custom to the exhibition of miraculous legend. In each case the body of work, the story acted by the real *dramatis personae*, is strictly realistic in tone and fact, and in purport contradictory to 'religion' (that is to say, to certain decadent superstitions); while the prologue and epilogue, in sharp opposition to the drama proper and therefore with manifest irony, assert *pro forma* the miraculous explanation which the facts tend visibly to invalidate and deny. The use of this method, not always in exactly the same way, but with modifications for different cases of the same general principle, is characteristic of Euripides, and is the true cause of a phenomenon, which candid and reasonable judges have always admitted to be perplexing,—the singular stiffness, formality, frigidity, and general artlessness which often appear in his opening and his conclusion. The final scenes in particular, the *coups de théâtre* with which the action is wound up or cut short, have almost always a conventionality of manner, a perfunctory style, a looseness of adaptation, a feebleness in thought and feeling, which contrast strangely with the originality, terseness, energy, and passion displayed in other parts of the work, and constantly prompt the critic to wonder, sarcastically or sorrowfully, at such a suicide of genius. It seems as if in the catastrophe the author, if we take him at his word, does his utmost to ruin the whole, and to prevent us from attaching any serious importance to his

representations. The case of the *Ion*, though the logical contradiction there is signally precise, is by no means the most
startling in opposition of colour. The 'divine' performances
which terminate the *Orestes* and the *Electra* seem to be nothing
better than burlesque, and have long been favourite exercises
for the derision of the poet's detractors. The epilogue of the
Andromache, if taken as conveying what the author really
took for the main point of his story, must lead us to the conclusion that this story is a hopeless tangle of accidents and
impossibilities, as Schlegel and his successors with much
complacency point out. Lucian knew more of the matter.
The true explanation of these phenomena, both in the epi-
logues and to a less extent in the prologues, is the obvious
explanation, that Euripides, when he seems not to be serious,
is not serious ; and that when he propounds for his meaning
something which seems no meaning at all, nor reconcilable
with what he has himself with apparent gravity put before us,
this can only be because he was compelled and expected to
use irony, and to present his real opinions and sentiments
under the veil of a penetrable disguise.

It is natural and necessary to suppose, as I have said, that
a method of this kind, practised for forty years of increasing
fame, among a small society who regarded themselves, and
not without some reason, as the sole arbiters of literary
criticism, the only people who understood their own poets
(not to say poets in general)[1], came before long to be a well-
understood convention. Experienced readers at Athens must
have known that in Euripides what had been spoken *from the
machine* was not to be taken seriously, was no true part of
the realistic drama, but a mere concession to the requirements
of a theological stage and to established superstition, which
must not be too openly defied. How completely this convention was in fact understood, and how frankly the author
counted upon it, is well seen in what we read at the conclusion
of the *Iphigenia in Taurica*.

This excellent piece, which for its symmetry, vigour, and
artistic construction has drawn praise from the most unfavour-

[1] Aristoph. *Frogs*, 809.

able judges, has for its termination a *theophany* to which, as we shall see, the poet himself has directed special attention. By a successful stratagem Orestes and Pylades have carried off from the temple of the Crimean 'Artemis' its chief treasure, an image which 'fell from heaven,' and rescued Iphigenia, Orestes' sister, who for many years had been compelled to carry on, as priestess, the barbarous rites of the place, while her friends supposed her to have perished as a victim at Aulis. The Chorus of Greek women, captives devoted to the same service as Iphigenia herself, have taken part in the plot and are at the mercy of the king Thoas, who threatens to punish them when the arrest and execution of the fugitives shall have left him at leisure. At this point Athena appears and forbids his projects. As for the fugitives, he will not overtake them, for destiny 'to which the gods and he are alike subject' has decreed that the image shall reach Attica. And for the women who are in his power, they are to be released and sent home by her order, with which Thoas observing that 'to hear the gods and disobey them is folly,' promises to comply. All is so far simple; but for the latter part of her injunction, that which relates to the Chorus, the goddess gives a reason which to readers who want to take her seriously appears to be, and in fact is, unintelligible. "As for these Greek women, that they be dismissed from Taurica I command for the sake of just principle—as having saved Orestes at the Areopagus by my judgement on an equality of votes—and with a view to consistency at least in the ruling, that he who obtains half the votes is victorious. Carry, son of Agamemnon, your rescued sister away, and you, Thoas, be not angry[1]." This passage, judged upon the received

---

[1] *Iph. T.* 1467

τάσδε δ' ἐκπέμπειν χθονὸς
Ἑλληνίδας γυναῖκας ἐξεφίεμαι,
γνώμης δικαίας εἵνεκ'—ἐκσώσασά γε
καὶ πρίν σ' Ἀρείοις ἐν πάγοις ψήφους ἴσας
κρίνασ', Ὀρέστα—καὶ νόμισμ' εἰς ταὐτό γε,
νικᾶν ἰσήρεις ὅστις ἂν ψήφους λάβῃ.
ἀλλ' ἐκκομίζου σὴν κασιγνήτην χθονός,
Ἀγαμέμνονος παῖ, καὶ σὺ μὴ θυμοῦ, Θόας.

There is a small question about the words, but not material, in *v.* 1470: see Dr England's edition. All the readings give the same sense.

assumption that Athena in a Euripidean machine is the same
sort of person as Athena anywhere else, and may be expected
to speak the language (if we may say so) of a *bona fide*
goddess, has been given up as desperate; and no wonder. It
was a rule in the Areopagus that upon an equality of votes the
defendant 'won' and was acquitted; and the rule was derived,
according to a tradition, from the decision to that effect given
by Athena as president of the court in the case of Orestes,
who tells the story to Iphigenia in an earlier part of the play.
But the principle has no possible bearing on the relations of
Thoas and the Greek slaves, who have not been tried, and
whom no one proposes to try.   And not only so: the topic is
irrelevant not merely to the particular point with which it
seems to be connected, but altogether.   The dramatic situation
affords no reason why the trial of Orestes should be mentioned.
And this would forbid us to accept, even if the appearance of
the text gave room for it, the common expedient of supposing
that something, which explained the allusion, has been lost.
Such a loss would naturally betray itself by grammatical dis-
continuity, but there is none: and besides no insertion could
serve the turn.   The decision in question had been given,
according to the story, and accepted by the Athenians long
before.   It has nothing to do with the disposal of the persons
or things concerned in the present action, which is the present
business of the goddess and has all been appropriately dealt
with, except the case of the women, before this astonishing
reference is introduced.   To their case it must refer, and yet
apparently it does not touch their case in the least.   What is
the explanation?

The explanation is that the author, who, as his readers
knew, cared nothing for his 'Athena' in her dramatic character
as a goddess, has here coolly made her his spokesman to
convey, in the poem as circulated for the purpose of reading,
a jesting allusion to the satisfactory result of a representation,
either the first or some other.   This play is one of three, with
the *Orestes* and the *Phoenissae*, which conclude with a few
lines purporting to be spoken by the Chorus not in their
assumed character as persons in the drama, but in their true

character as Athenians contending in a dramatic competition. The tag takes the form of a prayer to Victory, " O mighty lady, Victory, pervade my life, and cease not to give me crowns." We do not happen to know (so far as I am aware) what measure of theatrical success attended the *Orestes* and the *Iphigenia*; the *Phoenissae* obtained the second of the three prizes. But it seems to be implied by the very form of the prayer, that it is not exactly, as is sometimes said, an appeal made in the theatre to the judges, but a recognition, inserted afterwards, of the fact that on some sufficiently notable occasion the play had actually obtained one of these formal decorations. To ask that Victory ' may not cease ' to bestow crowns is language appropriate only to one who has been crowned ; it is gratitude expressing itself, according to the proverb, in a sense of favours to come, and if taken generally, without reference to the particular occasion, would have come rather absurdly from Euripides, who gained in fact (and it is not difficult to imagine why) a very small number of such public awards, far less than corresponded to his influence and consideration. In the case of the *Orestes* and the *Iphigenia* at least, it would be probable, apart from the tag, that they took prizes on some occasion, for both were famous as stage-pieces and are in fact excellent in this aspect. And the tag itself, as I have said, seems to admit no other meaning. It signifies a hope that the play may please readers as well as it pleased the judges, and that other successes may follow.

Now the ' victory ' of a play, in this special sense, was technically the victory of *the Chorus*, as is signified by putting the prayer in their mouths. Theoretically the dramatic contest continued to be, what it had once been literally, a contest between *chorus* and *chorus*, for which reason the person charged with the material provision for the performance, and credited with the theatrical success, continued to be called a *choragos* and to set his prize, if he got one, on a *choragic* monument, even when the weight of the contest had long been transferred to the actors or, in Greek phrase, *contenders*. And when Euripides makes ' Athena ' say that Thoas must release the

women, that is to say the Chorus, in deference to her well-
known principle that 'if you halve the votes, you are victorious,' he must be referring not to anything in the dramatic
situation, to which that principle is inapplicable, but to the
circumstances of the 'victory' signified by the final tag.   On
the occasion to which he alludes the votes of the awarders,
in regard to one of the prizes, must have been equally divided
between himself and another competitor, "which" says
Athena humorously "I at any rate am consistent in calling
a victory for our Chorus, and I command you, Thoas, to
treat them with the favour that they have deserved."   The
four verses in which she gives her reason must have been
added, with the tag, after the so-called 'victory.'   In the
theatre she probably contented herself with the *sic volo sic
iubeo* by which Thoas is in fact determined.

    To clinch the matter, if there be any doubt, we may
observe that the same thing *mutatis mutandis* has been done
in the *Orestes*, where the 'victory' commemorated by the tag
is duly prophecied, as we now read the finale, by the 'Apollo'
who on that occasion occupies the machine.   Orestes, he says,
as a murderer, must clear himself by the customary year of
exile, to be spent in Arcadia, "and thence you must go to
the city of Athens, and offer satisfaction for the blood of
your mother to the three Eumenides.   *The divine umpires
of the cause shall most righteously give you the advantage
of the vote among the hills of Ares; and there you are
destined to be victorious*[1]."   That the victorious *Orestes* of this
prophecy is not the person only or chiefly, but the play,
the modern reader would hardly suspect, if we had not the
Iphigenia to direct us; a similar prophecy occurs in the finale
of the *Electra*, where a theatrical reference is not to be thought
of.   But an Athenian reader would see it, for his ear would
be arrested at once by the strange expression *among the hills
of Ares*, in which this passage and that of the *Iphigenia* agree.
The seat of the court, as all the world knows, was not the

---

[1] *Or.* 1650   θεοὶ δέ σοι δίκης βραβῆς
                    πάγοισιν ἐν Ἀρείοισιν εὐσεβεστάτην
                    ψῆφον διοίσουσ'· ἔνθα νικῆσαί σε χρή.

hills, but the *Hill* of Ares. Euripides himself calls it so in
reference to this very matter in the *Electra*[1]. So does
Sophocles, so does Aeschylus, so did every one every day;
and though I will not say that no instances of the plural,
except only these two, can be found, it was certainly irregular
enough to be noticed, and my belief is that it would have
sounded to an Athenian very much as 'Tower *hills*' would
have sounded, when London had citizens, to a citizen of
London. But for the plural in these two places there is
reason, since the 'victories' with which the forensic victory of
Orestes in the legend is compared, were not gained in 'the Hill
of Ares,' the spur of the Acropolis which properly bore that
name. They were gained in the theatre, on the side of the
Acropolis itself; and by 'the *hills* of Ares' the poet signifies
the whole block, of which Ares with others was a protector[2],
using this form purposely in order to bring the scenes of the
victories under a common appellation. In fact the prophecy
of the *Orestes*, shaped as we read it, is just an allusion to the
smarter point of the *Iphigenia*[3]. Whether the finale of the
Phoenissae, where 'Orestes' and his legend could not be used,
having nothing to do with the matter, has been in any way
adapted to the tag, is a question which would take us too far
from our present subject. The *Phoenissae* is no theme for a
paragraph. The use of the tag does not of course require
such adaptation; nor can anything be inferred from the
absence of the tag where it is not found. The *Medea* has not
got it, and the *Medea* was one of a group which obtained the
third prize: but this means only that in the year 431 Euripides
had not yet made the tag; and indeed the witty employment
of it in the *Iphigenia* almost justifies the inference that it was
first made for that play. However this is all digression, and
we must return to the matter before us.

In the *Iphigenia* then at least it is certain, as I think, that
the poet, in preparing his play for circulation, has deliberately

---

[1] *El.* 1271 πάγον παρ' αὐτόν: see also *Iph. T.* 961 Ἄρειον ὄχθον, and *passim*.

[2] Aesch. *Eum.* 917.

[3] The date of the *Iphigenia* is not known, but it is almost impossible that it
should be later than 408, the date of the *Orestes*.

used the 'goddess' of the finale as the vehicle of a jocular allusion from himself to the external fortunes of some recent performance. But what does this imply? Surely nothing less than that in his view the goddess was simply and solely a stage-pretence; that her personality as an object of worship believed to exist was wholly immaterial to the purpose of his work; and that when she had performed her function of pleasing the gapers, citing a local legend or so for patriotism, and paying by her mere appearance the expected compliment to the 'sacred' character of the orchestra, he and his under-standing readers might do what they liked with her, and the less respectfully she was treated, the better they were likely to understand. It is not the fact of the allusion being made which proves this, but the tone and manner of it. The Electra of Euripides' play so called carries on with her slave a conversation which is pointed critically at the *Choephori*; but she does not thus cease to be a real character in the play, because the conversation is in itself appropriate to the supposed situation, and would have a meaning if the *Choephori* had never existed. It would be permissible to think (I do not think so but merely suppose it as an illustration) that when the Athena of the *Eumenides* commands the reconciled Furies to bless Athens 'with due regard to a victory where none hath lost[1],' the hope of a victory for the Chorus as performers of the trilogy was included in the poet's view. We might think this without abating from the faith of the poet in the divine personages whom he presents, because he might well hold, and doubtless did, that the favourable acceptance of the *Oresteia* was a good omen for the religion in which he believed. But when the goddess of the *Iphigenia* orders the barbarian king to release the slave-women in consideration of their choric success, and this with a jest on a maxim of the Areopagus, which was held to depend on her sanction as the immortal daughter of Zeus, she ceases to be 'Athena' or to speak to 'Thoas.' 'She' talks as a man in a mask to another man in a mask; and the only way of accounting for such

[1] *v.* 903.

treatment of her is to suppose that the author does not want us even to fancy her. She, and with her necessarily the whole finale from her appearance, stands confessed as a mere piece of theatrical machinery, a device introduced only with a view to the conditions of performance: and the reader is assumed to know this. It cannot be believed that Aeschylus or Sophocles would have so treated a divine personage figuring in one of their plays, or that Euripides would have done so, if he had not meant and been known to mean that her deity was irrelevant to the significance of his play as a work of serious imagination[1].

We have then the poet's authority, conveyed perhaps with unusual clearness (but not to my mind much more clearly than, for example, in the *Ion*), that ' Athena,' and if ' Athena,' if the national goddess, then *a fortiori* the anthropomorphic and legendary theology in general, is to be discarded from the mind when we read the *Iphigenia* ; that no such beings as the gods of tradition enter into the hypothesis about life and the world upon which his story proceeds. Nor are there wanting other indications to the same effect in the body of the play. The most remarkable perhaps is the well-known passage, brilliant with poetry and wit, where the fair Greek youths, Orestes and Pylades, sitting by the shore, are taken by some of the natives for gods[2]. " In a cavernous breach cleft by the strong rush of the waves, which gatherers of sea-purple use for shelter, one of our herdsmen saw two youths, and coming back on tip-toe, as one steps a ford, said ' Beware ! There are gods here: yonder they sit.' And at the sight one of us, a man of piety, lifted up his hands and prayed : ' O son of the sea's Leucothea, protector of ships, our lord Palaemon, be gracious unto us, if these that sit on the beach be perchance

---

[1] These statements were framed at a time when I had certainly not seen for years the passage, almost verbally coincident, and absolutely coincident in sense, which is cited hereafter from the *Zeus Tragoedus* of Lucian. I got them, so far as I was aware, simply from the text of Euripides' plays, read under the presumption that after all the author must have meant something. This coincidence is of no importance except to me personally, but perhaps I may be pardoned for thinking that there are some of my readers to whom it will not be without interest.

[2] *v.* 262 ff.

the Twins of Zeus, or darlings of Nereus, sire of that fair
band of fifty nymphs.' Whereupon another, an insolent
fellow, disorderly and rash, laughed at the prayer, and said
they were wrecked seamen, who had got into the cave for fear
of our custom, when they were told that here the stranger is
used for a sacrifice. The more part of us thought him right,
and we resolved to capture for the goddess the victims that
our wont awards her." Now few or none would suppose that
the author here did not see, what the imaginary narrator is
supposed too dull and self-conceited to see, that the incident
is a little triumph for 'the insolent fellow, disorderly and rash'
to whom the notion of gods appearing in human form seemed
laughable, who held in short the opinions of the author. That
this is the aim of the episode in itself is plain enough and
commonly recognized. But surely, in bare justice to the
author, we must go beyond this, at least until we see a
necessity to stop, and must hold that *prima facie* the whole
work in which such a passage is found is meant to agree with
it in colour and tendency. An offence in art is no more to be
imputed without proof than any other offence : and it would
be a gross offence in art to insert such a narrative as this
in a fiction which rested as a whole upon the hypothesis of
anthropomorphic religion. Be it noted that this proposition
has nothing to do with the creed of the author or the creed of
anyone. It relates solely to the belief that we are to *assume*
for the purpose of the story. Does this *assumed belief* cover
anthropomorphism and a world where Athena, Palaemon,
and the like exist and may sometimes be seen? If it does,
the author is unpardonable as an artist, whatever his opinions
may have been, for shaking the foundation of his structure.
It is a mere insult to your audience, in one scene of your story
to direct ridicule against the notion that the Dioscuri might
appear, and in the next scene to present, with all the air of
gravity, facts intelligible only on the assumption that on a
most solemn and important occasion Apollo did actually
appear. Of course I am aware that Euripides is now accused
of committing such offences perpetually. But upon what
enquiry? I doubt if there exists any critical work in which

the question, whether for instance the story of the *Iphigenia in Taurica* does indeed assume anthropomorphism, is so much as raised. And if anywhere it has been raised, it has left no trace on the received exposition, which takes an affirmative answer for granted[1]. But since that answer is an accusation, is this fair?

The truth is that the story of the play does not presume the fancies of anthropomorphism. It neither requires nor leads to the supposition that any such persons as Apollo of Delphi or Artemis of Brauron exist *in rerum natura*. The *dramatis personae* are believers in such deities, as Ion is and Admetus, but their experience, so far as it is shown to us by Euripides, goes to refute, not to support, their traditional faith.

We will take first the case of Apollo, whose Delphian oracle is, as usual, a prime mover in the mechanism. It is by the command of Delphi that Orestes undertakes the task of bringing a Crimean image to Attica, as a final means to rid him of the Furies of his mother. In this fact itself there is nothing miraculous or even uncommon. That the oracle was consulted frequently on cases of conscience, and was or had been able to impose dangerous and distant enterprises, is as indisputable as that there was a town of Delphi. Those who repaired to Apollo there did not in general see him; in Aeschylus Orestes does, but in Euripides the communication is made in the usual way through 'the voice from the tripod[2],' that is to say the prophetess. The question then is, how or whether it appears, from the story of the enterprise as related by Euripides, that this command was inspired by superhuman wisdom.

Now it is, to begin with, a strange and suspicious circumstance that the necessity for the enterprise has arisen through a failure, not to say a series of failures, on the part of Apollo,

---

[1] Dr England, for instance, relies upon it so implicitly, that in annotating the passage about the supposed apparition of the *Dioscuri* he treats the 'irony' of it as possibly 'not intentional.' If it be not, Euripides little deserves such labour and learning as Dr England has spent on him.

[2] *v.* 976.

which has placed the oracle, almost as much as Orestes himself, in a distressing position. The oracle had advised the murder of Clytaemnestra, the beginning of sorrows, and was therefore an interested party. Apollo had engaged, as might be supposed, to hold Orestes harmless. Primitive legend was content to represent him as fulfilling this promise by furnishing Orestes with a weapon, a bow or sword, to 'keep the Furies off.' But long before Euripides this symbolism had ceased to please; and a deeper feeling of the moral issues implied in the punishment of a criminal mother by a son was satisfied by the expedient of an expiatory period of suffering, followed by a trial before a court of divine justice, in which Apollo appeared for the defence and procured an acquittal. Notably this was the Athenian view and had been fixed imperishably by Aeschylus. But according to the story of Euripides (who invented, as there is every reason to believe, this expedition to Taurica), not only had the original counsel of the god excited the disapprobation of the world in general as well as of the Furies[1] (a view which the poet maintains not only here but also in the *Electra* and more violently in the *Orestes*); but the grand remedy of seeking divine justice at Athens, suggested to the tormented fugitive by the oracle itself and tested by him in a fashion which we will presently consider, *had failed.* According to Aeschylus, as we need hardly say, it succeeds in the object. The Furies are brought to submit to the verdict, and Orestes goes away triumphant. According to Euripides *some* of the Furies complied, but some, enough to make him as miserable as ever, continued the pursuit as before[2]. That is to say, the whole solemn proceeding of the *Eumenides*, Areopagus, Apollo, Pallas, and all, ended, so far as the true purpose of it was concerned, in —it is hard to find a term at once decent and appropriate. To be simple, nothing came of it.

Hereupon (proceeds this amazing continuation of Aeschylus) Orestes went to Delphi again, flung himself starving on the temple-floor, and swore that unless 'the god

[1] *v.* 713.   [2] *v.* 968 ff.

who had ruined him would rescue,' he would die where he lay.
It was under this pressure that 'the voice from the tripod'
commanded, as a final quietus, the present expedition to
the further side of the Euxine sea. Now considering all the
circumstances, it is not surprising that, when Orestes arrived
at his destination and found that (to aggravate the obvious
dangers of such a voyage to the end of the world) the
possessors of the image which he was to fetch had the habit
of offering visitors as victims to their goddess, he should have
suspected 'Apollo' of 'setting a trap' for him, of having
meant simply to remove his reproaching figure and memory
'as far from Hellas as possible[1].' It seems in fact that
nothing but success, obtained by the manifest will and aid of
the god himself, could justify any other construction of the
oracular motives. Let us see then what cause he has to
revise this judgement, what aid Apollo gives to the execution
of his command. The sort of aid that he would be expected
to give, the kind of signs by which, according to Greek belief,
his presence would be felt, we see, for instance, in the *Choephori*
of Aeschylus. There, as here, Orestes is sent by Apollo on a
dangerous enterprise, and accordingly the first and essential
step to his success is procured for him by means of a dream,
which is sent to his enemy. The dream is not only in itself
encouraging as a prophecy, but leads to action on the part of
the enemy which (under Providence) plays straight into the
plots of the divine emissary. Euripides has not forgotten
that such was the form in which, according to orthodox
Apolline religion, the divine approval and assistance should
present itself. Nay, he has well remembered, and taken care
to recall to his readers, that such is the form which it takes in
the parallel case of the *Choephori*. Not only does Iphigenia
receive a dream on the morning of Orestes' arrival, but that
dream has a sequel resembling the Aeschylean sequel down
to minute details. The result of the dream in the *Choephori*
is that Electra with a chorus of female slaves performs funeral
libations. The result of the dream here is that Iphigenia
with a chorus of female slaves performs funeral libations.

[1] *vv.* 67—103, 711—715.

The one ceremony takes place at the tomb of Agamemnon and is connected with a certain offering of hair, in the other ceremony we are reminded that it should take place, but cannot, at the tomb of Agamemnon's son, and should be accompanied by an offering of hair[1]. In short Euripides echoes Aeschylus precisely, and means to do so. The only difference is this, that whereas the dream of Clytaemnestra truly presages Orestes' victory, the dream of Iphigenia *presages his death*[2]; and whereas the Aeschylean dream makes his enterprise practicable, the Euripidean dream, by steeling Iphigenia's heart against the unknown strangers[3], goes near to nip his enterprise in the bud, and would have done so, if she had not, in spite of the dream and the rite performed in consequence, ascertained by enquiry that Orestes is alive, and the warning, as she reads it, *false*[4]. Now the dream of Iphigenia is, so far as I can see, the sole thing in the action of the piece in which, according to the notions of Greek popular religion, miraculous interference might be suspected; and here it certainly would be presumed, as it is by Iphigenia herself. If 'the gods' are not the senders of this dream so critically timed, the inference is that 'the gods' have no hand in the business. But to derive it from 'the gods' would be to suppose them adverse to Orestes, a *reductio ad absurdum* which throws us on the alternative that 'the gods,' that is the gods of the populace, have not any hand in the business. Nor does the author fail to dictate this inference expressly;

---

[1] Cp. *Iph. Taur.* 143—191 with the opening of the *Choephori* passim.

[2] It has been said, indeed, to reconcile with sense the current interpretation of the play, that the dream does not portend ill to Orestes, but is misinterpreted by Iphigenia. Even if this were so, it would be no defence, since Iphigenia is in fact misled and we are never told where she went wrong or how the dream can be read favourably. In the *Choephori* both interpretations are given, the misleading interpretation of Clytaemnestra and the true interpretation of Orestes. But in fact an interpretation consistent with the success of Orestes is not possible. Iphigenia dreams that she prepares for sacrifice, weeping, 'the sole pillar of her father's house,' seen in the form of a man. That she does not read this judiciously is true. She takes it to mean that Orestes *is dead*. What it does plainly suggest is that Orestes *is to die*, after certain rites performed on him by Iphigenia. And this is what really follows, so that the dream, as it happens, is true enough, only it cannot come from 'Apollo.' It is part of the author's irony.

[3] *v.* 348.   [4] *v.* 569.

for when Iphigenia remarks that after all there was no truth in the dream, Orestes gloomily adds that 'the deities famed for wisdom,' such as Apollo, 'are no less deceptive: divinity is altogether as confused as humanity, and if a man is fool enough to trust prophets, sensible men know what to think of his fate.'

From the nature of the case this is the nearest approach that a dramatist can make to furnishing direct and positive evidence on such a point. You cannot actually exhibit a person's *non-action*. Negative evidence can be given, and is given by Euripides, profusely. As I have already said, save the sending of the dream, which cannot be the work of Apollo, nothing happens in the story which even looks like his work. But the things which he might have done, which it is strange that he should not have done, which we are directed to think it strange that he should not have done, are plenty. Not a suggestion comes, so far as is indicated, from him as to the way in which his envoys are to cope with their fearful difficulties, neither at the time nor (which is perhaps odder in this case) beforehand. No doubt the gods are masters; they reveal what they like, and they conceal what they like. But Euripides thought (and surely with reason) that there is a point at which defective information, though not a ground for accusing Providence if we assume that a given message is providential, does become a ground for thinking that the message is not providential; and he indicates (rightly again, in my judgement) that this point is reached in the case before us. If Apollo dictated the command which sent Orestes and Pylades to Taurica, what did Apollo know about the conditions of the enterprise? He communicated nothing. The ignorance as to material facts in which his emissaries arrive is strikingly exhibited, together with Orestes' not unnatural sense of injury, in the opening scene. The oracle said nothing about the place (as we are expressly told[1]) except that *Artemis possessed there altars and*

---

[1] *vv.* 85, 977. Orestes lays stress on the fact that the precept of the god contained *no more* than he cites (*v.* 91), and finds it, on arriving, strangely insufficient.

an image which fell from heaven. What more than the fact
that there was such an image, no wonderful knowledge, did
Apollo know? Above all did he know—because here was a
fit occasion for him to enlighten an unhappy worshipper—that
Orestes would find there his sister Iphigenia, supposed to have
died a score of years before but in reality a captive in the
service of 'Artemis'? If he knew, why did he not say so,
foretell her assistance, and make the release of her a part of
his commission? We have no right to ask? We have not
only the right but, as readers of Euripides, the duty to ask ;
for Euripides has indicated that an uncomfortable feeling about
this lacuna in the oracle must necessarily arise from the facts,
even in a mind prepossessed by faith. After the recognition,
Iphigenia offers to put the image in her brother's hands and
remain herself to encounter certain death. Orestes, rejecting
this, and resolving to carry away both, encourages her as
follows : " Let me tell you my thought. If our plan had been
repugnant to Artemis, how could the oracular god have commanded my conveying of the goddess' image to Pallas' town
...and my meeting with you....Yes, putting all these things
together I have hope to win our way back[1]." "But the
meeting of the brother and sister," exclaim readers very
naturally[2], "was not comprised in the oracle!" "But it must
have been!" say others not less naturally. "Orestes mis-
took ; Apollo directed him, we may suppose, to Taurica

[1] *v.* 1012   γνώμης δ' ἄκουσον· εἰ πρόσαντες ἦν τόδε
                    'Αρτέμιδι, πῶς ἂν Λοξίας ἐθέσπισε
                    κομίσαι μ' ἄγαλμα θεᾶς πόλισμα Παλλάδος...
                    καὶ σὴν πρόσοψιν εἰσιδεῖν ;...ἄπαντα γὰρ
                    συνθεὶς τάδ' εἰς ἓν νόστον ἐλπίζω λαβεῖν.

The ambiguity of θεσπίζω between *command* and *reveal* is a difficulty for the
translator but a convenience to Orestes. In the last line I assume, in order not
to lay weight on a disputable point, that editors are right in choosing the variant
λαβεῖν. But I do not myself think it grammatical : ἐλπίζω λαβεῖν is not the
Greek of Euripides for 'I hope I shall obtain'; it would mean 'I *suppose* I
obtained.' The true reading is the alternative λαθεῖν, altered to λαβεῖν because
not understood. The meaning is then 'All these matters,' *i.e.* all the events in
Taurica, 'I put together as one, and suppose that it was our return (only) which
remained hidden,' *i.e.* of which nothing was revealed. This is exactly what
Orestes, still hoping in Apollo, is now painfully anxious to believe.

[2] See Paley's note.

where is an altar possessed by a sister, meaning *a sister of yours*, whereas Orestes took him to mean *a sister of mine.*" But of course this will not do, and others see that it will not do. We can know nothing about the oracle except what Orestes tells us, which is that Apollo said *altar possessed by Artemis*[1]. If we were to suppose misapprehension or ambiguity, we should be told so ; but no one hints it, not even (though that would not signify) Athena. Accordingly[2] it is once more time for that great defence of the faith that 'something is lost,' something which came before the words *and my meeting with you*, and to which Orestes refers when he speaks of 'putting all this together.' No, nothing is lost. The 'lacuna' is not in the text of the poet but in the wisdom of the oracle. When Orestes links to his sentence, with a weakness in the linking which betrays his hesitation, the words *and my meeting with you*, he does so because he naturally feels that, as things turn out, the oracle *ought* to have said—then *must* have said—then *did* say doubtless—or at any rate mean, that he was to meet his sister. And when he speaks of 'putting all this together' he includes his unspoken and indistinct thoughts, which bring him to the conclusion that all, it is to be hoped, may go right.

It is a pious conclusion : but is it logical and (what after all is the main question) is it justified by the event? Does Apollo bring the affair to the good issue which he is held to have promised? Not in the least. So far as 'Apollo' is concerned, so far as Euripides is concerned, and so far as we, his readers, are concerned, the expedition ends, as it was sure to end, in the destruction of the emissaries. They get on board with their booty, and they put off; but the barbarian king, knowing the voyage before them, regards their escape from his vessels as a mere impossibility, so much so that he is in no hurry about pursuit[3]. Nor, as it proves, is there need for pursuit. At the harbour's mouth the fugitives encounter 'a wind springing up with strange suddenness' which forces them back—an occurrence which should perhaps be added to

---

[1] *v.* 86.   [2] See Dr England.   [3] *v.* 1325.

the dream as an incident in the story conceivably miraculous, for the Taurians treat it so, referring it, as the ordinary super-stitious Greek would have done *mutatis mutandis*, to their own offended Artemis and to Poseidon, enemy of Orestes' house[1]; so that here again the unseen powers, the forces of nature, by whomsoever controlled are not controlled by Apollo. By him or for him nothing is done. The vessel grounds, and the natives make it fast. Nothing remains for King Thoas but to hunt down with boats and horsemen the miserable crew, and to enjoy a barbarous revenge.

Here, when all is over, appears not Apollo even now, but Athena; and the farce of the *Ion*, the farce of the *Alcestis*, the accustomed farce in short, is presented to orthodoxy as a peace-offering. The proceedings of Thoas are arrested by command; we are assured that the whole design, including (of course now) the escape of Iphigenia to Argos[2], is destined to success by the fiat of Apollo, and—but really it is not worth while to go on. Of 'Athena' the poet has told us what to think; and we can only remark with Thoas that 'when we hear a speaking god,' we naturally obey. Yes, *when we hear him speak*. With that proviso, anthropomorphic religion may be accepted...safely.

Of Apollo then in the narrative there is not a trace. The oracle of Delphi is there, and plays such a part as Euripides regularly chooses to give it, that is to say, a part of craft and pretension, cruelty and treachery. The inference from the whole facts, the only possible inference, is the one twice drawn by Orestes himself at earlier stages: 'Apollo,' or in other words the Delphians, finding that their counsel in the matter of Clytaemnestra was generally disapproved, and that their importunate victim was sinking under incurable remorse, made of his desperate faith a 'trap' to get rid of him, and sent him 'as far away as possible' upon an errand of which they knew no more than the one thing needful, to wit, that there was

---

[1] *v.* 1414. Modern editors, with their view of the play, are so much puzzled by these remarks that they strike them out,—a remedy which alternates with the 'lacuna.'

[2] *v.* 1440.

scarcely a chance of his coming back. They sent him to Athens, and it did him no good, so then they sent him...to Taurica. And so much for Apollo.

As for the Furies, their personality is literally transparent. In their case Euripides had an opportunity, of which he has promptly availed himself, actually to show on the stage 'the gods' so to speak 'not existing.' Both in this play and in the *Orestes* the Furies are hallucinations of a mind disordered by misery. Orestes, the murderer and outcast, sees them when he has fits, and no one else sees them at all. Such an access seizes him on the shores of Taurica, and he takes for his fancied pursuers some barking dogs and bellowing cows, upon which accordingly he falls sword in hand[1]. The meaning of this description is plain, and no one misses it. But it should have been seen also, and would have been seen long ago, if it were the fashion to credit Euripides with a consistent purpose, that the liability of Orestes to such temporary madness (as proved in this case) implies the worthlessness of his testimony as to anything which happened *according to him* at a time when the Furies were visible; and that therefore *we should dismiss to limbo the whole preposterous account which he gives to his sister of his visit to Athens*, or at least everything in it which is at all improbable or which connects itself specially with the presence of the imaginary fiends. That narrative is connected by the poet closely with a reference to the hallucination of the morning, which Orestes, according to the nature of his malady, still takes for a reality[2]. We know it was not. Why then should we pay him any regard, except in the way of pity, when he proceeds to relate how he and the Furies met at the Areopagus, how he took one platform and a Fury the other, how Apollo gave evidence, and Pallas sentence, and so forth? With a few stray dogs, with a rock and a statue, or with nothing at all except the silent hill and his own wild brain, he could make (and we know it) the whole proceeding. The solemnity celebrated in the *Eumenides* appears by this account as the invention of a madman, to be received with tears or frowns, with bitten lips or shrugging of shoulders, according to our interest in the patient, but true not one little

[1] *vv.* 281 ff.   [2] *vv.* 931 ff.

bit. The Pythia sent him to argue his cause against 'the nameless goddesses' at the Areopagus; and in the natural course of things he went through the experience—but without obtaining relief. All the same this was no bad suggestion, and the best thing, or rather the only good thing, which the Delphians, as Euripides tells the story, did in the course of it. Their mental pathology (in modern phrase) does indeed seem to have been the most solid part of their lore, which no one, not even Euripides, can have supposed to have had no points of superiority. It was—I should judge from what I read, knowing no medicine myself—quite possible and not unlikely that a *halluciné* such as Orestes would have left his 'Furies' behind him at the Areopagus; and indeed he was better; '*some of them stayed*,' but unhappily not all, and so the mad chase went on.

In his treatment of 'the Furies' Euripides is waging (with perfect consistency and propriety) literary as well as religious war against his opponents; for the Furies, or rather the visible shapes of them, were created by Aeschylus. Shadowy before, much more shadowy than most forms of Greek fancy, they seem to have become clearly personified and fully equipped for the first time in the *Eumenides*. Their costume, their attributes, their noises, beast-like and human, were (or at least the ancients believed so, and this comes practically to the same thing) of Aeschylus' making[1]. Euripides falls upon the whole frippery with as much vigour, though with a difference in the method, as Aristophanes did upon his. In the *Eumenides* their dog-like characteristics, their running on the scent of blood, their whining in slumber, their howls, are employed with a power inconceivable, if one had not seen it done. In the *Iphigenia* they are dogs still, the dogs of peaceable herdsmen, transformed by a lunatic. Nor does their dress escape. Critics misapprehend the poet's aim when they propose to soften into something more intelligible and more poetical the

---

[1] Pausanias, I. 28. 6. Pausanias is speaking of the images of the *Semnai* at the Areopagus, which evidently surprised him by lacking (for excellent reasons) the familiar attributes of the Furies. He derives from Aeschylus 'the snakes in the hair,' selecting this as the typical mark. So far as appears, there scarcely existed before Aeschylus, at least in literature, any such type as his fiends. The Erinyes of older allusions are tremendous but curiously formless.

crudeness of the Fury who is painted 'blowing fire and blood from her skirts[1].' The art-work of a madman is apt to want mellowness and lucidity ; and the like danger, Euripides could have added, waits on the poet or the dramaturgist who insists on putting the intangible into shape. The famous Aeschylean costume, with the snakes, robes red and black, and so on, though impressive, seems to have been reckoned somewhat too frightful[2]. The more sublime it was, the slighter the touch which would precipitate it into caricature ; and this touch the realist takes care to bestow. The sword again, which the Euripidean Orestes ' plunges into the flanks of the oxen,' is from the tiring-booth of the *Eumenides*, where Orestes at his first appearance, fresh from a bout with the gory monsters who harass him, sits at the sacred stone of Delphi, clear of them for the moment, with 'a sword *fresh-blooded* and dripping[3].'

It would take more space than the proportions of our present subject will allow, to exhaust the relation of the Euripidean Furies to the Aeschylean, even as it appears in the *Iphigenia* alone; and it is the same elsewhere. Some pages for instance would be necessary, if we began at the beginning, to show fully why Orestes speaks with a shade of impatience (the modern editors will not let him) when he says that Phoebus 'sent him on his own feet to Athens (aye, surely) to offer remedy of law unto *the goddesses that have no name*[4].' Partly it is that, in spite of the *surely*, even Athens

---

[1] *v.* 288 ἐκ χιτώνων πῦρ πνέουσα καὶ φόνον.

[2] The stories told of its untoward effect on sensitive spectators, though probably apocryphal, imply this criticism, which is moreover genuinely Attic.

[3] The current theory, that this is the sword of the murder, is impossible upon the facts. How could it be 'dripping' after a journey from Argos to Delphi? The sword here replaces the old 'bow and arrows,' which Apollo gave Orestes to guard himself. The story implies necessarily that he could by some means fight them off for a time, though, but for the Areopagus, they would doubtless have 'devoured' him at last. Needless to say, Aeschylus is careful to keep such fights well in the background. He hints them and no more, with sincerity, and also with discretion.

[4] *v.* 942   ἐμὸν πόδα

εἰς τὰς Ἀθήνας δή γ' ἔπεμψε Λοξίας
δίκην παρασχεῖν ταῖς ἀνωνύμοις θεαῖς.

In all recent texts the particles are altered.

could not give him relief. But partly it is because in the light of the failure there seemed to be something a little wild in the experiment; and what this was comes out, when he speaks of the legal satisfaction as offered to 'the goddesses that have no name.' The beings whom he thus describes (not very respectfully, as they did nothing for him), though they had not exactly a name, had a title, and a noble title; they were styled, for especial awe, *The Revered Ones (Semnai)*, and the title was applied to them in all ages as regularly as any name could be. They had a sanctuary-cavern near the Areopagus. Now the whole scheme of the *Eumenides* aims at conveying the suggestion, so bold and so little warranted by custom that Aeschylus never dares to assert it in words, that these beings and the Furies were identical, or that at any rate after the great trial the *Furies* or *Erinyes* somehow became the *Revered Ones*. It could be shown, if this were the proper place, that in truth, so far as there was a truth in the matter, this identification was built on almost nothing. The religious and mythical origin of the *Erinyes* and of the *Semnai* was widely different, and they had scarcely a point of contact. To help the union, Aeschylus brought in from yet a third source a name which, by hint again not assertion, he bestows on the combined 'Erinyes-Semnai,' the name of 'Eumenides.' At all this syncretism, which in Aeschylus is of profound religious importance and is managed with consummate art, yet an art not quite imperceptible, Orestes is made to point when he stamps the deities of the Areopagus so brusquely as 'the goddesses that have no name.' Of the new divinities compounded by the mystic chemistry of the *Eumenides*, it is literally true that 'they have no name,' and this for a reason at which Euripides, who held a different opinion as to the proper way of improving religious conceptions, had a right to direct a stroke, provided that it were done, as he does it, with appropriateness to the dramatic character used as the instrument.

To the report, which we are to take as wholly imaginary, of what passed in the sacred court, Orestes adds an account of the way in which the Athenians treated him elsewhere.

Here we have unfortunately no longer the advantage of knowing exactly how the matter was represented by Aeschylus and other like authorities. But upon the words of Euripides alone it is plain that here also his method is his own. Tradition derived from the visit of Orestes the custom that at certain religious feasts (*Choës*) mixing-bowls were not used but only separate cups, with other arrangements of the same kind. The original purpose of them had been, it was said, to avoid communication with the murderer. The account given by the Euripidean Orestes is that such arrangements were made (he, though hurt, not daring to question his hosts, but knowing only too well) because he was a matricide[1]: 'and I hear that from my misfortunes has grown an Athenian rite and that still it is their custom to respect the quartern cup.' But by this account, coming from such a witness, it is plain that the *origin* of the custom, as a piece of sacred history, is exploded. Why should we suppose that the custom of the cups was really then new, and introduced for the reason that Orestes gives? He does not say that any one told him so at the time. He says that he knew it *and dared not ask*. Afterwards he learnt that it was a ritual, and concluded, after the fashion of minds so ruled by persistent fancies, that it had 'become' one. Presumably it always was, and its use on the occasion of his presence merely a coincidence. The 'aetiological legend,' as it would now be called, is treated by Euripides like other legends. "About the *origin* of old customs" he says in effect "we do not at present know anything, and our tales are idle. The *Choës* began with

---

[1] *vv.* 953 ff.   εἰς δ' ἄγγος ἴδιον ἴσον ἄπασι βακχίου
μέτρημα πληρώσαντες εἶχον ἡδονήν—
κἀγὼ 'ξελέγξαι μὲν ξένους οὐκ ἠξίουν.
ἤλγουν δὲ σιγῇ κἀδόκουν οὐκ εἰδέναι
μέγα στενάζων—οὕνεκ' ἦν μητρὸς φονεύς.
κλύω δ' Ἀθηναίοισι τἀμὰ δυστυχῆ
τελετὴν γενέσθαι κ.τ.λ.

I think this punctuation, with parenthesis, preferable, but the sense is not affected by changing it. In the last sentence there is an ambiguity impossible to render, between 'my sufferings have become a rite' and 'were done as a rite,' a vital difference turning solely on whether δέ is *and* (with the first meaning) or *but* (with the second).

Orestes! Tradition says so; but who was the first authority
for the statement? Perhaps Orestes himself; and if so since,
according to the story, which you must take whole or not at
all, Orestes was a species of madman, what is the weight of
the evidence?" Readers who take these recollections of the
Euripidean Orestes for a sane account of things as they really
happened complain of them as rambling and bald, and even
try to improve them by cutting or shuffling the text. But
they are right and excellent if taken for what they are meant
to be, the outpourings of a maniac who has got for the moment
upon the dangerous topic. As for the imaginary meeting of
the Areopagus, Orestes' account of it is so arranged as to
convey by the very wording that he himself in his frenzy
played the whole scene, which stamped itself nevertheless on
his remembrance as an outward reality which he had witnessed.
The effect can hardly be transferred to a language so different
from the original as ours, but what he says, in Euripides
relieved of 'improvements,' is something like this: "When I
got to Ares' Hill"—*Hill* by the way not *Hills*—"and stood
to trial, taking I one platform and the other the principal of
the Furies, having spoken and received reply respecting my
mother's blood, Phoebus saved me by bearing witness; and
the equal votes were differenced in my favour *by Pallas with
the arm*[1]." This monstrous sentence, skipping wildly from
person to person, is itself a picture of the speaker's thoughts
on the subject, and reveals the ground of his belief. The odd
last words, though they may contain an allusion to some
legend not known to us, I believe to mean in themselves
simply that Orestes counted five fingers for one side and five
for the other, and *an arm* for the vote of the goddess. I could
allege illustrations for this, but it would be long and the point

---

[1] *vv.* 961 ff.   ὡς δ' εἰς "Αρειον ὄχθον ἧκον ἐς δίκην τ'
ἔστην, ἐγὼ μὲν θάτερον λαβὼν βάθρον
τὸ δ' ἄλλο πρέσβειρ' ἥπερ ἦν Ἐρινύων,
εἰπὼν ἀκούσας θ' αἵματος μητρὸς πέρι
Φοῖβός μ' ἔσωσε μαρτυρῶν· ἴσας δέ μοι
ψήφους διηρίθμιζε Παλλὰς ὠλένῃ.

Or διηρίθμησε, either, I think, possible. By omitting τ' and reading εἰπὼν δ', or
in some such way, modern recensions make 'better sense.'

is not worth it. With an actor's gestures such a meaning could be made instantly apparent.

It is scarcely necessary to remark that the natural import of this painful and striking scene is to shake or destroy imaginative faith not merely in the Furies but in all figures of the sort, Athena, Apollo, Artemis and all the pantheon. It is in the abstract possible to suppose that the same man at the same time *saw* one 'god' and merely *dreamed of* another; or that strange things which *A* dreamed of were elsewhere or at another time really seen by *B*. But practically these are not lines which any one would draw in such a case. From the belief that one *theophany* was the fiction of insanity it is indeed a long step to the generalization that all the evidence for theophanies would be found similar if it could be investigated. But where the one theophany was supposed a case of the gravest public and historic importance, all who got as far as the first step would hasten to stride the rest. And since without *some* theophanies an anthropo-morphic creed is baseless and not entertainable, the treatment by Euripides of the Areopagitic legend imports a general exclusion from his story of all such beings as the gods of popular tradition.

Except Apollo and the Furies, the only other such being whose action or supposed action affects the story is Artemis, to whom is attributed the escape of Iphigenia from the sacrifice at Aulis, and the transference of her to Taurica. The prologue, which is spoken by Iphigenia, consists of two parts, first a prologue proper, or relation of antecedents to the audience, and then the first step in the action, the 'telling to the sky' (a popular but, as is hinted, not very well ascertained remedy[1]) of Iphigenia's evil dream. In the first part she informs us how, brought on false pretext to Aulis, she "was lifted high over the piled wood, and the sword was about to slay me, when Artemis stole me away, giving the Achaeans a deer instead of me, and through clear sky brought me to dwell in this land of Taurica, where the strange folk have a

[1] *v.* 43.

strange king Thoas, who, setting a foot swift as wings[1], came
to this name because of foot-swiftness."

Now with regard to this story it is to be noted firstly that
merely by placing it in his conventional 'prologue' Euripides
implies, according to his practice in the matter, that it is to
be taken *cum grano*. These miraculous prologues like the
miraculous conclusions are given for mere stage-machinery ;
and, provided they bring us to the situation from which
the real action starts, how precisely we get there is of no
importance. And to the action of the *Iphigenia* it is not of the
least importance how the heroine was conveyed to Taurica ;
all that the *action* presumes is that she was carried there,
and believed herself indebted for rescue to Artemis. How
she travelled or what part 'Artemis' had really taken are
questions immaterial. We may suppose as we like. And
if this prologue had been put in the mouth of a 'divine'
person, of Artemis herself for instance, there would be no
reason to look further : that would mean in Euripidean
symbols, and we should merely have to say, that *this* account
at any rate is false, and the thing came to pass *otherwise*, it
matters not how, since we are concerned for the present with
nothing but the result.

But the fact that the miraculous story is put without
necessity in the mouth of a real person (I mean of course real
for the purpose of the action), and of a real person who took
part in it, persuades me that the poet meant us to take her
belief as *explicable*, and therefore presumably alludes in his
statement to a known explanation, one of that sort which,
under the influence of nascent rationalism and positive
enquiry, were springing up in all directions. Whether we
now can guess what this explanation was, or whether it is
worth while to guess what to the play as a work of art is
irrelevant, is another thing : but I feel some curiosity about
it, so perhaps the reader may also. Now in the story as
above cited there is one point which can scarcely fail to
rouse a passing wonder, that is to say, the stress laid upon

---

[1] *v.* 32 ὠκὺν πόδα τιθεὶς ἴσον πτεροῖς.

the apparently irrelevant remark on the derivation of the name *Thoas*. What can this be mentioned for, once and yet again, unless it throws some light on the matter with which it is joined? Here then we have to look. And first, what does the derivation mean? To 'set a foot swift as wings' is in Greek though not in English ambiguous, because *foot* happened to be the Greek term for the *sheet* of a ship[1]. Which swiftness was it then from which Thoas took his name, his own or that of his ships? The play leaves no doubt which was meant; it was that of his ships. About Thoas as a runner we hear nothing; but the swiftness of the Tauric ships is not only extolled by Thoas[2], but implied in the fact that the Tauric temple is served by women kidnapped from the Greek islands[3]. The peninsula is presented for what it historically was, a nest of rovers. The extraordinary swiftness then of these roving ships is for some reason highly important in connexion with Iphigenia's statement that she was transported from Aulis to Taurica by Artemis. Undoubtedly, for it is the whole solution. Euripides is alluding (lightly and without any expression of personal belief) to an explanation of the story, as of other such, after the fashion of infantine rationalism now represented by the book of Palaephatus, which tells us for instance that Actaeon was a spendthrift 'eaten up' by his pack of hounds, that Phryxus and Helle were taken over sea not by a ram but by a man called *Ram,* and that Pelops was a bride-stealer having a ship called *The Winged Horses* in which he carried off Hippodamia, whence the legend that he won her with winged horses in a chariot-race. It is worth notice that the prologue to the *Iphigenia* opens with the chariot of Pelops, to which however are given horses not winged but *swift* (*thoai*), so that the train is laid for

---

[1] e.g. *Iph. Taur.* 1135, πόδες ναὸς ὠκυπόμπου. The two meanings of the word are even played upon, as it were, by way of reminder, when Iphigenia says (*v.* 884) πότερον κατὰ χέρσον, οὐχὶ ναυσὶν ἀλλὰ ποδῶν ῥιπᾷ; 'Shall we flee by land, not with ships but with *feet that ply*?' It is only the fact that in Greek a ship had πόδας but not ποδῶν ῥιπάν which gives this expression point.

[2] *vv.* 1325 f.   [3] See the choric odes *passim.*

rationalizing upon *Thoas*. Legend said "When Iphigenia
was on the point of being sacrificed at Aulis, Artemis substi-
tuted a deer, which the sacrificers slew instead, still supposing
(by miracle) that they were slaying Iphigenia[1]. Meanwhile
the goddess carried her through the sky to Taurica and made
her priestess." Rationalism, through some early Palaephatus
playful or serious, said "Nothing of the sort! When the girl
reached Aulis and learned what was to be done with her,
anguish and terror drove her out of her mind (she was the
sister, remember, of Orestes). Odysseus and Calchas[2],
ashamed of the trick they had practised on her, and not
knowing what to do, smuggled her away and produced a
deer, into which *they said* she had been miraculously changed,
and which the ignorant multitude accepted accordingly.
Iphigenia was handed over, as troublesome people constantly
are, to a wandering slaver, who happened to be from Taurica
and to have a *ship called* (very naturally) by the name of the
Tauric goddess *Artemis*. The ship made a quick passage in
splendid weather (the *clear sky* of the legend); and when the
girl came to her senses again she found herself in the service
of the foreign temple. Out of what was told her and her
own confused recollection she put the story together, and
so with help of priestcraft it got into circulation." That
there is nothing improbable in the existence of this rationalizing theory or jest, will be admitted by any one who has
seen Palaephatus. But what, more than anything, convinces
me that Euripides knew, refers to, and assumes some such
version of the facts, is that in the play itself Iphigenia, after
alluding to the supposed sacrifice, goes on to recall in full
detail 'the miseries of that time *which she has not forgotten*,'
and these recollections, as will be seen, contain nothing after
her vain attempt, on discovering Odysseus' fraud of the
pretended marriage, to move the mercy of her father[3]. The
sacrifice itself, the substitution of another victim, her astonishing journey with the goddess, she never pretends to

---

[1] Cf. *Iph. T.* 176, 563.　　　　　　　[2] *Iph. T.* 24, 531 ff.

[3] *vv.* 361 ff. οἴμοι· κακῶν γὰρ τῶν τότ' οὐκ ἀμνημονῶ, κ.τ.λ. See also
vv. 850–867.

remember, and in the prologue she implicitly compares the whole story, as it stands now in her mind, to a dream[1]. She believes that a certain episode in her past was miraculous, but her recollection is limited precisely to that part of it which was not. The inference is obvious.

The reader is now in a position to judge whether the story of the *Iphigenia in Taurica* really requires the presumptions of anthropomorphic religion, and with how much justice the poet is accused of inconsistency, negligence, want of taste, and so on, for those parts of it which manifestly impeach those presumptions. In reality the play, so far from depending on any such hypothesis, cannot be fully understood and appreciated until every such hypothesis is put away. Not that in this respect the case is on a par with those we have previously considered. It is not so by any means. By ignoring the true realistic and rationalistic hypothesis, and taking as serious the poet's theatrical pretence of anthropomorphism, the *Alcestis* is dislocated, broken up, and partly effaced, while the *Ion* is ruined almost completely, becoming a heap of unpleasant and incomprehensible incidents, in which are imbedded fragments of a strange nobility. The *Iphigenia* suffers to a far less degree, its motives being to some extent independent of the question how the enterprise of Orestes and Pylades began and terminated. The admirable dramatic turns of the mutual recognition, the loyalty and gallantry of the two emissaries, the sisterly devotion of Iphigenia, are in themselves the same either way; the sequence of incidents is the same either way and equally intelligible. The result is that the *Iphigenia*, being one of the few plays of Euripides which are explicable on the current hypothesis, is one of the few, the same few, which are loved and studied, known and admired for their own sake, and apart from the collateral interests of Hellenistic philology and archaeology. But nevertheless it loses much. The deepest part, the real substantial

---

[1] *v.* 42 : after finishing the miraculous story of the past, she proceeds to 'the *new* phantoms which night hath brought with her,' *i.e.* the dream which she has just had.

tragic foundation, is cut away. Properly understood it is not a melodrama, it is a tragedy. Part of the pathos, and the profoundest part, in the resolute faith and invincible love of the two friends, is that it is *wasted*, materially speaking, as such qualities in the tangle of the world often are and will be. Orestes and Pylades are sacrificed (as Iphigenia has been sacrificed truly and not falsely before, and now is sacrificed again) to the relentless cruelty of a religion in danger. Orestes, drawing after him the far purer and more noble Pylades (such is the picture of Euripides), is sent to perish among savages, simply because Delphi has lost credit by what her believing sons have done at her bidding, and because one of them, tortured by a remorse which she has vainly striven to quiet, has become at last an intolerable reminder and advertisement of her reproach. In their fate is entangled the innocent and pious sister, whose life has already been wrecked by a like engine of politic superstition, together with a number of her humbler fellow-captives, who have no concern in the matter, but face death for Hellas' sake in order to give their lady a chance of escape. That is the 'moral' of the play, and it is a moral fit for tragedy. As for the 'tales of the sacristy' tacked on by the puppet Athena, they have no more to do with the tragedy than her green-room jests.

There is one point in the play which has excited particular interest among modern readers, partly because of comparisons suggested by the great modern writers who have borrowed the general theme and handled it in their own way. I refer, as will be guessed, to the morality of the unflinching deceit practised by the captives upon Thoas. Upon this, I venture to think, the light will fall with a certain difference, when we contemplate it under a right conception of the work as a whole. To own my mind, I confess that even under the current hypothesis, which leads us to expect in Orestes and his coadjutors objects fit for unqualified sympathy, I still should not see much to cavil at, as things go, in their behaviour towards the king. It is no doubt wrong to steal, wrong even for the captives of a slave-owning

prince, who is also a man-slayer and punishes by impale-
ment, to run away with his property; and doubly wrong
to achieve the robbery by shameless falsehoods which work
upon him through his respect for religion. Still it is a
thing which might be done, as things go, by human creatures
deserving on the whole not less than an indulgent acquittal.
Good Catholics, and good Protestants too, might have be-
haved very much so in the sixteenth or seventeenth century
to a chieftain of Barbary. Nevertheless I do not disagree
with the many critics who have felt that, if we suppose the
play really designed to lead us up in sympathy to the
success of Orestes, Pylades, and Iphigenia in their religious
theft, the author has shown some want of moral delicacy in
making it necessary for Iphigenia to do so much dull
hardened lying and enact without a qualm what upon her
own principles is an impious mockery. It cannot be said
that the Greeks would see no harm, and that Euripides
agreed with them; because Iphigenia herself, when her
conscience is awakened by signs that the scheme is not
favoured by the powers and is about to end in the ruin of
the contrivers, confesses that the theft is a bad business by
praying Artemis to forgive it[1]. These qualms, since she
could feel them then, she should have felt sooner, in order
to keep our perfect sympathy. And still worse, on the same
assumption, would be the way in which the project of
assassinating Thoas, in which there really is not the least
sense, is propounded by Orestes, and rejected by Iphigenia,
without a sign that either perceives clearly any objection
other than the extreme difficulty and danger of it[2]. Strangest
of all would it seem that Euripides should not have felt
the edge of the self-rebuke to which Iphigenia is led when,
in the midst of her fraud, she answers Thoas (who has asked
whether there is any need to chain the prisoners, since they
cannot possibly escape) with the words "Trust is unknown
to Hellas[3]!" She is certainly doing her best to illustrate
and justify the bitterness of the motto.

---

[1] *v.* 1400.   [2] *vv.* 1020–1023.

[3] *v.* 1205 πιστὸν Ἑλλὰς οἶδεν οὐδέν.

But we have in reality no need or right to suppose that Euripides thought the proceedings of the three conspirators altogether admirable, or desired to give that impression. The fact that Thoas, though for a savage he has merits, is a savage still, does not alter the fact that the proposed theft of the Tauric image is a bad business in itself and bad in the device employed. But the shame of it falls not so much on the agents as on the authority by which it is commanded, and to which the consciences of Orestes and his coadjutors are unhappily subject. Here, as usual, what comes from the great oracle is stamped (of course only according to Euripides) with the marks of baseness. To 'convey' the Tauric image to Greece, though this was not the real purpose of Delphi, was still a suggestion such as would naturally be attributed to Delphi by such an enemy as Euripides. It is a superstitious, immoral act, disgracing the 'religion' which recommends it. As for any notion of a moral difference between anthropomorphism in the Crimea and anthropomorphism in Hellas, Euripides is careful to exclude that notion. If 'Artemis' received human sacrifices on the shores of the Euxine, so she was in danger of doing, at the time when the story is laid, on the shores of the Euripus, as witness Aulis and the offering designed there by the highly respectable Calchas. The moral sense of poor Iphigenia revolts against such a goddess[1]; but this is only to say that she is better than her creed. The root of all the mischief (according to the poet) among Greeks and barbarians alike is the prevalence of low, false notions about the nature of the power which governs the world; it is the enthronement of idols, draped with the emblems and animated by the notions of ancient savagery, in the place of enlightening reason: and the most diligent cultivators of such mischief are the possessors and managers of the shrines which profit by it. Orestes, Pylades, and their abettors are entitled to pity as well as admiration for their courage and mutual loyalty, and to infinite pity, but by no means to admiration, for the useless, criminal, hopeless

---

[1] *vv.* 380 ff.

attempt to which they are condemned by the directors whom they have served too well.

As to the pretended conclusion, by which everything is abruptly turned upside down, not even those who take it seriously can avoid the perception of its flatness and futility[1]. It is impossible to think that the goddess plays a convincing or an impressive part. Euripides, we see, was especially well pleased with this particular finale; he has pointed forward to it by language which could not miss its meaning for accustomed auditors or readers, when Iphigenia, surveying the prospect as it appears after the recognition of her brother, and the apparently insuperable difficulties of escape by land or by sea, exclaims in despair, "Who, god or man, will disclose to an unhappy pair a means of release, *or by what unexpected way will he make the impossible possible*[2]?" Here not merely the substance but the wording reminds everyone of the famous *envoi*. But this, as seen in the *Alcestis*, marks the contrast of the 'divine' solution with the solid realistic knot : "that which was expected came not to pass, but for that which was not expected deity found a way." We are assured in short that this play is conceived on the accustomed model, and will have the usual double ending, the true and the theatrical. It seems also that the poet conceived himself to have expressed this relation of things with even exceptional happiness and simplicity. And so in fact he has. Nothing could be better for the purpose, if you know what it is, than the grotesque opposition between rebellious nature and the interference of Athena in person. In vain do the emissaries of Apollo implore

---

[1] See, for example, Dr England's endeavours to satisfy himself; *Introd.* to his edition, pp. xxiii–xxvi.

[2] *v.* 895

τίς ἂν οὖν τάδ' ἂν ἢ θεὸς ἢ βροτὸς, ἢ
τί τῶν ἀδοκήτων
πόρον ἄπορον ἐξανύσας,
δυοῖν τοῖν μόνοιν 'Ατρείδαιν φανεῖ
κακῶν ἔκλυσιν ;

Compare the close of the *Medea, Alcestis*, etc.

καὶ τὰ δοκηθέντ' οὐκ ἐτελέσθη,
τῶν δ' ἀδοκήτων πόρον ηὖρε θεός.

For questions (not material) as to the exact reading see Dr England's note.

that favour of circumstances without which their success and even their escape is manifestly impossible. Blind nature (or inscrutable Providence, if we so prefer) is not even impartial between them and their overwhelming foe. Deity, acting by those means which alone He is known to use, condemns and hands them over to a cruel death. Then, and only then, when we have been assured that the wind and the sea act we know not why, but at any rate *not* at the bidding of the god of Delphi, then an Olympian deity, *appearing in person*, requires and receives obedience. But that is to *expose* the goddess, not to exhibit her. Those who in the time of the poet still accepted her divinity did so because they saw or thought themselves to see in the working of fortune proof that she and her kindred powers, though unseen, did nevertheless control the forces of the world. Something might be done for such a religion by a story like the *Eumenides*, in which the Olympians come boldly on earth and act among men through a prolonged course of events. Imagination might thus be stimulated to believe that such things had been and might be again. Much more was done for such a religion by a story like that of the *Oedipus Tyrannus*, where common familiar forces, the forces of nature and circumstance, are seen to work out the command of Olympian deities who, as their wont unquestionably is, do not offer their persons to view, but speak by an accredited agency. But a story like that of the *Iphigenia*, in which all those superhuman forces, about whose existence there is no dispute, are seen to be at war with the Olympian command as alleged by the accredited agency, at war with it and victorious over it, a story in which the 'divine' purpose is saved only by the 'appearance' of a deity, who (as usual) does not appear until all is over,—such a story as this is deadly for the Olympian religion. Such a design, if the miraculous conclusion be really a part of it, is dull, frivolous, and without serious interest; it acquires a serious meaning only on the supposition that the miraculous conclusion is mere irony and pretence. It must be the work either of an 'atheist' or of a fool.

IPHIGENIA

211

The nature and use of the Euripidean stage-gods, and the relation between their prologizing or epilogizing—for to these functions they are with scarcely an exception confined—and the purport of the author as conveyed in the drama proper, a relation of such importance that without comprehension of it the works of the poet cannot be understood, is happily one of those too rare points of literary interpretation upon which we possess a clear, complete, and definite statement from a competent Greek authority. The formal work of ancient Greek scholarship, the result of Greek erudition in its classic age of the third and second centuries before Christ, is almost totally lost to us ; it seems indeed to have perished in great part during the shocks by which the world was recast into its Roman form ; and even the erudition of later and less trust-worthy times has for the most part gone into the same pit. Of the general estimation in which the various Greek authors were held by those who had adequate means to interpret them, we obtain considerable evidence in the frequency and tone of ordinary allusions. But of exposition we have little or nothing. It happens however that upon the matter now in hand we have the instruction of one who, notwithstanding his unpromising date, is universally and justly recognized as having conquered the centuries, as it were, and placed himself in spirit and thought more near to Atticism than any but the great Athenian artists themselves. I mean of course Lucian. Persons more competent than Lucian to understand and explain Euripides may no doubt and must have existed ; but there are few indeed, if any, more competent among those whose light can now be obtained. Now in the dialogue entitled *Zeus as Tragedian* Lucian has set forth the nature and function of the Euripidean stage-god in terms which so exactly tally with the views expressed in this book that I think I must (though unable to trace the fact) have learnt them from Lucian in the first instance. A 'Stoic' and an 'Epicurean,' neither of them (it should be said) a quite worthy representative of his school, are debating as to the reality of the Greek popular gods, the Stoic (Timocles by name) being of course for it, the Epicurean

14—2

(Damis) against, and the sympathies of their creator Lucian being altogether on the 'atheistic' side. The champion of the gods cites among other witnesses the poets, beginning with Homer, upon which ground he is as usual defeated, and proceeding to 'tragedy,' which for Lucian means mainly and generally Euripides.

Timocles. And Euripides again ! He also, it seems, in your opinion speaks without sense, when he puts the gods in person upon the stage, and exhibits them as rescuing the good people of the sacred story and damning the bad and irreligious like yourself !

Damis. Friend Timocles, you are a most respectable philosopher ; but if your conviction about the gods is based upon such tragedy as that, you must choose between believing either that at the time when it was written [the actors] Polus, Aristodemus, and Satyrus were gods, or that there was divinity in the actual masks, shoes, surplices, mantles, sleeves, false bellies, false chests, and other apparatus employed by them for the scenic pomp,—the second opinion being perhaps the most ridiculous. For where Euripides is expressing his own thoughts, unconstrained by the exigence of the performances, you may hear him say frankly this :

> " See'st thou aloft yon infinite of air,
>   Which keeps the earth in liquid arms embraced,
>   That, that is 'Zeus,' believe me, that is God."—

or again this :

> " Zeus,...whatsoe'er he be ; I know of him
>   But tales."—

and so on elsewhere[1].

---

[1] *Zeus Tragoedus*, § 41.

ΤΙΜΟΚΛΗΣ. οὐδ' Εὐριπίδης ἄρα σοι δοκεῖ λέγειν τι ὑγιές, ὁπόταν αὐτοὺς ἀναβιβασάμενος τοὺς θεοὺς ἐπὶ τὴν σκηνὴν δεικνύῃ σῴζοντας μὲν τοὺς χρηστοὺς τῶν ἡρώων, τοὺς πονηροὺς δὲ καὶ κατὰ σὲ τὴν ἀσέβειαν ἐπιτρίβοντας;

ΔΑΜΙΣ. ἀλλ' ὦ γενναιότατε φιλοσόφων Τιμόκλεις, εἰ τοιαῦτα ποιοῦντες οἱ τραγῳδοποιοὶ πεπείκασί σε, ἀνάγκη δυοῖν θάτερον, ἤτοι Πῶλον καὶ Ἀριστόδημον καὶ Σάτυρον ἡγεῖσθαί σε θεοὺς εἶναι τότε, ἢ τὰ πρόσωπα τῶν θεῶν αὐτὰ καὶ τοὺς ἐμβάτας καὶ τοὺς ποδήρεις χιτῶνας καὶ χλαμύδας καὶ χειρίδας, καὶ προγαστρίδια καὶ σωμάτια, καὶ τἄλλ' οἷς ἐκεῖνοι σεμνύνουσι τὴν τραγῳδίαν, ὅπερ γελοιότατον οἶμαι· ἐπεὶ καθ' ἑαυτὸν ὁπόταν ὁ Εὐριπίδης, μηδὲν ἐπειγούσης τῆς χρείας τῶν δραμάτων τὰ δοκοῦντά οἱ λέγῃ, ἄκουσον αὐτοῦ τότε παρρησιαζομένου

> ὁρᾷς τὸν ὑψοῦ τόνδ' ἄπειρον αἰθέρα
> καὶ γῆν πέριξ ἔχονθ' ὑγραῖς ἐν ἀγκάλαις;
> τοῦτον νόμιζε Ζῆνα, τόνδ' ἡγοῦ θεόν.—

καὶ πάλιν

> Ζεύς, ὅστις ὁ Ζεύς· οὐ γὰρ οἶδα πλὴν λόγῳ
> κλύων—

καὶ τὰ τοιαῦτα.

To this passage, if I were forging it for my own purpose, I could not desire to add a word. Clearly and precisely, as well as with excellent humour, Lucian has stated the truth, that the 'gods' whom Euripides brings on the stage, usually at the close of the piece and to bring about a ' divine justice ' adapted to the prejudices of the vulgar, must, on pain of stultifying the poet and destroying his sense, be taken as not being personages in the drama at all, but simply actors in a certain costume introduced for 'the exigence of the performances '; and that to take them seriously, to suppose them or their speeches to be part of what the author wishes us to imagine as real, is absolutely impossible if the poet is to have a meaning, as we may see by the nature of the opinions, the express contradiction of anthropomorphism, which he is constantly recommending to us in the body of his works. When an actor comes on as Ion or Orestes, we must of course, to follow Euripides' sense, ignore the fact that he is Polus dressed up, and suppose that he is the personage presented, a part of the play. But when at the close of the piece he comes on in the machine as Athena, then, to follow Euripides' sense, we must on no account allow ourselves to make any such supposition. The very appearance of such a figure, in such works as those of Euripides, can only mean that we are mocked, that the author is no longer speaking to us seriously and no longer appealing to our imagination. The so-called ' goddess ' is not, cannot be Athena; it is just Polus the actor, or, if you like that better, the dress which he has on ; he talks certain nonsense to satisfy bigots ; but once away from the performance and its ' exigences,' you have not the slightest concern with him. And not only does Lucian point this out, but he also shows, what is perhaps even more interesting, that already in the early Christian centuries this fundamental truth about Euripides had come, in the general decay of pagan learning, to be so little known, that the opposite error could plausibly be attributed to a reputable member of a learned profession, although it would be received with scorn in the dwindling circle of Atticists to which

Lucian himself belonged. In fact it was just because the truth was being forgotten that for once and at the last possible moment we find it stated. In the days of Aristotle, or Aristarchus, or Cicero, or even Quintilian, it is probable that no one, who was not writing a professed study or disquisition on Euripides (and we have scarcely a fragment of any such work), would have mentioned such an elementary principle. In literary history as in other departments of life, the least likely things to be stated are those which, being fundamental, every one is supposed to know. The time may yet come, if literature and learning should suffer another Oriental invasion, when it will have to be painfully learnt and proved that Pope was not an Anglican, nor Defoe a Churchman, nor Swift orthodox, nor Voltaire a Christian, and that to make sense of their works these negatives must not be forgotten. Happy if the gibe of some Taine or Macaulay born out of due time shall survive to confirm the observation.

This character of mere theatrical and conventional pretence, contradictory to the sense of the poet and transparent to the instructed reader, which Lucian rightly attributes to the machine-gods of Euripides, is nowhere better illustrated than by the Athena of our present play. We have noticed already the suicidal jest with which her harangue concludes, a jest which proves, in the very terms of Lucian's remark, that if there be any deity here at all, then that deity is not Pallas the daughter of Zeus, but the actor in *propria persona*. But the whole harangue, however pleasantly its tags of Attic legend, or plausible imitations of such[1], might sound in the ears of Athenian groundlings, is futile as a commentary upon the preceding action. Like the similar harangue in the *Ion*, it is on the face of it incredible.

---

[1] It is not certain, nor I think likely, that the legends are ungarbled, though the cults mentioned are doubtless genuine, and grossly savage they are. That offerings such as Euripides describes were made at Brauron, we may take for granted, but we need not suppose that the deity to whom they were made was commonly identified with Iphigenia.

So far as words will go, the goddess no doubt sends every one off to be happy ever after. But as in the *Ion*, so here, her prophecies hang upon the calm assumption that things are not as we know from the play that they are. All that she foreshows depends upon the condition that this time the Delphian oracle, which had so often deceived Orestes with the promise of cure, will be justified by success, and that his ' Furies ' will have departed for ever. Yet this essential thing Athena does not even assert, nor could we believe her, if she did. Had it been the intention of the poet that we should accept such a solution as possible, he would have prepared us for it. He would have shown us in Orestes such feelings to-wards the enterprise on which he is engaged as would lead us naturally to the conclusion, that the success of that enterprise in his hands might restore him to moral and intellectual sanity. But what Euripides does show us is everywhere the contrary. Nowhere does Orestes pretend the slightest enthu-siasm for the work on which he is sent, nor the slightest faith, except the 'faith' of despair, in the adviser who sends him. The modern expositors who accept Athena's promises, and therefore must needs assume, though without her guarantee, that Orestes is cured by stealing the Tauric image, are so shocked and astonished at the remarks upon that divine em-ployment which are put into the mouth of the agent (or rather the patient), that they expel them wholesale from the text. Three times in the course of the brief dialogue of forty verses, in which the brother and sister settle their plan, this curative process has to be applied. Three times the speeches of Orestes must be excised or altered, in order that he may not betray the loathing which, when it comes to the point of action, the larcenous business naturally excites in one who, miserable as he is, has not lost altogether the instincts of a man. ' How would it be,' says he to Iphigenia, when she has rejected the proposal to fall upon the king and slay him, 'how would it be, if you were to hide me in the temple?'—' Do you mean that we might then get safe away by the aid of darkness?'—'Yes,' says he bitterly,

' *the night belongs to thieves, as light to truth*[1].' But if Orestes is to be morally cured by his faith in Apollo and Apollo's command, such a blasphemy seems monstrous, so we draw a pen through it. Yet a few lines lower the same spirit breaks out again. The parts to be taken by the brother and sister in carrying off the statue have been now settled. 'And what part' asks Orestes 'is Pylades to have in our...massacre[2]?' The turn is startling, but perfectly natural. It is manifest that the scheme of Iphigenia must lead to bloodshed, as in fact it does ; that Orestes and Pylades must again be united in the infliction of wounds or death, and this, when all is said, on behalf of a cause not otherwise definable than as that of robber against owner. The mere deliverance of Iphigenia would of course have been just, though neither the king nor the people of Taurica are on any supposition responsible for her 'disappearance.' But the deliverance of Iphigenia might have been accomplished in the circumstances with ease and almost with certainty. It is 'by the taking of the image,' as Iphigenia says[3], by the attempt to comply with that base command which the oracle gave without either expectation or desire that it should ever be accomplished, that 'the escape is embarrassed,' and it is by this that the fugitives are put in the wrong. It is natural then that, when the crisis approaches, Orestes should feel,—it would be strange in the circumstances represented

---

[1] *vv.* 1024–1026.

    OP. τί δ' εἴ με ναῷ τῷδε κρύψειας λάθρα;

    IΦ. ὡς δὴ σκότος λαβόντες ἐκσωθεῖμεν ἄν;

    OP. κλεπτῶν γὰρ ἡ νύξ, τῆς δ' ἀληθείας τὸ φῶς.

For expelling the last two verses with Markland and others there is no reason whatever, except that undoubtedly the last 'makes against Orestes' plan instead of for it' (Dr England), which is (*ex hypothesi*) absurd. The objection that in a final sentence the optative with ἄν is a solecism errs in the assumption that ὡς here is final; it is causal (*since, because*), and ἄν is indispensable. As to the neuter σκότος, if it be wrong (*sed quaere*) we must replace σκότον. If the lines were not from Euripides, who should have inserted them, and why?

[2] *v.* 1046 Πυλάδης δ' ὅδ' ἡμῖν ποῦ τετάξεται φόνου; MSS.: πόνου, δόλου, λόγου, χοροῦ, etc. the commentators.

[3] *v.* 1018.

if he did not in his dark, perplexed, and unhappy manner
betray the feeling,—that after all, this act of robbery and
'massacre' is a strange sort of expiation for blood.   But this
feeling nevertheless, if we are to save the credit of 'Apollo'
and 'Athena,' we dare not let him reveal or entertain ; and
therefore instead of the 'massacre' he must say 'the task,' or
'the plan,' or 'the performance.'   But yet a few lines later
we have to be mending again, and this time with a bolder
hand.   The dialogue ends thus[1] : *Or.* 'Well, at all events my
ship has rowers who pull a brave stroke.'—*Iph.* 'Your care it
must be then that all the rest be well—save one needful
thing, that these maids should keep our secret.'—*Or.* 'Beseech
them then and find words to win their pity.   There is a
faculty for doing it in woman.   And the rest...perhaps...
—Let us hope that all will end well!'   The last sentence[2],
which wants nothing but punctuation to be as plain Greek as
can be, has been expelled.   Why?   Because the tone of
it reveals beyond misunderstanding that Orestes goes to
his task without any moral faith, and because to suppose this
is to condemn as absurd the sequel promised by Athena.
But he reveals it everywhere.   In the very sentence preceding, with its scarce suppressed sarcasm, he reveals the
unbearable distress of his nerves.   The first scene reveals it,
when at the sight of the temple which he has come to
plunder he breaks down, and is barely prevented by Pylades
from re-embarking for Greece.   And so by every kind of
suggestion, positive and negative, do all the scenes of
the play.   After all this it is mockery to put up a goddess of
pasteboard, whose predictions require us to imagine that this
broken man, brainsick with remorse and obloquy, having
tried in vain prescriptions really salutary, will be made sane
by the success of an enterprise in which he has not and never
pretends to have the slightest moral interest whatsoever.   A
disease like that of Orestes must be cured, if at all, through

---

[1] *vv.* 1050–1055.

[2] τὰ δ' ἀλλ'...ἴσως...—ἄπαντα συμβαίη καλῶς.   Taken as one sentence this is
unconstruable.   But the verse has really been rejected, as Dr England says, for
its 'sense.'

the heart. The remedy or remedies found for him by
Aeschylus content our imagination not merely because they
are sanctioned by heaven, but because they are remedies for
the heart. But what signifies it to the heart of this Argive
matricide whether a certain idol is in Taurica or in Attica?

There is no future possible for this Orestes; and when
Athena pretends that there is, she does but expose the
hollowness of her buckram deity. Nor is there any for
Iphigenia. She is appointed to become a priestess and
eventually a local deity in Attica. Whether this is unadul-
terated legend, or whether (as seems more probable) the
identification of the local deity with the sacrificer of Greeks
was invented by Euripides himself, he lets us know what we
are to think of it. Priestess or not, Iphigenia must always be
the woman who had lived by offering up her countrymen
on behalf of barbarians, pitiable but horrible, as Orestes views
her before she is found to be his sister[1]. In the raptures
of the recognition this is forgotten, but it would be remembered afterwards and remembered always. Nor does
the sister, any more than the brother, approve in her conscience the oracular command. She thinks it a sin[2]; but
it is, as she believes, the appointed means of saving her
brother, and that for her is enough.

Of the three principal actors in the play the only
one who has a desirable future, the only one for whom the
miraculous escape secured by Athena could be a boon, is
Pylades; who also stands alone in accepting, with a faith so
implicit that it cannot be called assent, the injunctions and
assurances of the Pythian oracle. Orestes may quail at
impossibilities and groan at a crime; Iphigenia may confess
herself a sinner; Pylades never hesitates, never doubts, never
reflects[3], and herein lies the interest of his character. We
are moved to ask what is the weight of this remarkable
exception from fears and scruples *prima facie* so legitimate.
And Euripides gives us the measure. When Pylades, entrusted with Iphigenia's letter to her brother, has given her
his oath that it shall be duly delivered, he insists upon one

---

[1] *vv.* 617-621.   [2] *v.* 1400.   [3] *vv.* 104 ff., 716 ff., and *passim.*

reservation, that if the ship be wrecked and the letter with Pylades' own property be thus lost, then he Pylades, should he escape with his life, shall not for non-delivery of the letter be guilty of perjury nor liable for it to divine punishment[1]. Mechanically this precaution of his is useful in the scene, by leading Iphigenia to give a verbal repetition of her message ; but by the technical skill which Euripides, as Aristotle implies, has nowhere more admirably shown than in this play, it serves another and a much more important purpose. It is a revelation of the man. For here at least in common fairness Euripides must have the benefit of his reproach. Whatever else may be said of the casuistry of his Hippolytus, 'the tongue hath sworn but the mind remains unbound,' it proves at any rate that Euripides was not likely to propound the casuistry of Pylades for anything but what it is, the reflexion of a man honest indeed and brave to the last breath, but stupid and bigoted to the same extreme degree. To ask whether such a man believes or approves the dictates of the religious authority under which he has been reared is a needless question. Of course he does, and can do no other till he is laid in his grave. Pylades is the sworn servant of Delphi in the same fashion and for the same reason that he is once and for ever the adherent of Orestes. He has a big heart, but no mind : and of such is the realm of Apollo. Apart from this he has no importance, and his fate (his real fate, not that preposterously sketched by Athena), pitiable though it be, is but a small addition to the disaster of the others. Many a man, though healthy, wealthy, and happily married, has died not unhappy with less consolation than Pylades would find in falling by the side of Orestes. The only end morally tolerable or physically possible for the story as pictured by Euripides is that to which it is already conducted when 'the machine' appears and excuses us from further attention. Nothing remains to imagine but the manner of the fugitives' deaths, and over this it was better, as well as necessary, to draw a veil.

---

[1] *vv.* 753 ff.

If the tear of mere sentiment is to be shed over their fate at all—though the poet is thinking and we ought to be thinking of other and more terrible things—then most of all the hapless handmaidens, whose unpaid and unpurchasable devotion is a moral trait more beautiful than any exhibited by the chief personages[1],—they should have the best of the weeping.   Nor is it without significance that even 'Athena' is not allowed to save these most pitiable of the oracle's victims except by a fiat so crudely arbitrary that she can scarcely speak it for laughing.

In reference to the precise point of the character belonging to the Euripidean 'god,' it is possible and likely, for reasons above given, that the existing remains of ancient literature contain no other statement than that of Lucian ; though this cannot be presumed until the whole has been read (as I must confess that by me it has not) with the fact in mind and with attention awake to it.   But with regard to the general aim of Euripides we have the contemporary evidence of Aristophanes, and with regard to his general method of pursuing his aim we have that of the highest-sounding authority in the whole of ancient criticism, the authority of Aristotle himself.   It happens that the play on which we are engaged is one, unhappily it is almost the only one, upon the construction and purpose of which, as a whole, the opinion of Aristotle can now be ascertained.   The occasion is therefore suitable to do what in a book of this kind we may be expected to do ; to say something of what is or what should be inferred respecting Euripides from the notices of him which appear in the *Poetic*.

The references made in the *Poetic* of Aristotle to the dramatists of the fifth century must be read and interpreted strictly in connexion with the plan and purpose of the work, and cannot be separated from it without injustice not only to the poets but still more to the critic.   To give an estimate of these or any writers is not his object, nor does he attempt it.   The scope of his treatise (or rather sketch for a treatise), so far as it relates to tragedy, is to define the end of play-

---

[1] *v.* 1075.

writing and to deduce from this end suggestions for the better practice of the art. And the general drift of his argument, together with the incidental illustrations, is to answer in the negative his question 'whether tragedy has as yet perfected its proper types or not.' It appeared to Aristotle (and so far as we have the means of reviewing his materials it would seem that he was right) that there was no tragedian, including in the negative those revered poets of the previous century from whom his illustrations are drawn, whose general practice could be recommended as a safe example of method upon the principles maintained in the *Poetic*. This opinion, though not anywhere stated in so many words, is conveyed as clearly as it decently could be by a man of any modesty who was not himself a tragedian. An indication sufficient in itself is the fact that, while he expressly and repeatedly designates the author of the *Iliad* and the *Odyssey* as a sufficient model for composers of narrative poetry, he does not name or suggest anyone as filling the same office in relation to dramatic poetry : and the negative is confirmed by the general bearing of his references to particular dramatists or dramas.

In regard to Aeschylus, if this negative cannot be proved explicitly, that is only because the critic exhibits it in a more efficient manner, by scarcely citing him at all. That a scene in the *Choephori* stood high, though not in the first rank, among scenes of recognition or discovery ; that Aeschylus showed better judgement than some other writers (not named nor deserving to be named) in not attempting to frame his *Niobe* so as to include in the plot the entire legendary history of that personage ; and that a certain verse of Aeschylus had been admirably corrected by Euripides ; this, apart from merely historical notices, is about all that is said of him ; the truth being that in the latter part of the fourth century Aeschylus was far on his way to that limbo of a *magni nominis umbra* in which (strange as it seems to us and strange as it is, though explicable) he remained for the most part throughout antiquity. In the *Poetic*, as in Aristotle generally, the notice bestowed on Aeschylus is very little compared with that given to Sophocles, and *a fortiori* nothing compared with that given to Euripides. Of that opinion respecting the comparative merits and importance of the three, which has prevailed or tended to prevail in modern times, there is no trace to be found in Aristotle, or, speaking broadly, in any ancient literature except the temporary and ineffectual polemic of Aristophanes. As to Aeschylus, it may be said with confidence, that if he had received any further notice (we may almost say any) in the *Poetic*, he would have supplied, as from the strict Aristotelian point of view he is fitted to supply, illustrations of defect.

Passing to Sophocles we arrive at something more definite. It is the key-note of Aristotle's theory and pre-cepts to insist on the supreme importance of the plot, of subordinating the structure and every element in it to the essential purpose of setting in the strongest light a single tragic event or situation, the *motif* of the piece, as it would now be called. This being his doctrine, we should naturally suppose from such remains of older tragedy as we have, that if it supplied him with any one satisfactory illus-tration, that illustration would be the *Oedipus Tyrannus*. Exactly to this extent and no further we are actually carried in the *Poetic*. That even the *Oedipus Tyrannus* is a perfect illustration of his principles, or as good as might be desired, Aristotle does not say, nor must we make him say, for it would appear not to be true. Better illustrations of the method (which is not at all to say better plays or plays which Aristotle would have more esteemed) have been pro-duced, one at least far better, by those who had the advan-tage, immense for this purpose, of reading Aristotle before they wrote. However he cites the *Oedipus Tyrannus* five or six times, twice as often, that is to say, as any other play, and always with strong commendation ; and had he been bound to name an extant model, though in fact he is careful not to do so, he would evidently have much preferred this play to any other. But this approval or comparative approval is awarded to the *Oedipus Tyrannus* itself and solely, not at all to the general practice of Sophocles. Such an extension is forbidden, not merely by the constant recurrence of this one example (which would be worse than misleading if others equally or nearly as good were at hand) but expressly. Other plays of Sophocles are cited, the *Electra* among those which we have, the *Tyro* and the *Mysians* among those which are lost; but they are cited for defects, for points which, strictly in reference to his theory, Aristotle notes as either comparatively or absolutely disadvantageous. The mass of the poet's work, including very many plays which Aristotle could be shown to have read with admiration and interest, is passed over, for the immediate purpose of the treatise, with an intelligible silence. Apparently it did not supply, and this is certainly true as far as we can now see, a second *Oedipus Tyrannus*.

Nor did the works of Euripides: and to say this is to sum in one sentence the score or so of references to him which the treatise contains. That Aristotle, like his contemporaries in general, was deeply interested by Euripides, and found his works, on the average, more attractive than those of any other dramatist, is shown by the frequency of allusion, in which everywhere Euripides has a decided pre-eminence. In the *Poetic* itself he has all the honour which, from the nature of the case and relatively to the purpose of the work, it was possible that he should have. A play of his, the *Iphigenia* which we are now considering, is three times cited with approbation, and this in a book where very few other plays receive such notice at all, and hardly one (with the exception of the *Oedipus Tyrannus*) more than once; and this same play is selected for the still higher distinction of being compared with that imaginary example, perfect in the mere article of method, which then, as the author implies, had still to be produced, but now may be actually seen, as nearly as one man's idea is likely to be seen realized by the hand of another, in the *Athalie* of Racine. Indeed so far as can be judged from the indications of a treatise which is but a skeleton, and that broken, the *Iphigenia in Taurica* would have been the play which, next at a long distance after the *Oedipus Tyrannus*, Aristotle would, under careful reservations,

have recommended as a lesson to the attention of the playwright. Further it may be said of Euripides (and, I think,
of no one else) that not one only but two at least of his
dramas are mentioned in the *Poetic* for points of method
emphatically praised ; the *Iphigenia in Taurica* as exhibiting,
with the *Oedipus Tyrannus*, the 'absolutely best' way of
managing a discovery, and this same *Iphigenia*, with the
Cresphontes also his, and the *Helle*, for the 'absolutely best'
species in another classification. But with these five or six
exceptions, few but proportionally very many, the references to Euripides imply the judgement on him, relatively
to the question of method and solely in this relation, which
is passed by the like implication on his compeers. About
six of his plays are cited for points of structure not good
or not best, and the mass, as in the case of Sophocles, are not
cited at all. And if in one place—we must say 'if,' for the
passage is obscure and disputable—it were said of Euripides
generally that 'his management is faulty,' this would be but
to sum up what upon the strict principles of the *Poetic* is
true and is alleged by Aristotle respecting the whole
dramatic art of the fifth century. It would not import any
particular condemnation of Euripides ; and indeed such a
meaning would be excluded by the unparalleled compliment,
declaring that Euripides 'appears to be the most tragic of
the poets,' which is attached to the censure and must be
extended or limited together with it. There is however
reason and authority for maintaining that both the blame
and the praise of this passage have a much narrower import,
and that the large interpretation of them must be added
to the misunderstandings of which perhaps, as recent expositors have shown us, no merely secular book has been so
fertile as this unlucky treatise[1]. And at all events that

---

[1] Aristotle is maintaining (*Poet.* xiii. 4 ff.) that in the best tragedy 'the
change of fortune should not be from bad to good but reversely from good to
bad.' διὸ καὶ οἱ Εὐριπίδῃ ἐγκαλοῦντες τοῦτ᾽ αὐτὸ ἁμαρτάνουσιν, ὅτι τοῦτο δρᾷ ἐν
ταῖς τραγῳδίαις καὶ πολλαὶ αὐτῶν εἰς δυστυχίαν τελευτῶσιν. τοῦτο γάρ ἐστιν,
ὥσπερ εἴρηται, ὀρθόν. σημεῖον δὲ μέγιστον· ἐπὶ γὰρ τῶν σκηνῶν καὶ τῶν ἀγώνων
τραγικώταται αἱ τοιαῦται φαίνονται, ἂν κατορθωθῶσιν, καὶ ὁ Εὐριπίδης, εἰ καὶ τὰ
ἄλλα μὴ εὖ οἰκονομεῖ, ἀλλὰ τραγικώτατός γε τῶν ποιητῶν φαίνεται 'Hence they

Aristotle had no such charges to make against Euripides as those with which modern criticism abounds, can be proved by the clearest evidence which the case admits. Aristotle is emphatic, and properly so, in condemnation of such plots as he calls *epeisodic*, ' in which the episodes or acts succeed one another without probable or necessary sequence.' Now if he had read his Euripides as Euripides has been read in modern times, instead of giving that poet almost if not absolutely the most prominent place in the treatise, he might very briefly have excused himself from paying any attention in such a work to a composer who repeatedly, habitually, and almost always, would appear to ignore this rudimentary precept of the art. It would have been enough to say of him that he was the author of the *Alcestis, Andromache, Troades, Orestes*,

are in error who censure Euripides just because he follows this principle in his plays, many of which end unhappily. It is, we have said, the right ending. The best proof is that on the stage and in dramatic competition, such plays, if they are well represented, are most tragic in their effect; and Euripides, faulty as he is in the general management of his subject, yet is felt to be the most tragic of poets.' (Prof. Butcher's translation in *Aristotle's Theory of Poetry and Fine Art*.) The words 'general management of his subject,' though justifiable, indicate perhaps a larger scope than is *necessarily* contained in the original : ' though otherwise managing not rightly ' is a verbally sufficient rendering, and the question is, what does that mean. Prof. Butcher (p. 283), discussing the description 'the most tragic of poets,' properly insists upon the importance of reading it in connexion with the context and " with the preference of the poet for the true tragic ending." I cannot but think that this just limitation is the key not only to the complimentary part of the passage, but to the whole of it. It is improbable that Aristotle, who offers in the *Poetic* no general estimate of any other tragedian, nor even hints for such an estimate, would there offer a general and comparative estimate of Euripides ; and it is surely incredible that, if he had wished to enter upon a subject so important (as the treatise itself would prove it), he would have raised and dismissed it in the tail of a paragraph. His intention here is limited, as usual, to the particular point, the matter of *endings* happy and unhappy; and he means no more than that " an ending thoroughly and without qualification unhappy, such as those of the *Medea, Hippolytus, Hecuba, Troades*, and other plays of Euripides, produces on the stage, if properly represented, a powerful effect, and inclines us to regard the poet as the greatest master of his art, even though, it may be, the play or the closing scene itself is open to criticism," as upon the principles of the *Poetic* all these plays actually are, and most if not all of their 'endings.' The possibility of a much larger construction should be set down either to a slight carelessness in the composition, or to some injury of time ; and since half the paragraphs in the work require similar allowance, it must be available here.

Phoenissae, Heraclidae, Madness of Heracles, Ion, Electra, Suppliants, etc., etc., etc.　It is certain that, when the *Poetic* was written, the *Alcestis* for instance and the *Andromache* were two of the most admired pieces in the Greek repertory.　Why is it that Aristotle nowhere conveys or hints a caution that these works, and most others of the same author, are essentially 'epeisodic,' or in other words scarcely deserve in point of art to be called plays ?　Surely because he did not think so.

What he thought and said is that Euripides did not, any more than the other dramatists of the great age, furnish by his general practice or in a single case a perfectly satisfactory example of the Aristotelian method.　He saw not only this fact but the cause of it.　The truth is that the tragedy of the fifth century, all of it, is based in part upon principles practically, though not perhaps theoretically, inconsistent with those of the *Poetic*.　We cannot have all good things at once: elevate one object and you depress another.　Which is most important in a drama, the aesthetic effect, which may be approximately the same for men of different times, or the moral and intellectual effect, which must be calculated mainly for the particular age of the production ?　Aristotle would declare for the aesthetic effect, and he may be right ; but it is hard to say by which of the four men who represent to us the drama of the fifth century, Aeschylus, Sophocles, Euripides, and Aristophanes, this position would have been most strenuously denied[1].　According to Aristotle, provided that the imagination of the expected audience is prepared to accept *pro tempore* the story adopted by the dramatist, the question of its truth is immaterial ; if an objection should be raised on this head, it will be a sufficient reply that such is the story, 'this is what is said.'　And this, adds the author consistently, "applies to tales about the gods.　It may well be that these stories are not higher than fact nor yet true to fact : they are very possibly what Xenophanes says of them.　But anyhow 'this is what is said.'"[2]　Sound

---

[1] See Butcher, *Aristotle's Theory of Poetry and Fine Art*, pp. 205 ff.

[2] *Poetic*, xxv 7.　Xenophanes is cited as the first and typical enemy of popular Greek theology.

doctrine perhaps, or sound as far as it goes. But whoever insists on reading the poets of the fifth century as if they had held this doctrine, for him the *Oedipus* will lose half its depth, the *Choephori* all its strength, and the *Alcestis*, with Euripides generally, will be once and for ever unintelligible.

And of this opposition Aristotle was perfectly well aware. It is brought out precisely in the brief comparison, unhappily too brief like the rest of the book, which he makes between an *Iphigenia* framed on his principles and our actual *Iphigenia* of Euripides. "The general plan," he says, "of the *Iphigenia*"—of his ideal *Iphigenia*, that is to say—"may be thus seen":—

A young girl is sacrificed; she disappears mysteriously from the eyes of those who sacrificed her; she is transported to another country, where the custom is to offer up all strangers to the goddess. To this ministry she is appointed. Some time later her brother chances to arrive. (The fact that the oracle for some reason ordered him to go there is outside the general plan of the play. The purpose again of his coming is outside the action proper[1].) However, he comes, he is seized, and when on the point of being sacrificed reveals who he is. The mode of recognition may be either that of Euripides or of Polyidus[2].

It will be noticed that, in the words here printed as parenthetical, Aristotle, with our *Iphigenia in Taurica* before him, marks out as elements in it, not belonging to what he considers the essence of an *Iphigenia*, precisely those matters which, as we have shown, are included and emphasized by Euripides in pursuit of his antitheistic purpose. The motive of the oracle in sending Orestes to Taurica, and the nature of his errand there, are matters which, as Aristotle saw, are raised by Euripides to the rank of essentials; and upon this he remarks, that if you aim at his aesthetically ideal *Iphigenia*, in which everything shall be strictly subordinated to the *motif* (as we should say now) of the brother's escape from a tragic fate, these Euripidean elements must not be made prominent, nor indeed allowed at all within your limits. The motive of those who send the brother is irrelevant to the

[1] Or 'outside the plot.'   [2] *Poetic*, xvii 3, trans. Butcher.

typical or 'general' conception of the subject, that is to say, to the brother's narrow escape ; and the errand which brings him is a trivial circumstance, such as you will put not in your 'action proper' but in your prologue, so as to have done with it. All which is perfectly just and unobjectionable upon the assumptions of the treatise ; and whoever desires to produce the 'typical' or 'general' *Iphigenia* should certainly comply with the directions. But what is *not* just, what is deplorable, what is not supported by Aristotle, but is nevertheless now universally done, is to read the *Iphigenia* of Euripides as if Euripides had aimed at producing some such *Iphigenia*, as if the brother's escape had been the true interest for him and his readers, and to neglect those non-typical developments of the story in which for Euripides lies the very kernel of his thought and lesson. In modern expositions of the *Iphigenia in Taurica* the vice of Orestes' errand is firmly ignored, and *the motive of the oracle*, the ultimate and vital question, is necessarily allowed to drop out of sight. It was not thus, we see, that the works of Euripides were read by Aristotle ; and so long as they are read thus, half the power of them will remain sealed up, and the admiration of the ancient world will remain a mystery.

It is no part of our purpose now to estimate the value of Aristotle's theory in itself, and to do so in a by-way would be impertinent. A mere personal feeling may perhaps be expressed without impropriety.

While acknowledging of course the good sense of Aristotle's remarks on play-writing, and reverencing the deep thought which lies behind and about them, I own that (Racine having died with his *Iphigenia in Taurica*, alas, projected only) I am not very impatient to see the 'general,' typical, ideal *Iphigenia* produced ; and I doubt it would not be (to me) so interesting or so valuable as the local, temporal, by no means typical *Iphigenia* which Euripides wrote for the improvement of believers in Apolline inspiration. I even think that there is some admixture of error and danger, as in all human thoughts, so in this notion of a universalizing quality residing in adherence to the 'type' or *motif* of the story; or at least that to insist on it involves some correlative neglect of other universalities not less important to the power of literature. In one sense Euripides' play is not 'universal,' nor a work for all time ; we should like to be sure that there are any such works ; it is a work for Athens in the fifth century before Christ. But in another way it is no less universal than superstition, and this seems universal enough. It is curious that the play in which, as is generally agreed, Aristotle's precepts have been in the main most nearly realized, the noble and glorious *Athalie*, is yet in another way the most strictly local and temporal of great literary products, since it cannot be understood completely without restoring in imagination the convent of St Cyr and the court of Louis XIV. After all, a human mind is not universal. Let a man generalize himself and his thoughts as he will, his time and his place will not let him go, and with their help, not in disregard of them, will be done the best that he can do.

But neither with the virtues nor with the defects (if such there be) of Aristotle's speculation are we now concerned. Our present business is not to appraise the *Iphigenia in Taurica*, but simply to explain it. Be it assumed that there would be higher merit, or merit of a better kind, in an *Iphigenia* framed with the object of setting in a strong light the narrow escape of a brother from dying by the hand of his sister; and that it is an abuse of this *motif* when Euripides (who after all invented it and had the *patria potestas*) subordinates it as a detail to the general purpose of an assault on the pretensions of the Pythian oracle. That does not touch the fact, to which, as well as to his particular judgement upon it, we are pointed by Aristotle, that this, and nothing else, is the thing which Euripides has done, and that, if we are to read him with understanding, in this sense and no other he must be read.

A word may here be added in conclusion[1] upon the recent performance of this play in Cambridge, or rather upon the light obtainable from it on the question, whether the interest

[1] February, 1895.

of the play can be maintained in separation from its true religious 'atheistic' purpose. This of course was what we attempted, what must be attempted in presenting a play of Euripides to any large audience which could be collected at the present time. It was played, according to the current hypothesis, as a melodrama, a story of incident, leading up to the *theophany* accepted as the *dénouement* really intended by the author. I am the last person competent to pronounce an impartial judgement on such an experiment. I can only say for myself that both the spectacle and the criticisms of the public seemed to me, like the performance of the *Ion*, to confirm the opinion in which, as I conceive, I follow the authority of Aristotle and of Lucian. So taken, the play has indeed much merit; that is to say the real purpose and the supposed purpose coincide to an unusual extent. But so taken it is not worthy, and to an average assembly it cannot appear worthy, of an author who claims to stand with Aeschylus and with Sophocles. There is thus no depth in it, nothing solemn, nothing to show that here was a man to whose voice all humanity ought to listen. Nor is it even altogether intelligible. The condition and character of Orestes, for example, his panic terror, his increasing gloom, his bitterness, all this, with many another trait and turn in the piece, provoked the astonishment of able men, who knowing nature and the stage, but being without prejudices about Athens or about Euripides, were compelled to say, as they did, that the author, whatever his merits, might have executed his purpose better if he had been a little instructed in his art. And to this there is, as I believe, no other possible reply than that the fault is with us, the expositors. We shall cease from the injury of presenting him as a tiro in his art only when we confess that hitherto we have in the main misapprehended his purpose[1].

---

[1] In this essay I have intentionally abstained from noticing the play of Goethe on the subject, which does not, I think, throw much light on the particular questions which I discuss. I would not leave the impression that I have the bad taste not to admire it.

EURIPIDES IN A HYMN

"Yes, dear Van! that is how you should behave. Imply things."
GEORGE MEREDITH.

IT has been the object of the foregoing essay to show
that the *Iphigenia in Taurica* rests, like the works of the
poet in general, upon a hypothesis, in relation to the
Olympian anthropomorphic religion, purely 'atheistic,' that
no such person as Apollo is required or admissible as an
agent in the story which the dramatist presents. The
dramatis personae are believers in Apollo, to their sorrow
and confusion; the dramatist does not pretend, or barely
pretends, to believe in him at all. We are not however
bound to infer from this that the poet must hold himself
altogether unconcerned in the variations (if we may say so)
of orthodoxy, in the disputes which had arisen or were liable
to rise between different worshippers of Apollo. On the
contrary, nothing could suit his purpose better than to bring
such divisions into light. It was one of the chief difficulties
by which polytheistic paganism was embarrassed, so soon
as the spread of intellectual training created a demand for
system and regularity in belief (for a 'creed' in short, to use
the familiar term), that the existing traditions, having been
designed in separate pieces to suit the interests of separate
religious centres unconnected one with the other, insub-
ordinate, and even sharply antagonistic, could scarcely be
fitted into a harmonious whole without sleight or violence
not easy to be practised under the eyes of the enemy.
What paganism wanted, but naturally never could get, was
an oecumenical council, or a supreme court of theological

appeal. Aeschylus no doubt would gladly have given such a function to the Areopagus, nor is it inconceivable that half Hellas might have been brought to consent. But since the dearest pleasure of the other half would have been to flout their decisions, and that other half would have been supported, not steadily but with practical efficiency, by an authority of no less pretension than the oracle of Delphi, catholicity would have made a bad beginning, or rather no beginning at all. The *Iphigenia* exhibits proof, among other things, that Euripides was alive to the disadvantage which his opponents were under in having to mould a creed out of elements mutually repugnant, and was ready to avail himself of an opportunity to accent their divisions. The recognition of this may throw some light on the purpose of a poem introduced with manifest abruptness and lack of juncture, facts which ought, on ordinary principles of art, to signify a design on the part of the author to arrest attention and encourage us to look beneath the surface. I refer to the ode in honour of the Pythian Apollo, which forms the third *entr'acte.*

The Chorus of the *Iphigenia* consists, as we have before seen, of Greek female slaves attached to the service of the Tauric temple. They have been procured according to the normal custom, Greek as well as barbarian, from kidnappers or man-stealers, by whom they were torn from their homes and sold[1]. From the circumstances of the case, from the fact that their enemies could strike only from the sea, it is natural to suppose that those homes were in the coasts and islands of the Aegean, and in fact this clearly appears when we see that their recollections and sentiments centre upon Delos, its hill of Cynthus, its legend of Leto, Apollo, and Artemis, its sacred trees, memorial of the holy travail, its 'round water' and musical mystical swans[2].

Now it is nothing extraordinary that such women, when for a brief moment, by the success of the imposture practised upon Thoas and the carrying of the Tauric image by Iphigenia to the coast, the supposed design of the Delphian

---

[1] *vv.* 1106 ff.　　　　[2] *vv.* 1096 ff.

Apollo appears to have some chance of success, should give vent to their sympathy, as soon as they find themselves alone, by a song in honour of the deity in his Pythian aspect. It is however by no means to be assumed without consideration that this song must needs be altogether such as a Pythian authority would have approved. Not even the dramatic character of the singers demanded this; for it was not to Delos, nor to worshippers trained in the tradition of Delos, that a well-informed Greek would have been likely to apply, if he wished to hear the genuine voice of Pytho. Whatever the prehistoric relations of the two shrines may have been—and probably the time was not so very remote when those relations were but slight—their interests in the fifth century were far from identical or even harmonious. Delos was in a certain sense the religious centre of the Athenian empire. The conduct of Delphi towards the makers of that empire had been, and was during the chief part of Euripides' career, such as made it hard to reconcile Athenian patriotism with the claims of the Delphian Apollo on the respect of the pious. Moreover a choric ode was not, could not be, so strictly bound by the requirements of dramatic character as a scene in dialogue. It was by its nature, according to the fully developed scheme of choric drama, a pause in the action, something not detached exactly from the action, but ready to be detached[1]. In this particular case it is manifest that the author was not anxious to lay stress on the dramatic function of the ode, but rather wished to present it in isolation as a thing to be considered apart. Nothing would have been easier than to turn the praises of the Pythian Apollo so as to bear directly on the

---

[1] The well-known judgement of Aristotle that 'the Chorus too should be regarded as one of the actors; it should be an integral part of the whole, and share in the action, in the manner not of Euripides but of Sophocles,' the only judgement between the two which is pronounced in the *Poetic*, is correct on the assumption; but we should not forget to add that choric drama is a form of art much too narrow in its limits, and that nothing but the necessities of the ancient theatre would have justified the retention of a chorus at all. Modern art has produced one thoroughly satisfactory choric drama, *Athalie*, and probably will not produce another.

success which, as is too cheerfully believed, he has forwarded
and is about to secure.   But on the contrary Euripides
prefers generality, and has inserted a hymn which would
have the same appropriateness (whatever that may be) in
any circumstances favourable, or so supposed, to the credit
of the Pythian deity.   The presumption is then, that the
purpose of the ode is to be found in itself, the dramatic
situation serving for little more than a pretext to place it.

At all events it is the fact, that in the legend here
related concerning the foundation of the Pythian oracle,
stress is laid on every aspect of Pythian tradition and
Pythian history which, as we know from the counter-example
of Aeschylus, judicious defenders of the oracle in the fifth
century would most gladly have thrown into the shade.
We have already seen that when Euripides was composing
the *Iphigenia* his attention was naturally directed to the
Choephori and *Eumenides*, which dealt in part with the same
incidents as his own play, but with aim and spirit precisely
opposite.   Now the prologue to the *Eumenides* consists of
a sacred history of Delphi, propounded by Aeschylus, perhaps
with authority, perhaps as a tentative suggestion of his own,
through the mouth of the Pythian prophetess figuring as a
character in the play.   Every single important trait in that
sacred history is historically false, and contrary, as Aeschylus
must have known, to tradition.   Indeed it is propounded for the
very purpose of overlaying and replacing tradition, all being
done of course in perfect sincerity and on the principle, which
has had its weight with historians of greater scientific pretension, that in such matters as these edification is the measure of
truth.   And if, after carefully studying the prologue to the
Eumenides, we go to the Pythian ode in the *Iphigenia*, we
shall perceive that the later composition asserts, with a perceptible under-current of mockery, precisely those features
of antique legend which Aeschylus is bent on denying and
dissolving away.

Those who, like Aeschylus, would have fain made Delphi,
and Apollo as prophet of Zeus, the centre of a sort of catholic
paganism, in which every thing repugnant to a high morality

should be explained away, and the anarchy of the savage pantheon replaced by an edifying subordination, did not find in old Pythian tradition a material by any means tractable. The cult of Delphi was the product, not merely of different religious elements, but of elements which had been in violent conflict, and this fact was stamped, with the ingenuous simplicity of preachers who saw no harm in it, on sacred history. It was said, and no doubt with perfect truth, that Apollo, not the original possessor of the oracle, but an invader, had taken possession of the country as his worshippers did, by simple force. No feat of his was more famous than the slaying of the dragon-guardian, which represented and protected the interest of the old earth-deities.

Nor was this old 'Chthonian' or subterranean cult the only foreign religion which Phoebus had encountered on the site of Pytho. The Bacchic religion, a worship wholly distinct from the Apolline and in its general character even inconsistent with it, had a hold on Parnassus, nor is it certain whether Apollo or Bacchus was in this particular case the first-comer. As between these two deities matters were settled, neither by force confessed, such as was used towards Earth and her children, nor by force disguised in civil form, as when Poseidon, the old elemental deity of the underground waters, was said to have been bought out; but by a sort of partition *per my et per tout*, both Apollo and Bacchus remaining 'seized' of the whole. The Delphian temple bore on one side Apolline emblems, on the other side Bacchic, and the ritual year was divided between them. In the central and characteristic element of the local doctrine, the communication of truth from the deity through a person 'possessed,' the trace of bacchic origin is strong; and in fact it would seem, if we compare Apollo as he was at Pytho with Apollo as he appears in general elsewhere, that he became master of Pytho only by admitting to his patronage, or rather to his alliance, a partner of such character and power that he transformed Apollo himself.

Now it could hardly escape any thoughtful man, when systematic and scientific reflexion had so much as begun to

have any influence,—at any rate it certainly did not escape
Aeschylus, that for such a savage theology as this there was
only the choice between transformation and annihilation.
Aeschylus was as anxious as Euripides himself to moralize
theology, and scarcely less anxious for regularity, fixity, and
system in thought : he only differed—but the difference was
as a wall reaching from heaven to earth—in thinking that
these results might be attained without cutting religion loose
from the old sanctuaries, that not only Zeus might be proved
(this did not require so much effort) a tolerable representative
of supreme order and supreme morality, but that with proper
explanations, symbolic interpretations, and so on, the pantheon might come in as subordinate powers. Only of course
it was a first necessity to change the mythology; in 'gods'
who robbed one another, fought one another, maimed, imprisoned, nay, slew one another for no better motives than
the passions which produce similar events among mankind,
in these gods assuredly Athens was not going to believe much
longer. The mythology of Pytho was full of such gods,
having been shaped by savage imaginations which saw no
harm. Aeschylus, seeing the fatal harm, proceeds with as
much assurance as Pindar, and with a far profounder sense of
what the situation required, to get rid of the mischief by
just asserting for true tradition that which in his judgement
ought to be taught.

The religious scheme of Aeschylus, carried out thoroughly,
would have ended in what a modern would call monotheism.
Zeus, as we see in the famous passage of the *Agamemnon* on
the solution of mysteries by trust[1], Zeus, when this course of
thinking had been worked to its completion, would have been
'God' in a wholly different sense from that in which the same
term applied to beings like Athena and Apollo. They though
superior to man are still, like him, children of the Supreme,
creatures and subjects of his will. Both of them without any
pretension refer their authority, wisdom, and power to Him
by whom they are commissioned. If Apollo is true, that is
because Zeus puts the word in his mouth; if Athena is

[1] *vv.* 170 ff.

mighty, that is because to none but her has Zeus committed
his thunder. It is upon such principles that Aeschylus has
re-faced or rather re-built the unsatisfactory mythology of
Delphi. The wisdom of the oracle is to be the wisdom of
Zeus and of no other; no other is to advance or to have
advanced in the past any claim inconsistent with his supreme
disposition. First at one stroke[1] the poet sweeps away the
whole chain of stories, which implied the historic truth that
Apollo and his religion had appropriated Pytho, as a material
possession, by force. On the contrary, the oracle, that is to
say the cave and its appurtenances, had descended to him
(according to Aeschylus) by regular and peaceful succession
of inheritance or gift, any tale to the contrary being by a
side-glance expressly denied. And as for the oracular power,
this he held direct from the Supreme, by no intermediary
derivation even of the legal and friendly sort. The notion
that the wisdom of Pytho depended at all on the place, or
that Apollo became a seer by acquiring the property of his
predecessors, is emphatically excluded ; 'fourth in succession
of time, he *speaks* for his *father*, for Zeus who inspired his
mind with knowledge and set him in his seat.' So far all is
fairly simple. But the question remained, what was to be
done with those other deities, representing strata or phases
of religious belief other than the Apolline, whose share in
constructing the religion of Delphi as it actually stood was
visibly confessed in its art and ritual? Above all, what was
to be done with Bacchus and the Bacchic element? To admit
this as an actual constituent would have necessarily destroyed
the unity of conception at which Aeschylus aims. For as to
asserting that Bacchus, where he came, came by peaceable
means, that was a hopeless idea. That the religion of Bacchus
was a militant, invading religion, provoking everywhere strife
and resistance, was a truth known not merely by legend but
by direct experience. The religion of Bacchus was still recognized in the fifth century for a comparatively modern thing.
It had by no means yet been completely accepted—indeed it
never was—by the older cults into whose domain it had

[1] See the prologue to the *Eumenides*.

thrust itself. And if Apollo shared Delphi (as in fact he did)
with Bacchus, Bromius, or Dionysus, the only presentable conclusion was that he had done so because he could not help
himself. Accordingly Aeschylus, with great audacity but true
religious logic, denies Bacchus altogether for a partner in the
cult. In order to do this with the preservation of respect
or at least a formal compliment to the facts, he had used
a device of which it would be most interesting to know
whether it is altogether his own or whether he had any
Delphian authority for it. The Pythian prophetess draws a
sharp distinction between two classes of deities, to whom she
owes different observances. To some she gives *prayers*, to
others only *mention*. The recipients of the prayers are the
possessors former and present of the shrine, whose claims, as
we have seen, all merge eventually in that of Apollo as
representative of Zeus. The recipients of mention are deities
adjunct to the shrine or connected with it by some remini-
scence ; these, who for more security are again made explicitly
subordinate to Zeus, are Athena, patroness of a famous chapel
outside the second precinct, Poseidon, giver of waters,—and
Bromius or Bacchus. By this arrangement Athena receives
full justice ; indeed it may be doubted whether a Delphian
prophetess, speaking not in the Athenian theatre but at
Delphi, would have given her quite so much. Poseidon has
something less than justice. He was really recognized, as we
know from other sources, for a former possessor, and had his
altar in the inmost sanctuary accordingly. And Bacchus,
with a view to whom, as Aeschylus uneasily betrays, the
whole of this classification is designed, is treated with extreme
injustice. Of him, whose story was figured, parallel to that
of Apollo, in the sculpture of the temple, who had like Apollo
his part in the Delphian calendar, the prophetess has nothing
to tell but that 'he holds the region' (Parnassus that is to say
and its upper cavern, not that of the oracle) 'he holds the
region, *as I do not forget,* ever since his deity led the army
of bacchants, and devised against Pentheus the death, as it
were, of a hare'—an event of which the date in relation to
the other history is left by the narrator unfixed, though no

one could fail to suppose, as is no doubt the intention, that it was comparatively recent, and in no way affected the establishment of Apollo as previously set forth. The observance thus rendered to Bacchus, as a deity of Delphi, is accurately defined by the prophetess herself, who is plainly not without some reasonable apprehension that others may think it insufficient: *she has not forgotten him.* No, certainly not. The religious Athenian poet, confronted by the demands of scientific system, but anxious to reconcile them with antique traditional devotion, has not forgotten, and is not able to forget, that in a Delphian mythology some place must be found by the harmoniser and unifier for the recalcitrant divinity of Bacchus. He has not forgotten him; and we may believe, if we can, that he would not have done so, had he dared.

Now such was the aspect of Delphian tradition, and such the manner of dealing with it which had been recommended to pious Athenians, hovering anxiously between 'religion' and 'science,' by their favourite instructor, when Euripides, in a work of which the general hypothesis denies, as his wont is, the divine authority, wisdom, and goodness of Delphian inspiration, finds opportunity to celebrate the acquisition of Pytho by Apollo in a hymn to the following effect[1]:—

"Glorious is the son of Leto, whom once on a time she bare in Delos' fruitful dell, golden of hair, skilled in the lyre and in the well-aimed bow, his pride. From the sea-girt crags, leaving proud memory of her travail, she carried her youngling to the unstinted springs of Parnassus, summit possessed by Dionysus' inspiring power[2], where a snake of spotted skin and ruby eye, coiled in the shade of a leafy bay, a prodigious monster of Earth, kept watch over Earth's oracular cave. But thou, Phoebus, thou yet a babe, dancing yet upon thy mother's arm, didst slay the monster, didst invade the oracle divine, and hast thy seat on a golden tripod, chair

---

[1] *Iph. T.* 1234 ff. I take no notice here of textual questions. There are none of material importance.

[2] τὰν βακχεύουσαν Διονύσῳ Παρνάσιον κορυφάν: the actual hill is treated as if it were, like a bacchant, a being 'possessed' by the god.

of unfailing truth, dealing to men oracular speech from the sanctuary, where hard by Castaly's stream thy palace is placed at the centre of earth.

"Now Themis, daughter of Earth, had been dislodged by Leto's boy from the place of divine response; so thereupon Earth gave birth to nocturnal apparitions, which in dreams would commonly tell to men all things that should happen, according to their order first and last, while they lay asleep in the black darkness upon the ground; and thus, in jealousy for her daughter, she took from Phoebus the oracle's reward. So the lord god sped him on swift foot to Olympus, and curling his infant arms about the chair of Zeus, besought him to rid his Pythian house of Earth's vengeance and the nocturnal dreams. Zeus smiled to see the child come with such quick eagerness to recover the golden riches of his service, and shaking his locks made promise that he would put an end to the voices of the night. So taking away from human kind their nightly vision of truth, he gave to Apollo his rewards again; and many a *gallant* welcomed to the chair finds encouragement...for mortality in the prophetic chant[1]."

I am sorry to rob this graceful and witty story of half its charm by giving it in the nakedness of prose, but I fear to misrepresent something, if I essayed verse; nor could I pretend to convey the exquisite lightness and *ripple* of tune— I can find no other word, and must take the risk of seeming affected in the use of this—which gives to the original a kind

---

[1]   πολυάνορι δ' ἐν ξενόεντι θρόνῳ
         θάρσῃ...βροτοῖς θεσφάτων ἀοιδαῖς.

Compare Aesch. *Ag.* 62 πολυάνορος ἀμφὶ γυναικός (Helen). The insinuation is a commonplace and the plot of the *Ion* is partly founded upon it: indeed, though probably undeserved in the main and in spite of one or two historic examples to the contrary, it was invited by the grotesque Pythian theory of inspiration. To call the chair of a woman θρόνος πολυάνωρ is *prima facie* a gross insult. The peril of the adjective (which a writer with a sensitive ear could then hardly have used except in one sense) is illustrated also by Aristophanes (*Birds* 1313). 'Before long some human being will be calling our city *polyanor*,' says a bird gaily. The remark, otherwise flat, seems to be aimed at some poet who had actually raised a laugh by forgetting that for a feminine subject (πολυάνορα τὰν πόλιν) the epithet is not happy. Here the possibility of an innocent interpretation is barely saved by the last words.

of elfish effect. But without these aids the mere substance is sufficiently plain in its purpose. It is from first to last a stroke of malice, struck as with a cat's paw, velvet and clawed. It brings into prominence, under the guise of a mock legend (there is no reason to suppose that the main part is a real myth, though it may be) just so nearly resembling the genuine products of religious fable as not to be on this ground open to objection, precisely those aspects of Delphi and Delphian history which a friend, such as Aeschylus, would have suppressed and disguised. In the first place the principal theme of the story is a matter on which Aeschylus would not have dwelt for worlds, the immense *profits* which Delphi brought to the proprietary, that is to say of course, to Apollo. According to this truly Voltairian chapter of sacred history, the dispute between Phoebus and his predecessor was entirely a question of fees. The credit of the oracular cave was the foundation of a fine business, an old-established house with a magnificent connexion. When Apollo turned out the family of Earth, the head of that family tried to make the concern worthless by cheapening the commodity sold : so long as knowledge of the future could be generally acquired by simple dreaming, the sacrifices and offerings at Delphi naturally ran short. Hereupon Apollo invoked the interference of his almighty father, who, much amused at his precocious avarice, gave an injunction against the expropriated rival and restored the threatened monopoly. The whole conception and treatment is exquisitely diverting ; but it would be absurd as part of a work really devoted, as the false finale pretends, to the celebration of a success achieved under the command and sanction of the oracle. Of course the vast wealth of Delphi, and the fact that all the town, from the chief priests to the beggars, lived upon the pilgrims, the upper orders in splendid state and the masses in indolence,—all this admitted of explanation or justification for religious minds. But it was not an aspect of the oracular function on which a wise believer could dwell with pleasure, or without misgiving. It will be seen that in the *Eumenides* Aeschylus, though he does not say that consultation was free, is most careful in wording the invitation of the prophetess to say nothing to the contrary; the sacrifices and all the apparatus of approach are simply ignored[1]; while for opposite reasons the *Ion* is throughout explicit on the material aspects of the cult, the graduated offerings for admission at different stages[2], the thank-offerings and banquets, the gorgeous buildings, vessels, tapestries, statues, paintings and all the treasures of the sacristy. It is enough to reveal the true character of this Euripidean hymn that it represents Delphi as essentially an institution for profit.

Consonant with this design is the historical account which the poet is pleased to favour. In this part he had traditional authority; the story of the Pythian snake, which implies in itself that Phoebus came in as a conqueror, is as old as the 'Homeric' hymns, and doubtless far older. Here, as we see, Euripides emphasizes, and enriches with suggestions of his own more or less in the primitive manner, all that story of conflict which Aeschylus so peremptorily dismisses in the interest of a more elevated theology. As a matter of historical fact, if that were the question, there is every reason to think that the traditional (and Euripidean) version corresponds to the truth, and that the cult of Apollo, a late arrival as compared with the cave-worship, stone-worship, and water-worship upon which Pytho was based, did really impose itself only after a struggle and under some compromise. But Euripides liked to tell the story in this shape not because it contained truth, but because it was a rock of offence to cultivated consciences unwilling to break with an old and venerable superstition.

Still more significant is the comparison between the Aeschylean and the Euripidean story in respect of the Dionysiac or Bacchic element in the Pythian religion. Aeschylus, as we saw, practically thrusts it out altogether. In the interests of theological unity he will have only one source of the oracular inspiration, Zeus, and only one

---

[1] *Eum.* 30 ff.

[2] *Ion*, 224 ff. For the rest see that play *passim*: the subject is never dropped.

recipient or channel, Apollo. As for any connexion which may exist or have existed between Pytho and any other subordinate power, it is mere matter of history, matter of *meution* or record, interesting may-be in itself, but in no way touching the vital theory of the sacred function. Contrary on every point is the story of Euripides. As he puts the matter, Apollo is not, properly speaking, a prophet at all. The inspiration belongs to the place, to the oracular cave, and, if we are to trace it deeper, it would seem to come either from Earth or (much rather) from Dionysus, by whom the whole sacred mountain is 'possessed' or 'inspired,' like one of his bacchants into whom the god has entered. The seat of wisdom thus already created and established, Phoebus, being strong himself and backed by omnipotent strength, appropriates it, for the sake of the profit, and defends it against competition. As to Dionysus it is not certain, nor does it matter for art, where exactly the historical truth lay as between the two representations. It is certain indeed, as already said, that whatever may have been the truth, it was not the account of Aeschylus. That Bacchus was much more important to Delphi than he chooses to admit is known for a fact; nor is there, so far as I know, any proof that Euripides may not be following tradition, and tradition substantially true, when he implies that the Pythian *inspiration*, the communication of divine truth *by personal possession of the prophetess-recipient*, was in origin Bacchic and not Apolline at all. The cult of Dionysus as a whole was of later growth in Hellas than the cult of Apollo. But it does not follow that this was the order of their importance, or even of their appearance, in a sanctuary more ancient than either. However with historic truth we are not at present concerned; in any case, with or without historical warrant, Euripides chooses to give priority, and much more than priority, to the Dionysiac element. And his purpose in this, as in the whole scheme of his hymn, a purpose perfectly legitimate in itself and pursued in the most appropriate way, is to emphasize the embarrassments of the traditional polytheism, to insist on the radical impossibility of reconciling the claims of high thought and high morality with the preservation in any form of theology saturated with the notions of savagery. The age of Aeschylus and Pindar, and the earlier age—we might probably add, if our information were not so small—of Solon and Stesichorus, had held that the proper method was to recast the legends in shapes acceptable to feelings more refined than those of the primary inventors, in a word, to bring Apollo up to date. By the time of Euripides historical enquiry and speculation in general had advanced sufficiently far to make evident for many minds the hopelessness and fundamental illegitimacy of this proceeding. Apollo could no longer be brought up to date without being improved clean away. For the philosophers and their followers legend and religion were once for all divorced : and it is entirely in accordance with the philosophic or rationalistic aim of Euripides' play that, in what he offers for a Pythian hymn, he should present and develope in his own sense precisely those aspects of legend which religion could no longer digest.

What excuse there may have been for putting such an ode into the mouth of a Chorus, who in their dramatic capacity are supposed believers in the god, is not so easily determined as we might suppose. The women have been trained, we are given to understand, in the tradition not of Delphi but of Delos. Now it is very probable that if you had enquired at Delos in the fifth century for an account of Delphi, the picture would have differed notably, and not favourably, from a representation by the hand of a Pythian. The two sanctuaries were so far from sisterly concord that during much of the century they were nearly or actually at war. The Euripidean ode, as a satire on Pythian greed, would no doubt have been hooted at Delphi, or rather could not have been sung there without exposing the singers to the imminent risk of being 'flung from the cliff' ; but we could easily suppose that the same circumstances which procured it a welcome in Athens procured it connivance in Delos. However, to say the truth, I cannot think this question of dramatic character very important. The choric odes of a Greek drama cannot in any case be regarded purely and

strictly as speeches by the Chorus as acting personages; if
they were so regarded, they would be absurd. Where exactly
the limit of detachment should be drawn, and whether in any
case it has been exceeded, does not seem a vital question.
What is truly a vital question, absolutely vital, is whether
the effect of the ode, *however produced,* is in itself concordant
with the general spirit of the drama. This question we may
answer in the affirmative for the case before us, provided that
the play be supposed hostile, not friendly, to the traditional
anthropomorphic theology with which the interest of Delphi
was bound up. For such is the spirit of the ode ; and this is
the reason why it seemed worth while to devote a few pages
to the separate examination of it.

'LAST SCENE OF ALL'

(*PHOENISSAE*)

THE purpose of the investigations, which we have pursued in this volume, has been to throw some light on the strange and unparalleled perplexity of Euripidean art, as proceeding apparently, without harmony and without discrimination, upon contradictory hypotheses. On the one hand we have the fact that *prima facie* his plays, like those of his two great rivals, seem to be illustrations of sacred legends, in which the gods and miracles of anthropomorphic religion are assumed, at least for artistic purposes, as truth, forming the machinery of the story, giving the conclusion to which it points, and controlling the sentiment which it raises. On the other hand we have the equally visible fact that the plays are full of incidents and language pointing directly to the opposite conclusion, stimulating an adverse sentiment, consistent only with disbelief in the traditional religion and rejection of the anthropomorphic gods. The result is a confusion, a want of unity, which, if accepted as the final base for a judgement of the author, degrades him at once to a level of thought and feeling altogether below that of his alleged compeers, and indeed below that of the ordinary practitioner in literary fiction, thus causing us, if we consider the matter clearly, to wonder how his contemporaries, and still more the generations which immediately followed his death, can have entered, as they certainly did, into the delusion that this was an artist worthy of the very highest rank. The answer which we have offered is briefly, that of the two conflicting elements one is real and one pretence. The rationalism is genuine fiction, if we may use this term for convenience; the orthodoxy is pretended fiction, a mere theatrical trick, required in the first instance, and to some extent throughout, by the peculiar conditions of the tragic stage at Athens, but maintained in part out of a natural love for duplicity, ambiguity, irony, and play of meaning, which was characteristic of the people and the time. For contemporary readers, and especially for those incredulous philosophic circles upon which the poet rested for support, the two elements were always easily separable, and in the latter stages at least of the poet's career the method of union was developed into a typical fixed convention; so that an accustomed reader of Euripides not only knew that something must be subtracted from the published work in order to arrive at the author's true meaning, but also knew precisely where that something would be found. The facts of the story were treated as a sort of problem, of which for theatrical purposes the author offered, in regular form, a miraculous and orthodox solution. This solution was known for a pretence, and marked as such with increasing boldness by the manner in which it was handled by the poet himself. To reach the genuine thought, which the theatre did not admit except on condition of reserve, the reader had simply to reject the pretended solution, the superfluous 'divine' machinery, and interpret the significance of the facts in themselves either by his own wit or by such help as, in the relations of Athenian society, he could obtain without any difficulty.

I now propose to consider whether from this side any light can be thrown on one of the most curious historical enquiries presented by Euripidean criticism. Will it enable us to explain the questionable shape in which we find the *Phoenissae*? It will be well to say at the outset, lest the reader should be misled and disappointed, that with the main part of that play, with the story itself and the manner in which it is told, this essay will have no concern. I shall not here even discuss the relation between Euripides' way of presenting the episode of the Theban brothers, and that of

Aeschylus, for instance, or any other. With Eteocles and Polynices we shall have little or nothing to do. And this perhaps is fortunate; for my own feeling is that of all the poet's extant works the *Phoenissae* is that in which we should be most sensible of the defects in our material for a judgement. I do not see how it is possible to be sure, or even to believe, that we have materials for rightly estimating the *Phoenissae.* What we do know for certain is that the play is a professed piece of criticism. In more than one place we find situations and expressions, of which the significance would be lost to us, but for the accident that we are fully acquainted with the *Seven against Thebes.* Here therefore we have actual proof of what, as I think, a reader accustomed to the methods of art in general must frequently suspect without proof when he peruses Euripides ; that the author assumes our acquaintance with something in literature extraneous to his own text, something of which too often we can only say that it is beyond our reach. Clearly we have no right (in the fragmentary state of our information) to assume that only the *Seven against Thebes* is necessary for a complete understanding of the *Phoenissae* because that is all or nearly all the literary equipment which we happen to possess. I note this in passing for a reflexion which may and ought to carry us far, far enough to suspend decision in many a case where it has been pronounced ; having done so, we will go on to our proper and immediate subject.

It is notorious that the *Phoenissae* in its present shape exhibits, for a Greek play, a remarkable looseness of connexion, and this effect is found on consideration to lie mainly if not entirely in two points, the beginning and the end. The objection here, we may say to avoid confusion, has no resemblance to those which we have been considering in other cases. There is no conflict of realism and fancy, of rationalism and miracle. From first to last, prologue, drama, and finale, all is fact of the common visible world, independent of any theory, orthodox or unorthodox, as to the unseen powers. The point of objection is simply that some of the scenes, or more exactly two of the scenes, are not connected with the next parts of the play in that close and careful manner which the severity of Greek art would lead us to demand. The point is taken correctly, or nearly so, by the author of a remark in a Greek prefatory note or *hypothesis*[1]: "The action is very rich in stage-exhibition, indeed it is superabundant; the scene in which Antigone looks forth from the terrace is no part of the plot; there is no purpose for the admission of Polynices (into Thebes) under a safe-conduct; and the departure of Oedipus into exile, with its tag of irrelevant lyrics, is a useless adjunct." I cite this dictum not as an authority —there is nothing in these prefaces to indicate that the compilers of them were entitled to particular respect on a literary question—but as a *prima facie* judgement by a reader guiltless of theory. On one point indeed his judgement is disputable and, as a fact, not generally supported. Whatever else may be said of the scene in which Polynices and Eteocles meet, it cannot fairly be said that there is no motive for the invitation to Polynices, by which alone their mother brings the meeting about. Her natural and obvious motive, as alleged by herself[2], is to make a last attempt at reconciliation before the encounter of arms; the truce is in place, and properly related to the central interest of the play. Nor is it true—if that is what the critic means—that the conference of the brothers is without *result*. It is a sufficient dramatic result in itself, that the effort to reconcile them does not succeed, and that by means of it their unappeasable antagonism is exhibited in a natural and appropriate manner. Here therefore the critic has over-stepped the mark under the seduction of fault-finding; but his other two points are fairly made and supported by common consent. The scenes in question, judged by the Attic standard, are tacked in or tacked on with a strange looseness of fit. The scene 'in which Antigone looks forth from the terrace[3]' is the first of

---

[1] τὸ δρᾶμά ἐστι μὲν ταῖς σκηνικαῖς ὄψεσι κάλλιστον, ἐπεὶ καὶ παραπληρωματικόν· ἥ τε ἀπὸ τῶν τεγέων Ἀντιγόνη θεωροῦσα μέρος οὐκ ἔστι δράματος, καὶ ὑπόσπονδος Πολυνείκης οὐδενὸς ἕνεκα παραγίνεται, ἔτι τε ἐπὶ πᾶσι μετ' ᾠδῆς ἀδολέσχου φυγαδευόμενος Οἰδίπους προσέρραπται διακενῆς.

[2] *Phoen.* 81 ff.   [3] *vv.* 88 ff.

the play, following immediately on the prologue. The girl
comes out under the care of a slave-guardian to indulge her
curiosity with the spectacle of the beleaguering army, in
which the divisions and principal personages are pointed out
by her attendant. As a method of exposition, and a device
for introducing these personages to the audience, the scene is
passable ; or rather it would be, if they played, as in fact they
do not, important parts as individuals in the drama which
follows, and if it were not certain that all which Antigone
learns in this dialogue was already familiar to the Athenian
play-goer. But whatever its merits or demerits as an exposition, the critic above-cited speaks truly when he says that it
is 'no part of the plot' or 'action'; and he is also right (so
far as extant evidence shows) in his tacit assumption that this
is a notable infringement of the rules imposed by Attic taste.
The excursion of Antigone has neither preparation nor sequel;
in the body of the play she scarcely appears, and her intrusion
upon the scene, when it occurs, involves the story in a singular
embarrassment. Not until the finale, when after lamenting
her brothers she accompanies her father into exile, does she
do anything which seems to be wanted ; and the part which
she then plays, so far as it is relevant to the drama, would be
as intelligible (to say the least) without the expository scene
as it is with it. Moreover—and this brings us to the critic's
other point—this her final appearance is associated with yet
another notable breach of the expected unity. • It is accurately
true, as he says, that 'the departure of Oedipus into exile,
with its tag of irrelevant lyrics, is a useless adjunct' to the
play as a whole. According to the story of Euripides, the
blind and dethroned Oedipus had been kept by his sons in
a sort of imprisonment. When they have fallen each by the
other's hand, and their mother by her own, the captive creeps
forth from his darkness to encounter the corpses ; and to
crown his misery the new king Creon, to be rid of his
accursed presence, expels him from the city to wander as he
may. The situation is undeniably pathetic, and the pathos
of it is increased, rather than diminished, by the faithful
adherence of his daughter, who rejects a princely husband in

order to accompany him. But for an Attic dramatist, or
indeed for any dramatist, it is an astonishing blunder that
having reached this climax he should fritter away the whole
effect of it by a dropping fire of mutual lamentations between
the father and daughter, not merely prolix as a whole, but in
detail so curiously irrelevant to the situation as to be scarcely
even intelligible.

Such are the facts of the case, as noted by the Greek
commentator, who is content to note them without further
remark. His abstinence, if designed, is perhaps prudent; but
when we consider all the circumstances, we must think it
strange if he felt no inferential suspicion, and shall pardon or
praise the modern readers, who have not only felt but expressed it. That the play has suffered *interpolation*, that the
form in which we have it does not exactly correspond to the
original design, but contains something, ascertainable or not,
which was intruded after the scheme had been fixed and
completed, is an opinion which, with whatever divergences of
detail, has been supported, I believe, by every critic of recent
times. The form which I shall give to this opinion may not
answer exactly (I am not aware that it does) to the statement
of any previous supporter; but I believe there is nothing in
the next three paragraphs which will be found surprising by
those who are acquainted with the general current of commentary.

When we consider that these two scenes, each of them
liable for a separate reason to the charge of offending against
unity, of being an irrelevant excrescence upon the true stem
of the play, are found one at the beginning and the other at
the end (that is to say, precisely at the places where extraneous addition is easiest), and further that the two scenes
have a certain correlation, the first serving to bring the person
of Antigone into a prominence for which the rest of the play
does not furnish sufficient reason, while the second erects the
destiny of Antigone into a prominence for which the rest of
the play does not furnish sufficient reason, we do not take
a long or a rash step in connecting the phenomena and
referring them to a common origin. It is simplest and most

natural to suppose, without prejudging the distinct question
of authorship, that the two scenes are in fact what they
appear to be, additions to a work which was first designed
and completed without them. Moreover it happens that in
the case of the initial scene, against which the internal
evidence of alienage is perhaps the less strong, there is
external evidence amounting to proof, that it has been thrust
between parts which were once in juxtaposition. The prologue, spoken by Jocasta, contains no reference to Antigone
except the mention of her birth and name. It concludes
with a statement that Polynices has accepted the invitation
to a conference, and a prayer that the result may be peace.
Common sense and common practice would lead us to
suppose from this that the conference itself is to be the com-
mencement of the action. And accordingly, as soon as the
Chorus have been introduced and have completed their *ode of
entrance* (which again ignores Antigone and by its conclusion
fixes our attention once more on the contest of the brothers),
as soon, that is, as the stage is ready for action, the scene,
which would be the first, if it were not for the excursion of
Antigone, presents to us the arrival of Polynices and proceeds
in due course to the conference[1]. We cannot easily believe
that the prologue was designed to introduce not the scene
that it does properly introduce, but another scene beginning
with the statement that Antigone has received her mother's
permission to quit the accustomed seclusion of a Greek
maiden and take an excursion upon the terrace, an indulgence
of which her mother, who has barely quitted the scene before
Antigone enters, has not thought it necessary to speak. Nor
can we omit to notice, as an anticipation upon the matter of
authorship, that if the excursion of Antigone be the work of
the original designer he has committed an odd oversight in
not making a corresponding change in his prologue. Between this scene and its immediate sequel, the entrance of
the Chorus, a connexion of a sort has been made: by the
approach of the Chorus Antigone, says her attendant, is
compelled in modesty to retire again. With what precedes

[1] *v.* 261.

the scene no connexion is attempted. We are left to suppose, what is in rigour supposable, that Antigone has met her mother and obtained the alleged permission just inside the door. In short the adjustment of the scene is exactly what it would be, had it been inserted by some one who had not full authority over the text. Be that however as it may, and whether the insertion is the work of Euripides or some other, the fact of insertion seems as clear as evidence can make it. Nor are there wanting indications in the body of the play, as well as in the opening and finale, that it has been retouched after completion by some one who had a careful eye for Antigone. Framed as the piece now is, with Antigone figuring sole at the head of it and Antigone figuring again with her father as the main interest of the close, it would be intolerable that between these points the heroine should do nothing and never be seen. Accordingly she is seen and she does do something, but the closer we look, the more we shall doubt whether her appearance and action were reckoned upon when the plot was originally drawn out. When Jocasta is informed that her sons are on the point of settling their quarrel by a duel to the death, she resolves, as a last effort, to go forth and throw herself between them. As we now read the play, although she is exhorted to do this by the messenger who reports the situation, yet thereupon, instead of flying instantly to the field, as the situation seems to demand, she spends some precious minutes in summoning, to accompany her, her daughter Antigone, who receives the command in a brief dialogue of nineteen lines[1], the sole occasion on which she presents herself between the first scene and the last. Now this sole appearance bristles with circumstances of suspicion. In the first place Jocasta has two daughters, as she tells us in the prologue. But she does not think of taking Ismene. It is not natural that she should wait for any one; but she waits for Antigone, and Antigone only. And further, as the scene now runs, the Chorus are fully informed of Jocasta's intention. It is discussed in their presence between her and her daughter. But curiously

[1] vv. 1264—1282.

enough, the same phenomenon occurs here which we have noticed already on the first appearance of Antigone. The context ignores it. When the mother and daughter are gone on their errand, the Chorus bewail the crisis, the fratricidal duel, and the agony of the mother, at considerable length[1], not only without reference to the daughter, but without betraying the least suspicion that the mother proposes to interfere between the combatants. They speak exactly as they might if Jocasta, on hearing of the project, had rushed away without a word, which is just what she naturally would have done, when the thought of interfering occurred to her. What follows is stranger still. Creon, brother of Jocasta, enters in search of his sister. The Chorus tell him that, having received news of the proposed combat, she left the house, and Antigone with her; and this is the end of their information. Even now they say not a word which shows knowledge of her intention to go on to the field of battle, and this although Creon is asking where to find her. The facts, as they report them, may suggest it as an inference; but why, if they know it for certain, they should not plainly say it, I at least am unable to imagine.

However in this manner Antigone is got on and off again as companion to her mother; and accordingly in the report afterwards given of what occurred in the field we find Antigone present there. But so little is she expected (if we may put it so) by the disposer of the facts, that her presence, nowhere serviceable, becomes at a certain point the cause of embarrassment almost ludicrous. The mother arrives at the place only to find her sons dying, and slays herself upon their bodies. Now then, if ever, is the time for the daughter to perform. Unfortunately just at this moment according to the story the battle, suspended by the single combat, is suddenly resumed, and the maiden in one verse must be hurried off; 'meanwhile Antigone slipped away from the host[2].' Every one is struck by the feebleness of the effect, and it is hard to disagree, as a matter of taste,

---

[1] *vv.* 1283—1306.
[2] 1465 κἀν τῷδ' ὑπεξῆλθ' Ἀντιγόνη στρατοῦ δίχα.

either with Valckenaer and others who wish to omit the verse and let Antigone shift for herself unnoticed, or with Hermann and others who maintain that the poet, having taken her there, was bound to get her away again. Nor is this the only example of the kind: in two other places the fact that Jocasta is accompanied by Antigone is indicated in a single unnecessary verse[1], and one of them is turned so ill that all wonder how the poet, supposed to be writing at large, could be guilty of such clumsiness. Everything in short combines to indicate that here, as at the first appearance of Antigone, her part has been enlarged against the intention of the first designer. A glance through the narrative will show that by a few modifications it might be relieved of her inconvenient presence; and though 'to restore the original' would in such a case be a chimerical attempt, it is not, as I think, too much to assert that the scene has been retouched, with the purpose, as before, of preparing us better for the independent interest now invited to the heroine in the finale.

As to the finale itself, the *prima facie* impression which it makes on the reader is precisely that indicated by the observation of the Greek commentator, that 'the departure of Oedipus into exile, with its tag of irrelevant lyrics, is a useless adjunct.' It is clear that by the sudden transference of the interest from the fall of the brothers to the future of Oedipus and his daughter, and by the extension which is given to this new theme, the finale ceases to serve as a finale. In the prospect thus opened the retrospect is lost, and the end comes not as a close, but simply as an interruption. Moreover in order to bring about this conclusion, the course of the story has to take a sudden and (for more than one reason) strangely improbable twist. Since the blind old king is now dismissed to long wanderings, which are to end at Athens, it is inevitable that he should be provided with a companion, and this

---

[1] 1323 κόρη τε μητρὸς Ἀντιγόνη κοινῷ ποδί, 1430 σὺν παρθένῳ τε καὶ προθυμίᾳ ποδός. This last for elegance of expression can be compared only to the famous description of Mr Pickwick's partner at whist, going home 'in a flood of tears and a sedan-chair.' Almost every edition, after Valckenaer, omits it: but this, as an isolated remedy, is illegitimate; we must answer first the question why it was put in.

companion is Antigone. But Antigone had another destiny. According to the play written by Euripides on her story and bearing her name, she was afterwards married to Haemon the son of Creon, who figures as her lover in the *Antigone* of Sophocles[1]. Now in the *Phoenissae*[2] Creon announces his intention to make this match, according to the disposition of Eteocles, who thus before his death had confirmed, as king of Thebes, the right of Creon and his family to the contingent succession. Were it not for the actual sequel, we should certainly suppose that Euripides, here as elsewhere, was preluding or referring to a story of his own, the story of his *Antigone*. But in ten verses all this elaborate design is abruptly dropped[3]. Antigone declares her resolve to accompany her father, and threatens, if forced to wed, that her husband shall find in her 'a Danaid' or Bride of Lammermoor. With a prudence or timidity unexampled, I should think, in the history of ambitious fathers, Creon takes this threat as decisive: " Go, thou shalt not murder my son ; depart from the land "; and so Oedipus and his daughter 'with their irrelevant lyrics' set forth together for Athens. Nor is the marriage of Antigone the only important project which is thus cut short. The most famous function of Antigone in story, as all know, was the burial of her brother Polynices, contrary to the sentence which deprived him of funeral rights as a traitor. It seems impossible to doubt that in the *Phoenissae* as originally designed this function was anticipated as a sequel. Creon, announcing the decree against Polynices, is confronted by her in this play just as he is in the *Antigone* of Sophocles, and as the herald is in the *Seven against Thebes*[4]. And accordingly in the *Antigone* of Euripides her burial of Polynices was combined in the plot with her marriage to Haemon. But how it is to be reconciled with the present conclusion of the *Phoenissae*, we ask in vain. It is true that Antigone in 'the lyrics' reiterates her resolve

---

[1] See the 'argument' to that play, and remarks on it in Jebb, *Introduction*, p. xxxviii.

[2] *vv.* 1586 ff., *v.* 1638.   [3] *vv.* 1673—1682.

[4] *Phoen.* 1644 ff.

to perform the interdicted rite, even if it costs her life; but what chance or possibility there is of her accomplishing such an act of rebellion in Thebes and also accompanying her banished father, as we see her at the *exodus* in the act to do, the dramatist does not enable us to conjecture. The play in fact ends, without closing, in a plaiting of incompatible motives[1], and the cause of the whole mischief is visibly 'the departure of Oedipus into exile with its irrelevant lyrics.'

It has been already said that, while there is a general agreement among modern critics in thinking that the play has been retouched, there is much difference of opinion when it comes to the pointing out of single 'interpolations.' The fact is that, unless the change be of a very simple kind (such as the insertion of a whole complete and separate scene), exact analysis is impossible, neither is it necessary to the validity of a general conclusion. For my own part I take it as certain (and I should expect to this extent the agreement of every reader who will view the question broadly and will not require unattainable and improper exactness of detail) that the truth of the matter is innocently touched by the Greek critic already quoted, when he speaks of 'Oedipus' banishment' as an 'adjunct,' or more precisely 'a piece tacked on[2].' No one, I will venture to say, who is accustomed to literary compositions, can reasonably doubt that the *Phoenissae* as originally designed did not conclude, as it now does, with the joint departure of Oedipus and Antigone on a wandering exile which is to end at Athens. Possibly (though this is a distinct question) it did not assume removal of Oedipus at all; according to the best accredited tradition,

---

[1] In *vv.* 1643—1646 the complication of strands becomes almost perceptible to analysis.

> AN. ἀτὰρ σ' ἐρωτῶ τὸν νεωστὶ κοίρανον
> [τί τόνδ' ὑβρίζεις πατέρ' ἀποστέλλων χθονός;]
> τί θεσμοποιεῖς ἐπὶ ταλαιπώρῳ νεκρῷ;
> ΚΡ. Ἐτεοκλέους βουλεύματ' οὐκ ἐμοῦ τάδε. κ.τ.λ.

In the reply of Creon and what follows, the question in brackets is ignored, and Valckenaer accordingly omits it. The debate turns upon the king's order respecting the corpse, not at all on the banishment of Oedipus. This is but one example of what the reader will find on attentive perusal in the whole finale.

[2] προσέρραπται, Paley's certain correction of προσέρριπται.

the 'Homeric' tradition, Oedipus died and was buried at
Thebes itself. Or possibly again Euripides may have adopted
here the version of which there are traces in the *Oedipus at
Colonus* of Sophocles[1], that the curse-laden man, for certain
intricate religious reasons, was compelled to end his days, and
was eventually buried, not in but just outside the territory
covered by the name of Thebes. My own opinion, if one
may have an opinion on what is not susceptible of proof, is
that this latter account, or something like it, was adopted for
the original *Phoenissae*. There are reasons for thinking so.
But I prefer not to enter here upon any such speculative
question. Our present concern is with the conclusion of the
play not as it was or may have been, but as it is now and
once was not. The existing finale (to emphasize the point
once more) fixes our attention on the joint future of Oedipus
and Antigone, going forth to wander together. For this
finale the play was not designed; ethically and mechanically
it is an inapplicable termination; and almost all those signs
of disturbance which by common consent the play now
exhibits, are accounted for by supposing, what we are
forced to suppose, that some one, having determined to
append such a finale, set himself to make in the body of
the work just the minimum of alteration which seemed
indispensable. To enlarge the part of Oedipus was impossible. The appearance of the blind prisoner in the
conclusion depends for its effect upon being his first appearance. But it was not impossible to command attention from
the first for Antigone, and to enlarge her action so as to
diminish at least the inconsistency of her singular importance
at the close: and this is what the reviser has done. His
purpose is visible in the very first line that he writes, *Thou
tender daughter of Oedipus and glory of his house*[2]: nothing in
the main action of the play explains why Antigone should be
thus addressed, but the address is exactly adapted to prepare
us for the daughter's heroic devotion to her father, as exhibited
in the existing conclusion. More might be said to the same

[1] *Oed. Col.* 396 ff.
[2] *v.* 88 ὦ κλεινὸν οἴκοις 'Αντιγόνη θάλος πατρί.

purpose on points of detail ; but it will be better to leave the matter upon the broad basis of general impression. This, I think, will be enough to satisfy us as to the truth of a proposition in which, as was said before, there is nothing which the course of modern commentary, taken as a whole, does not harmoniously tend to support.

We turn now to the proper question of this essay, whether from our point of view any light can be thrown on the purpose of this remarkable transformation. Here we may say at once that the manner, in which the transformation is executed, proves an executant who would not have treated the play as he has, without some very strong and defensible motive. We are perhaps too apt, in speculations of this kind, to help a theory by the convenient hypothesis of a wondrous simpleton, who did the mangling, blundering, or whatever it is that we require. In this case at any rate no such hypothesis is entertainable. Even in those parts of the play which are most open to suspicion, the handiwork, as Paley justly remarks in one or two places, is not only good in the main but thoroughly Euripidean. The performance, to give a negative illustration, does not in the least resemble those *rifacimenti* of Shakespeare, which were produced in the seventeenth and eighteenth centuries. It does not seem necessary to enter upon details, which will best be appreciated by reading the whole work. I will only say that in my judgement there is no sign in the text of any operator to whom we can reasonably or consistently attribute such literary incompetence, as would be implied by blindness to the result of what has been done. The author of the finale must have seen, as well as we can see, that he had done some mischief. That he was deeply versed in Euripides and genuinely interested in his fame, is a position which may be defended when any one will attack it : the scene on the terrace or the final lyrics might be the poet's own, if only they were found somewhere else. We are driven then to the conclusion, as alone accounting for the facts, that the existing finale was in the view of the transformer worth the cost of it. He must have had, as already said, some very strong and defensible motive for exhibiting in a Euripidean play the banishment of Oedipus and Antigone. I hold that this motive is discoverable and even patent. I take the close of the *Phoenissae*, understood as it was meant, to be one of the most pathetic passages in the history of literature; with all its inaptness, or rather by virtue of its inaptness, it would make the play eternally interesting even if, which is not the case, the play had no other claim on our notice.

To reach a position from which we can judge what intention the reviser is likely to have had, we must now settle a point reserved, that is to say, whether we can suppose that the transformation and the original design are by one and the same hand,—that Euripides altered his own play. This is not to be rejected without consideration, not even upon the ground that the changes are to some extent injurious. It is not an unknown thing for an artist to spoil his own work. But we have already noticed some signs which in this case would make the supposition difficult. The imperfect junctures by which the insertions are betrayed, could be accounted for, if the original poet did all, only by extreme and scarcely credible carelessness. If we suppose a second hand, they are accounted for naturally by the fact that a second hand cannot be perfectly free. The appearance of the product on examination suggests of itself, that there was a desire on the part of the interpolator to limit his alterations to the minimum required by his purpose, a feeling not easily attributable to a poet revising himself. This however I should not consider conclusive; but it is confirmed by other evidence. One thing we may say positively from internal evidence respecting the composer of the finale. He knew the very last works of Sophocles; and one of his motives, not the least efficient, was to pay, as he has done, a compliment to Sophocles or to his memory. The last speaker[1] is Oedipus, who turning, as it were, to his countrymen appeals to their recollection of his services in the following terms: 'O famous citizens of my native land, behold, this is Oedipus, who read the famous

---

[1] The tag indicating the 'victory' of the play is scarcely to be reckoned a part of it.

riddle, and was a man very great. I, who alone subdued
the power of the murderous Sphinx, now, a citizen no more,
myself am pitiably banished from the soil. But why do I
lament it, and in vain bewail? For what is imposed by gods
a mortal needs must bear.' These verses, as every one knows,
by their long emphatic metre, here abruptly introduced, recall
the close of the *Oedipus Tyrannus*, and the two first repeat
almost word for word the two first of the corresponding
passage spoken in that play by the Chorus[1]. To strike out
the passage from the *Phoenissae*, to omit the two first lines,
or the second line, or otherwise to trim away the allusion, is
surely to overlook the fact, that the person who framed it as
it is could have no possible motive for doing so except the
express desire of recalling the *Oedipus Tyrannus*, and recalling
it with honour. To suppose that the composer of this finale
could not have done without the verses, all six or any two, is
impossible. So far from helping him, the two verses borrowed
from Sophocles are mechanically rather an embarrassment, for
they involve in the sequel a change from the third person to
the first. Nor would any one else but the composer have a
motive for putting them in, if he had not done so. They are,
they must be, a deliberate quotation from Sophocles, which,
made as it is gravely and appropriately, is a signification of
respect. Similarly, or at least with the same apparent purpose
of directing attention to Sophocles, the composer has managed,
not without difficulty, to find a place in the speech of Creon
on the refusal of burial to Polynices, where it is just possible
to put in almost unaltered a line of Sophocles' *Antigone*[2]. It
does not help the sentence, on the contrary it makes a rather
difficult construction; it does not illustrate the rest of the

---

[1] *Oed. Tyr.* ὦ πάτρας Θήβης ἔνοικοι, λεύσσετ', Οἰδίπους ὅδε
ὃς τὰ κλείν' αἰνίγματ' ᾔδει καὶ κράτιστος ἦν ἀνήρ. κ.τ.λ.

Phoenissae. ὦ πάτρας κλεινοὶ πολῖται, λεύσσετ', Οἰδίπους ὅδε
ὃς τὰ κλείν' αἰνίγματ' ἔγνω καὶ μέγιστος ἦν ἀνήρ.
ὃς μόνος Σφιγγὸς κατέσχον τῆς μιαιφόνου κράτη,
νῦν ἄτιμος αὐτὸς οἰκτρῶς ἐξελαύνομαι χθονός. κ.τ.λ.

[2] *Phoen.* 1634 ἐᾶν δ' ἄκλαυστον, ἄταφον, οἰωνοῖς βοράν. Of course the verse
has been struck out, but this is not to explain it. Klotz retains it, but does not
account for it.

speech, having not one word in common with it; it serves in short no purpose, and cannot have been brought there with any other motive, except to bring Sophocles himself before the recollection of the audience. All which becomes significant, and leads us to the matter of our immediate enquiry, the date of the present finale, when we consider, what of course is obvious, that the story of the finale is the story of the *Oedipus at Colonus*. It was Sophocles in that play who gave, for the first time as it seems, general fame and recognition to the local tradition of Colonus, his own birth-place, that it was the final refuge of Oedipus, the place of his death and burial; it was Sophocles who had shown Antigone, as she appears in this finale, as the devoted guide of the wanderer. And it is to the play of Sophocles, not to the legend which it celebrates—even if that was sufficiently known before the play to be the subject of an allusion—that the composer of the finale refers.

Oed. Now, daughter, comes the fulfilment of a prophecy by Apollo.

Ant. What prophecy? Canst thou mean other woe to be added yet?

Oed. That wandering I must come to my death in Athens.

Ant. Where? What tower in Attica shall give thee reception?

Oed. Sacred Colonus, home of the rider-god[1].

The reference here is not to the legend, but to the *Oedipus at Colonus* direct, as appears in the form of the question, 'What *tower* in Attica will give thee reception?', or, as it might be rendered, 'What wall[2]?' So far as I know—I speak under correction—'sacred Colonus' had neither *wall* nor *tower* nor anything about it which would naturally suggest the word *pyrgos* as a description of it. It lay out in the country; and its hill, enclosures, groves, shrines, and statues had no fortification of any kind. But what the writer has in his mind is the opening scene of the Sophoclean play, where the place at which Oedipus pauses to rest is first fixed by Antigone's remark to her father that '*the towers* that guard the city, to judge by sight, are far off, and *this place is sacred* to all seeming.' The 'wall' that the author has in view is the

---

[1] *Phoen.* 1703—1707.   [2] τίς σε πύργος Ἀτθίδος προσδέξεται;

wall of Athens itself, seen from Colonus at some distance ;
but he could not have put this for a description of Colonus, if
it were not that what he really has before his mental eye is
the verse and the scene of Sophocles. From all this taken
together—and more might be added—it is plain that in
composing the finale he had Sophocles, and the *Oedipus at
Colonus* in particular, specially in view. But in that case we
need not go further to show that he was not Euripides. The
form of the literary compliment paid to Sophocles is not such
as is commonly used, or perhaps could properly be used,
towards a living writer. It is not like Euripides, or perhaps like any writer, to pay such a compliment at the
expense of an inconvenient alteration in his own original
design. And lastly it is much more probable than not that
he never read the *Oedipus at Colonus*[1], to say nothing of the
likelihood that, if it reached him in Macedonia, he would
have employed his dwindling days in altering the *Phoenissae*
to suit it, instead of finishing (let us say) the *Iphigenia at
Aulis*. The *Phoenissae* in its present shape contains the work
of another hand, added after the death of Sophocles and the
circulation of the *Oedipus at Colonus*, and later therefore *a
fortiori* than the death of Euripides himself; and this, or
something like it, with whatever modifications of detail, I
take to be in general the received opinion.

Nor is there any difficulty in receiving this hypothesis as
accounting sufficiently for the mere production of the play in
its present shape. During the last years of the fifth century
and the early years of the fourth, at the time when the popu-
larity of Euripides' works was at the height, they must have
been brought out repeatedly (indeed we know that they were)
by his family and, in a modern phrase not here inapplicable,
his literary representatives ; and it would have been surprising

---

[1] As to the date of the *Oedipus at Colonus* see the full discussion in Jebb's
introduction. If it was not known until the posthumous exhibition of it on
the stage in B.C. 402, the revision of the *Phoenissae* was after that. But it
may have been made public earlier. However an exact date is not required :
we can scarcely suppose that the *Oedipus at Colonus*, not performed till 402,
was sufficiently known to be the subject of public allusion before Euripides retired,
about 407.

rather if they had never seen occasion or thought themselves required to make temporary changes for the immediate purpose. But there remains, untouched by this presumption, the question why, in the case of the *Phoenissae*, this make-shift work should have been preserved, why it should have become classical, and why we have an interpolated play instead of the original play, as it was originally exhibited by the poet some years before his death. The case, as far as appears, is unique; for the patching of the *Iphigenia at Aulis*, unhappily not finished and (still more unhappily) brought to its present form by persons of whom some could not even observe the rules of verse, is not a parallel case. In saying that there is no parallel, I do not of course mean to assert that there is no interpolation in other works of Euripides. As a fact I believe that there is very little in them of interpolation properly so called. But at any rate nowhere else except in the *Phoenissae* do we find evidence worth notice of remodelling comparable in extent and bold-ness to that which is visible here. On such a point the general impression of fairly competent and attentive students is the only decisive test; and by this test the *Phoenissae* is sharply distinguished. There are other plays in which, with some ingenuity, a case for supposing more or less extensive interpolations may be made out: it may be thought that there never was or will be a literary work in which, with some ingenuity, such a case might not be made out. But in the *Phoenissae* it needs no making out. The facts are so patent, and the interpretation of them, broadly taken, so inevitable, that even a reader innocent of any theory on the subject, a critic like the author of the Greek argument, who seems scarcely to perceive the bearing of his observations, is led as it were in his own despite to speak of a certain part as 'tacked on.' That it should have been 'tacked on' is not very surprising, but by what interest did the supposititious work, in spite of palpable inconvenience, usurp and hold the place of the original and genuine?

The answer to this question I myself consider to be scarcely less patent than the question itself. Whether it has been previously given, I am not prepared to say; I may have overlooked it. The dialogue of Oedipus and Antigone, meaningless as drama, is intelligible only as allegory. The final scene of the *Phoenissae* was preserved, with its concomitants, for its profound and pathetic interest as a piece of literary history; because it was composed in the Euripidean circle, and understood by contemporaries, as a sort of last 'Epistle to the Athenians' from the poet himself. The 'Oedipus' of the finale is not the king of Thebes, and the 'Antigone' of the finale is not the Theban heroine, to whose dramatic fortunes the 'wholly irrelevant lyrics' of the father and child cannot even be applied consistently. The 'Oedipus' is Euripides himself, and his 'daughter' is his spiritual offspring, his poetry. His 'exile' is no imaginary banishment from Thebes, but the actual retirement of the aged poet from the beloved city where, overcome by weariness and the near approach of death, he had no longer spirit to carry on his life-long war on behalf of intelligence and sense. The scene is in a certain way more tragic than any pure fiction could be, but it appeals not really to the interest which might be excited in the future of Oedipus by the foregoing drama, but to that generous and not transitory emotion of gratitude and regret which, as we know by testimony, broke out in Athens, when it was known that the Athenian, who more than any other had formed the minds and inspired the ambitions of the Athenians then in their meridian, had been laid, like Aeschylus before him, not in Attica but in a foreign soil.

Oed. Now, daughter, comes the fulfilment of a certain *prophecy by Apollo!*

Ant. What prophecy? Canst thou mean other woe to be added yet?

Oed. *That wandering I must come to my death in Athens.*

Ant. Where? What tower in Attica shall give thee reception?

Oed. Sacred Colonus, home of the rider-god. Come then, come lend thy blind father help, since thy will it is to share my banishment.

[1]*Ant.* *To banishment, alas! Reach me thy loved hand, mine aged sire. Thou art the ship, I the speeding wind.*

[1] Here begin the 'lyrics' of which the Greek argument complains.

Oed.　Behold, my child, I go.　Be thou, unhappy, the guide of my feet.

Ant.　Unhappy am I now, yes, unhappy, beyond any maid of Thebes.

Oed.　Where shall I set my failing steps ?　My staff, child, here !

Ant.　So, so, step so, and so; how weak, even as a dream !

Oed.　Fie, fie on him that sends me forth thus old from my native land !　Sorrow, sorrow, hardly borne !

Ant.　Why borne ?　Why borne ?　Doth not Justice regard the evil, doth she not punish in men the want of understanding ?

Oed.　This is I !　I who climbed to triumph of poesy heaven-high, by reading the Maiden's riddle not understood !

Ant.　The reproach of the Sphinx !　Recallest thou that ?　Nay, speak no more of those successes past.　This was the fate, alas, that awaited thee, to quit the land of thy birth and die, O father, where ?　Tears of regret shall I leave to the maids that love me, when I go forth far from my native ground to wander a maid forlorn !

Oed.　Alas, for a helpful soul !

Ant.　Aye, for the sake of my sire's distress[1] it will win me a fair renown.

[Woe for the foul wrong done to thee, and to my brother, whose outcast corpse hath no burial.　O father, e'en if I must die for it, I will, when 'tis dark, put earth on the uncovered wretch.]

Oed.　Let thy maiden companions see thy face.

Ant.　No, I have wept enough.

Oed.　Then to the altars with prayer !

Ant.　Nay, I am sick of my sorrows.

Oed.　Go then at least to Bacchus, to the holy ground on the hills reserved for his maenads' feet.

Ant.　Bacchus !　Ah, he it was for whom in time past I draped myself with the Cadmean fawn-skin, and trod on the hills the sacred paces of Semele's choir, doing for gods a service not requited !

Oed.　O famous citizens of my native land, behold this is Oedipus, who read the famous riddle and was a man very great.　I, who alone subdued the power of the murderous Sphinx, now, a citizen no more, myself am pitiably banished from the soil.　But why do I lament it, or in vain bewail ?　For what is imposed by gods a mortal needs must bear.

If this scene be read as applying really to the hero and heroine of the play, there is scarcely a single point in it which is properly or intelligibly put, scarcely one significant expression which is not either forced or irrelevant.　Referred

---

[1] ἐς πατρὸς συμφοράς, literally 'looking to,' 'considering.'

on the other hand to the misfortunes of the poet and his
art, all is correct and clear. Why for example should the
legendary Antigone be moved by the exile of the legendary
Oedipus to invoke the wrath of heaven against 'the want of
understanding[1]'? The supposed offence of Creon is simple
cruelty, not the want of intelligence: and if in general it is
possible to regard moral offences theoretically as errors of
judgement, that is no reason for confusing the ideas in a
special case which is not an error of judgement. We are told
therefore to read 'want of understanding' in the sense of
'outrage': yet Oedipus takes it in the strict sense[2]. Or
what again can 'Oedipus' mean, when he says that 'by
reading the riddle of the Maiden' (that is, of the Sphinx) he
'climbed to triumph of poesy heaven-high[3]'? It is true that
the Sphinx was said to have chanted her riddles in metre, as
oracles and other profound sayings were commonly chanted,
and is therefore spoken of frequently as a 'singer,' 'minstrel'
or the like, while the riddles themselves are called her 'un-
musical songs,' her 'poesy unmeet for the lyre,' and so on[4].
It is also true that Oedipus was commonly supposed, as in
such a fairy-tale he naturally would be, to have replied in
metre[5]. But did ever any one regard Oedipus on this ground
as essentially an artist, like Orpheus, or describe his success
as a 'triumph of song,' 'a triumph of the muse'? It does not
appear that Sophocles applies to Oedipus any such language,
or Euripides anywhere else; and wherever such language
might be found, we should take it for a sign that the writer,
if he really had the legendary Oedipus in view, intended to
speak lightly and by way of a jest. But of such an intention

---

[1] βροτῶν ἀσυνεσίας.

[2] ἀσελγείας schol., and see Paley's note. It does not appear that ἀσυνεσία
is ever used by Euripides in the sense supposed, or would be likely to suggest
itself to so good an imitator. And here the context is decisive against it:
ANT. οὐχ ὁρᾷ Δίκα κακούς, οὐδ' ἀμείβεται βροτῶν ἀσυνεσίας; ΟΙΔ. ὅδ' εἰμὶ μοῦσαν
ὃς ἐπὶ καλλίνικον οὐράνιον ἔβαν, παρθένου κόρας αἴνιγμ' ἀσύνετον εὑρών. Surely
it is impossible to take ἀσυνεσίας and ἀσύνετον in alien senses, when the one is
suggested by the other.

[3] μοῦσαν ἐπὶ καλλίνικον οὐράνιον ἔβαν.   [4] e.g. Phoen. 807, 1028.

[5] See the alleged riddle and reply in the Arguments to the Oedipus
Tyrannus.

our present writer cannot be suspected : he is serious beyond question, and passionately serious.   Yet the language that he uses, taken naturally and according to the usage of the time, signifies (as Paley for instance says truly and by instinct) 'to aspire *to literature,*' and not (as Paley adds by afterthought, in order to satisfy the sense) 'to ascend to lofty victorious wisdom.'   The triumph of 'Oedipus,' according to our author, was a poetic and literary triumph : *ergo* his 'Oedipus' is not the legendary hero, but some one utterly different.   And in the next sentence this becomes, if possible, plainer still.   'The reproach of the Sphinx !' says Antigone 'Recallest thou that ? Nay, speak no more of those successes past[1].'   *Reproach*, that is to say *glory.*   Such was the simple theory of some Hellenist in the bolder ages, when interpreters were not embarrassed by words.   But *reproach*, for all that, is not *glory* ; what the writer means, as the more scrupulous moderns say, is plainly that the Sphinx, because none could answer her, was a reproach *to Thebes* ; and the implication is, that the public service pleaded by Oedipus against an ungrateful country lay in taking this reproach away.   But yet what an ineptitude is this, if the reference be really to the legend ! What was this 'reproach' to Thebes, or the ridding of it, that the boon to Thebes should be laid on this, and not simply on the ending of the Sphinx herself and her murderous depredations ?   The language is not adapted to the legend ; and it is plain, as before, that the reference is to something else.   Next we have Antigone saying, with pathetic emphasis, that her father is quitting his country to die—they know not where[2].   Then what of Apollo's prophecy, just before mentioned, that he is to die at Athens, or more exactly at Colonus ?   If 'Oedipus' be the Oedipus of legend, then we must take it from the author that this was a true prophecy. Why then should Antigone be made to speak as if she had never heard of it ?

---

[1] Σφιγγὸς ἀναφέρεις ὄνειδος ; ἄπαγε τὰ πάρος εὐτυχήματ' αὐδῶν.—Schol. ad loc. τὸ ὄνειδος, ἀντὶ τοῦ τὸ κλέος. See Paley's note.

[2] φυγάδα πατρίδος ἄπο γενόμενον, ὦ πάτερ, θανεῖν...ποῦ ; (or θανεῖν που). The interrogative seems better, but the sense is the same either way.

We now turn to the fortunes of 'Antigone,' and still the confusion grows. The pathos of her situation, it seems, lies in parting from her maiden companions. They will weep for her when she is gone. Her father begs her to see them once again before she goes, and to visit the places (among them as it seems the 'hills' of Thebes, though what hills at this moment she can visit, he does not say, nor what he proposes to do meanwhile), where with other girls like herself she had celebrated the worship of the Theban gods, especially Bacchus. All this, to cite the Greek critic yet once again, if applied to the preceding drama, must be dismissed as wholly 'irrelevant lyrics.' A finale, as a finale, should be occupied with the persons and themes of the drama, not with other persons and themes of which nothing has before been made. There is in the drama mention of persons whom 'Antigone,' if she were really Antigone, could not at this moment forget, of whom she must have spoken, if she was to speak within the limits of nature and credibility. What of Eteocles? What of Jocasta? They are dead it is true, but even their bleeding corpses, which a few minutes before she had hoped to bury, might call for a word of farewell. And what, above all, of *her younger sister*[1], her only sister, sole remnant now with herself of her father's house? Ismene is not dead. Ismene is to be left (at least so we must understand) in Thebes, for Creon to deal with as he thinks fit. Yet neither Antigone nor Oedipus himself so much as mentions her name; only 'maiden companions' and 'dances in honour of Bacchus,' matters in which the spectator of the drama, as such, has not the smallest interest. The whole scene, taken as relative to the play and to the dramatic situation of the legendary personages, is a string of irrelevance. It seems impossible that anyone with wits enough to write verses should have offered this dialogue as really representing what passed between Oedipus and Antigone when about to quit Thebes under the

---

[1] *Phoen.* 57. She is mentioned here no doubt for the sake of her part in the sequel, that is to say in Euripides' *Antigone*. The corpses are addressed in the foregoing verses (1693—1702) but *not with words of farewell*; that passage, like all the rest up to the departure (*vv.* 1703 ff.), except a few lines here and there, belongs to the original work, and takes no account of the departure.

circumstances described in the *Phoenissae* : inconceivable too, that by way of a climax he should put on a purposeless quotation from Sophocles, and then should not quote him right.

But the true reason why this poet (for a poet he was, and no mean one) has pointed by the whole topic of his scene, and especially by the stately and melancholy cadence of the close, to the recollection of Sophocles, is because Sophocles, like the gentle man that he was, though he had never, so far as we know, been intimate with Euripides, and certainly was no partizan of the cause for which Euripides fought, had chivalry enough and courage (for at the moment it must have wanted some courage) to speak peace to the grave of genius and to rebuke the malice of bigotry, when he heard that Euripides was dead. According to the familiar anecdote, he not only put on mourning himself, but directed his actors and chorus to appear without the accustomed emblems of festivity ; and it is added that at the sight the sensitive people burst into tears[1]. Without assuming that these details are exactly correct, we may safely suppose that Sophocles showed respect, and that his doing so was felt to be a thing of importance, since the memory of it survives in the poor scraps of biography which are left to us. Probably nothing was more efficient in generating and stimulating the kindness to Euripides' memory, which in the next year after his death, the implacable Aristophanes confesses to be the sentiment of an overwhelming majority. That Aristophanes himself, or at least the zealots whose views it sometimes suited him to express, did not much approve nor even very well comprehend the moderation of Sophocles, may be inferred not only from common experience, but from the faint and dubious compliment (as it seems) which he pays to the tragedian's temper, so easy, he says, that Sophocles, if he had a chance to escape from Hades, would probably let it pass[2]. He thought of him, as Steele thought of Addison or Somers, as a person of excellent intentions but unhappily wanting in spirit. But in the Euripidean circle his calm generosity excited, as well it might, something more than a passing

[1] Life of Euripides.   [2] *Frogs*, 80.

gratitude. By choosing a familiar passage of Sophocles, the
close of his most famous work, as the model for that in which
'Oedipus,' that is to say Euripides himself, should appeal
from the stage to the remembrance of his renown, and plead
his painful removal from Athens as a propitiation of those to
whom in the combat of life he had given offence, the author
of this finale, speaking evidently as with authority[1], repays
the debt by an acknowledgement respectful, public, and
solemn as the manifestation on the part of Sophocles had
been, and joins as it were the hands of the dead rivals in
a pledge of perpetual amity. And if this be not a fine and
becoming thought, a just and noble payment of a noble and
just obligation, then where may these qualities be found?
Nor is it without reason that the composer, while borrowing
the words of Sophocles so far as to ensure recognition, adopts
them nevertheless with some modification. The Chorus of
the *Oedipus Tyrannus* addresses itself to the 'dwellers in our
native Thebes': but the 'Oedipus' of this finale, as long
before this has become plain, is not speaking to imaginary
Thebans, but to his own true countrymen, the Athenians
assembled in the theatre of Athens, and to them therefore his
address is directed by the adapter in the anonymous formula:
'O famous citizens of my native land.' Still more to the
purpose are the subtle changes made in the following verse.
'Who *knew* ($\mathring{\eta}\delta\epsilon\iota$) the famed riddle and was a man *most
mighty* ($\kappa\rho\acute{\alpha}\tau\iota\sigma\tau\sigma\varsigma$)' says Sophocles. 'Who *read* ($\mathring{\epsilon}\gamma\nu\omega$) the
famed riddle and was a man *very great* ($\mu\acute{\epsilon}\gamma\iota\sigma\tau\sigma\varsigma$),' says the
adapter, in each case just letting the phrase fall to the natural
tone of common speech, from which Sophocles, rightly for
his purpose, has raised it[2]. It becomes more 'real' and
therefore more Euripidean; it is not Sophocles who speaks,
but Euripides with Sophocles in his thoughts.

All that is said in the finale by and of 'Antigone,' idle
and tiresome if referred to the daughter of Jocasta and sister
of Ismene, becomes full of sense and pathos when referred
to the spiritual daughter of Euripides. If 'Oedipus' is

---

[1] He was probably the poet's own son (or nephew) and 'literary executor.'
[2] See Jebb *ad loc.*

Euripides, the poet in his public capacity, his child and inseparable companion is naturally his 'work' or poetic art. The figure is a commonplace and used by Euripides himself[1]. The 'virgin companions' who love her are the other 'muses,' the other poetic and poetry-loving spirits of Athens: and they will weep for her, when she is gone, as the muse of Sophocles did. The rite of Bacchus, which it was her practice to celebrate, is the service of that Athenian theatre and theatric festival of which Bacchus was in fact the patron and symbol. And when she complains that this worship of hers, as a service to religion, was ill-requited, she makes the claim which Euripides would have made and constantly does make, that, in extricating the conception of deity from the follies and atrocities of legend, he was defending 'the gods' against human perversity, not assailing them, as was perversely supposed. When she predicts that her 'helpful soul' or 'serviceable wit[2]' will be praised hereafter 'for the sake of her sire's misfortunes,' she anticipates that rebound of feeling in favour of Euripides and his work, of which her creator intends to avail himself. If she ignores 'the prophecy of Apollo,' that is because she is her father's true daughter, and therefore regards such a prophecy as vain and presumably false, which in fact, applied to the veritable 'Oedipus' of the finale, it manifestly is,—not the truth but the reverse of the truth. He is to die 'in Athens'; but this is just the very destiny which he should have had, yet will not. To the author of the finale Delphi is still, as it should be, what it was to Euripides; it was not the business of Euripides' representatives to retract on his behalf the opinions to which he had given his life. Everywhere the recognition of the true 'Antigone' makes light out of darkness. To one thing only she refers in this finale which concerns her fictitious interest, and does not concern the real, and that is the burial of Polynices. At least we do not see (though with our scanty knowledge of the facts it would be rash to found much upon that) how the muse or poetry of Euripides should have an unburied brother.

---

[1] τὸν θ' ὑμνοποιὸν αὐτὸς ἂν τίκτῃ μέλη κ.τ.λ., *Supp.* 180.

[2] τὸ χρήσιμον φρενῶν.

For this reason in the foregoing translation that passage is distinguished from the context. The reader will perceive that it interrupts the connexion; for the topic in hand, both before and after, is the farewell of Antigone to her maiden friends. We may suspect that originally it was not there, but is due to the well-meaning mistake of some one who thought that these lyrics should contain at least something relevant to the play. On the other hand the author himself may possibly have been tempted to try an impracticable combination. If so, this must be cited as his only mistake, and it is of little importance.

But 'Antigone,' or the muse of Euripides, is after all but a secondary figure. The main interest of the scene lies in 'Oedipus,' and in the light which this allegory throws on the notion of Euripides and his work entertained by those who best knew and best understood him. Both the choice of this comparison and the treatment of it agree exactly, as will, I think, be admitted, with the view which these essays are written to recommend. The fault alleged against his enemies, the cause of the ill-will before which he at last retired, is laid in 'want of intelligence.' His poetic fame is based, his claim to gratitude grounded, on his triumphs over 'the Sphinx,' whose 'unintelligible riddles' he read, whose reproach he took away from his country, and whose destroying power he checked. Upon the principles propounded in this book all this is natural, obvious, and transparent.

The Sphinx or 'Virgin Maid,' who like Antigone and the other virgins of the scene is a 'muse' or literary type, stands for the only such power which she could properly represent, *the spirit of mystery and darkness*, regarded not with the reverent eye of a friend, but by a champion of the opposite powers, of reason, daylight, and simplicity.

For the Athenians of the fifth century, the spirit of mystery was represented by art such as that of Aeschylus, art in which the miraculous stories of orthodox tradition were accepted as realities, not the less true, but rather the more deeply true, because inexplicable to reason. Neither Aeschylus of course nor those who agreed with him would have described this spirit as that of a sphinx, because this is to mark it as inhuman and pernicious. But this is precisely the aspect in which to Euripides, as a rationalist and combatant for rationalism, the spirit of mystery or, as he would have said, of superstition, did actually appear. According to him this spirit was a monster of darkness 'preying' upon the intellect of the nation ; according to him it was 'a reproach' to the intellect of the nation, that those discreditable ancient falsehoods, in which the power of that spirit was bound up, should be taken for articles of faith, and set forth with splendour and pomp of imagination, instead of being resolutely explained away and reduced to the true elements of the veritable world out of which in times of darkness they had been first compounded. To Euripides a miraculous legend was even as a riddle of the Sphinx, an insult to human understanding and an engine of deadly mischief. To 'solve the riddle,' to vanquish the art of superstitious mystery by an art of reason and common sense, which translated the mysterious fable into terms of real life and thus took away from it the power to befool men any more,—this (he thought and his friends thought after him) was to fight the battle of intelligence and illumination, and to relieve at least one city in Hellas from the disgrace of submitting in passive stupidity to be devoured for want of an answer.

From the manner in which this allegory is engrafted upon the revived *Phoenissae* we should naturally suppose that it was not then put forward for the first time, but that, amid the various gossip occasioned by the death of Euripides, a complimentary comparison to Oedipus, in the character of an intelligent patriot repaid with exile, had become more or less notorious. And of this we have some confirmation elsewhere. It will explain, for one thing, the strange statement of biographies, that his parents had been resident in Boeotia, and even that his father was a native Boeotian[1]. The silence of Aristophanes proves that there is no truth in this, and indeed it is denied by the ancient biographies themselves.

[1] See Suidas, *Euripides*, with Dindorf's notes in the preface to the *Poetae Scenici*.

It must have sprung, like many other fables in the same documents, from misapprehension, and it shows that Euripides was at some time called a Boeotian in jest. If shortly after his death, and at the time when rumour was most busy with him, his friends were in the habit of describing him as an Oedipus, the occasion for such a jest is apparent. And further this comparison also accounts for a certain strange excursion in the *Frogs*. It explains why Aristophanes falls with such a fury of ridicule upon the innocent and unimportant couplet which stood at the beginning of Euripides' *Antigone*[1]: 'There was a man Oedipus, who prosperous at the first became afterwards the most miserable of mankind.' What there is here to attract attention, or why these words should be picked out from all the openings of Euripidean plays to receive notice unique in form, extent, and emphasis, we ask at present in vain. Aristophanes has nothing real to allege against the verses, and there is nothing real to allege. The burlesque version of the legend of Oedipus, which he there puts into the mouths of Aeschylus and Dionysus, does not really justify censure either of the expression or of the thought. It might have been directed just as well against the *Oedipus Tyrannus* itself. The comedian, as indeed he allows his Euripides to say, is talking nonsense, and must be aware of it. And unless there was at the time a motive for degrading the figure of Oedipus in association with that of Euripides, it is nonsense without purpose; but it is legitimate and sensible nonsense, if the couplet had become charged by quotation in Euripidean circles with a meaning beyond its own, and had come to imply a compliment to the author which was at the same time a reflexion upon Aristophanes himself.

The union of Sophocles with Euripides, presented in the finale of the *Phoenissae*, would be ennobled and completed, from a catholic point of view, if we were able to trace in it a sign of reconciliation possible, at any rate beyond the grave, between Euripides and Aeschylus himself. But this perhaps would be to ask too much of allegory, if not of charity. It

---

[1] *Frogs*, 1180 ff.

is still beyond our common capacity to make peace between
Oedipus and the Sphinx. And yet there was between the
representative men, between Aeschylus and Euripides, a
pathetic resemblance, at least in their fortunes, which the
author could not here forget and has not forgotten. 'I, who
alone subdued the power of the murderous Sphinx, now, a
citizen no more, *myself* am pitiably banished from the land.'
It is plain that the effect here of the word *myself* is to suggest
a parallel between the speaker and his opponent. But as
between Oedipus and the Sphinx, as figures of legend, where
is the parallel? 'Having conquered the Sphinx I am now
conquered myself' is the paraphrase of Paley, and this is
sense. But the text says 'Having subdued the Sphinx I am
now *exiled* myself'; which is not sense, unless in some
fashion 'the Sphinx' can be thought of as exiled. And
'exiled' the Sphinx of this passage actually was, in the
same sense and under the same circumstances as the Oedipus
of this passage; that is to say, Aeschylus like Euripides with-
drew in his last years from the city which he adorned and
loved, and never came back. In each case there is every
reason to suppose that the exile was not altogether voluntary;
and that, as Aeschylus was tired out at last by the struggle
against innovation, and driven to abandon a people whose
aspirations, under the guidance of the teachers who formed
Euripides, were daily becoming less compatible with the
doctrines of the *Eumenides*, so Euripides was tired out at
last, and perhaps scared, by the resistance and threats of an
orthodoxy which, a few years after his flight, exacted a not
more cruel expiation from a yet more illustrious servant of
truth.

Such were the aims, the doctrine, *and the method* of
Euripides as conceived by himself and his contemporaries;
nor without this conception is it possible to read him truly
or do justice to his powers. Naturally we are not in the
least required to subscribe to the Euripidean view of the
universe, to the Euripidean estimate of mystery, either as
an element in art or an element in life. It will perhaps have
appeared in the course of these essays that I should by no

means subscribe to it myself; at any rate this will be known
to those who may have done me the honour to read what
I have elsewhere written about Aeschylus. We are not called
upon as critics, or as lovers of art, to take for our own the
creed of any given artist, or to enlist under any of the
banners which continue to war for the empire of men's
minds. I see not why, for the purpose of enjoying art, we
should take a side in the quarrel; and there are many reasons
why we should not. To understand and enjoy the art of
Euripides we need not accept his views; but we must know,
feel, and remember what they were. *His stories assume that
'the gods' do not exist*; and unless we are alive to this, unless
we keep it *always* before us, the best of Euripides, the essence
of Euripides, must be sealed up from us. I have not any
wish, I should think it an affectation, to disguise the importance which in my judgement attaches to the propositions for
which I here contend, so far at least as it matters whether
Euripides is understood or not, justly praised or unjustly
decried. It concerns only ourselves. 'Doth not Justice re-
quite us for want of understanding?' Of existing criticism
on Euripides a considerable part is mere irrelevance and
misapprehension. Learning and even genius are copiously
spent in proving that he did not rightly pursue what was in
fact the very opposite of his aim, that he does not assist his
readers to imagine things which he was determined, if it were
possible, to prevent them from imagining. Of his extant
works some of the finest are so completely perverted by false
explanation that practically they have ceased to command
attention except from students of language. His rightful
place among the creators of noble pleasure, the champions
and benefactors of mankind, is either logically refused to him
by those who see what the current expositions really imply,
or illogically and doubtfully conceded by those who do not.
All is confusion, vexation, waste of spirits and time. Euripides was a soldier of rationalism after the fashion of his
time, a resolute *consistent* enemy of anthropomorphic theology,
a hater of embodied mystery, a man who, after his measure
and the measure of his time, stood up to answer the Sphinx.

ABSTRACT OF CONTENTS

ALCESTIS

The legend, pp. 3–5. Analysis of the play, 5–6. Paley's criticism, 7. Altercation with Pheres and intoxication of Heracles, their aesthetic effect, 8–10. Defence of Admetus, not maintainable, 11–15. Defence of Heracles; *Balaustion's Adventure*; Browning changes the character, substituting that of the *Madness of Heracles*, 15–23, 40 f. The true Heracles, professional athlete and soldier, 23–26. Greek view of drunkenness, 27. The bargain of the Fates, how limited, 28–30. The 'hospitality' of Admetus to Heracles, properly condemned by Euripides, 31–45. The 'unity of time,' a misleading fiction, 45. Funeral custom in Athens, 46–48. Funerals on the stage, 48 f. The funeral of Alcestis, 49–57. True bearing of the scenes with Heracles and Pheres, 57–63. Breaks in the action, absence of Chorus, 64 f. Final scene; disguise of Alcestis, its aesthetic effect, 66–68. Dialogue of Heracles and Admetus, 68 f. The finale, 69–71. προσειπεῖν, 70. συνέστιος, 71. The finale not conceivable as representing reality, 71–77. Explanation of this; the purpose of Euripides is to expose the legend as untrue; the finale is ironical, 77–82. This form of construction typical and regular in Euripides; the Euripidean 'tag,' 81, 119, 209. Contrast of ancient and modern theatre, 82–83. Religion of Euripides, and his relation to the theatre, 84–89. Disguise practically necessary to him, 89–93. Its moral danger; censure of Aristophanes, 93 f. Its special attraction for the Athenians, a consequence of their national character, 94–97. Its usefulness to wit; examples from the *Alcestis*, 97–101. Consequent method of exhibiting the popular gods; generally detached from the action proper, as in the *Alcestis*, 101–102. Difficulty of realizing Euripides' point of view from our habituation to another manner (the Alexandrian) of treating the Greek legends, 103–105. The prologue to the *Alcestis*, Apollo and Death, 105–109. Effect of Euripides on readers, and specially through discussion; great importance of this, shown by Aristophanes, 109–112. General view of the play as it might be expounded by the 'Euripides' of the *Frogs*, 112–119. Interest not centred on Alcestis, but on the resurrection, 120–122.

Disorganization in all the scenes produced by misplacing it, shown in commentaries, 122 f. The death-scene, 123–126. The intoxication of Heracles, 126. Dramatic advantage, to imitation of nature, of obscurity permissible to a certain degree, 128–129. Manner of Alcestis' burial; supposed oversight of author, really part of design, 129–137.

ION

Parallel in construction between *Ion* and *Alcestis*, 139–140. Prologue of the *Ion* compared with the finale; the failure of Apollo's design, 140–147. The prologue and finale, as in the *Alcestis*, ironical, 147–149. The action of the *Ion*; abstract, 150–154. The finale no *dénouement*, 154–156. The action of the play really proceeds on the assumption that there is no Apollo, the oracle being a fraud, 156–158. The fraud of the cradle and tokens, 158–162. Summary of the story, disengaged from the miraculous prologue and finale, 162–164. Result of the attempt to carry out logically the current hypothesis, 165–169. *Ion* and *Lourdes*, 169 f. The fraud of the cradle resumed, 171–174. The tragedy of faith, 174. Difficulty of performing Euripides at the present day, 175 f.

IPHIGENIA IN TAURICA

Finale of the *Iphigenia*; proof of the true character of a Euripidean god from stage-jest put in the mouth of Athena, 179–182. Parallel case of the *Orestes*, 182–183. Ἄρειοι πάγοι, 182. Ridicule of anthropomorphic religion in reference to the Dioscuri; inference from it to general intention of the play, 185–187. The story does not assume the existence of Apollo, 187–195. 'Lacuna' in the oracle, as to the meeting of Iphigenia and Orestes, 192. Trial before the Areopagus, contrast with the *Eumenides*, 188. Iphigenia's dream; contrast with the *Choephori*, 189 f. The miraculous wind, 193. The motive of the oracle, 194–195. The Furies; hallucination of Orestes; inference from this as to his account of the scene at the Areopagus, 195–201. The Furies in Aeschylus and in Euripides; their costume, etc., 196 f. The *Semnai* θεαὶ ἀνώνυμοι: point of this designation in reference to the *Eumenides*, 197–198. Legendary origin of the *Choës*; Euripides explodes it, 199–200. Artemis, her supposed part in the transference of Iphigenia to Taurica; rationalistic explanation, after the manner of Palaephatus; the name *Thoas*, 201–205. Summary. True purpose of the play;

necessary to its effect as a tragedy, 205–206. Moral quality of
Orestes' enterprise, and of Iphigenia's plot, 206–209. The pretended
finale, its flatness and futility; allusion to 'the Euripidean tag,' 209–
210. The stage-gods of Euripides, not to be regarded as personages
in the drama; statement of Lucian, 211–214. Inconsistency between
the finale and the play; character and condition of Orestes, 214–218.
And of Iphigenia, 218. Character and fate of Pylades, 218 f. And
of the Chorus, 220. Euripides and the *Poetic* of Aristotle, 220–229.
General purpose of Aristotle in the *Poetic*; his criticism of the
dramatists negative, 220–221. Aeschylus, 221–222. Sophocles,
222–223. Euripides, 223–226. 'The most tragic of the poets,'
225 n. General opposition between Aristotle's principles and the
tragedy of the fifth century, 226–227. Illustrated by Aristotle from
the *Iphigenia*, 227. Question as to the limits of Aristotle's theory,
228 f.

EURIPIDES IN A HYMN

The variations of orthodoxy useful to the dissenter, 231–232.
The Pythian ode in the *Iphigenia*; importance of its isolation as
an *entr'acte*, 232–234, 244 f. Religious character of the Chorus as
connected with Delos, 233. The ode contrasted with the prologue
to the *Eumenides*, 234–244. Aeschylean history of Pytho, its general
character, 234 f. Tradition of contest between rival deities, how dealt
with, 235. Aeschylean Zeus, 236 f. Bacchus at Delphi, 238. The
ode, 239–240. Satire of Pythian avarice, 241. Euripidean history
of Pytho, 242–244.

'LAST SCENE OF ALL'
PHOENISSAE

General result of the preceding Essays, 246–247. The critical
problem of the *Phoenissae*; *prima facie* appearance of interpolation, 247–251. The personage of Antigone and the banishment of
Oedipus, not appropriate, 251–259. Date of the change; not made
by Euripides, but suggested by the *Oedipus at Colonus*, 260–263.
Motive and interest of the change; the existing finale allegorical,
263–276. Euripides as 'Oedipus'; allusions elsewhere, 273–276.
The Sphinx and Aeschylus, 276. Conclusion, 276 f.

CAMBRIDGE: PRINTED BY JOHN CLAY, M.A. AT THE UNIVERSITY PRESS